Relating Carol Shields's Essays and Fiction

Crossing Borders

"This anthology is a must for fans of Carol Shields. Nowhere else will you find such lively, informed discussions of her writing craft or so quickly discover why her work was beloved by literary critics and the reading public alike. This anthology's fascinating, wide-ranging examination of the literary forms Shields used—novels, short stories, plays, essays and biographies—is a major contribution to an appreciation of one of our literary giants."
—Susan Swann, Professor Emerita, *Department of English, York University, Canada*, author and co-founder of the Carol Shields Prize for Fiction

"*Relating Carol Shields's Essays and Fiction* brings together some of the most longstanding and experienced critics of Canadian Literature between covers in wideranging and thorough analyses of the singular accomplishments of Carol Shields. Focusing on her essays, short fiction, novels, and reviews, they gauge the many ways Shields most effectively used and experimented with her inherited forms. Altogether, a compelling portrait of a great writer at work emerges."
—Robert Thacker, Charles A. Dana Professor of Canadian Studies and English Emeritus, *St. Lawrence University*

"In this collection of fourteen articles, prominent scholars read Carol Shields's short stories and novels through the lens of the writer's illuminating essays. In examining the policies and practices of fiction and her own experience of the writerly life, Shields's essays afford invaluable insight into her fiction. Original in its focus and range, this volume expands our understanding of Shields's visionary approach to 'writing as an act of redemption'."
—Ruth Panofsky, Professor of English, *Toronto Metropolitan University, Canada*

"This new collection of essays on Carol Shields is a welcome addition to the body of critical work on this esteemed author. Longtime fans of Shields among the general reading public—as I am—will be as receptive to this study as academics already well-versed in the field. The new perspectives help to keep alive a talented writer who left us far too young."
—Judith Ruderman, Professor Emerita of English, *Duke University*

"This is a wonderfully rich collection of essays on one of Canada's most important writers. Lucid, innovative, and brilliant, these essays read Shields' writing through her non-fiction, illuminating how the author's inner thoughts and beliefs shaped her craft. A significant contribution to Canadian literary criticism, the collection features essays written by an impressive array of scholars. It provides lively and insightful interpretations—a must-read for all those interested in Carol Shields and Canadian literature."

—Laura Davis, Professor of English, School of Arts and Culture, *Red Deer Polytechnic, Canada*

"There is something for every fan or scholar of Carol Shields's work in this engaging collection of essays. An impressive array of top scholars in the field covers a wide range of topics, showcasing the many dimensions of Shields's work, not just as an award-winning novelist and short story writer, but also as an essayist, book reviewer, and inspiring creative writing teacher. This book is an important contribution to Shields's literary legacy."

—Sarah Wylie Krotz, Associate Professor and Director, *Canadian Literature Centre, Department of English and Film Studies, University of Alberta, Canada*

"The fourteen contributors to this edited collection explore intricate and playful connections between Carol Shields's essays and fiction, highlighting the innovative experimentation of her writing—her blurring of fact and fiction, curiosity about narrative shapes, and writerly activism. In this powerful and engaging volume, highly regarded scholars come together to study the complexity of the feminist, postmodernist, and metafictional qualities of Shields's work and to celebrate one of the most generous and compassionate voices in Canadian literature."

—Margaret Steffler, Professor Emerita, *Department of English, Trent University, Canada*

"A superb collection, which brings together all the foremost Carol Shields scholars. Their contributions shed new light on Shields's novels and short stories by reading them through and against her non-fiction writing. Like Shields's own work, these essays are innovative, playful, strange and imaginative."

—Faye Hammill, Professor of English literature, *University of Glasgow, Scotland*

"This essay collection, written by a stellar group of Canadian literature specialists, is a love letter to the late Canadian writer Carol Shields, who died about twenty years ago. The essays revisit Shields's prolific career—short story writer, novelist, book reviewer, teacher and biographer—through the lens of her posthumous collection, *Startle and Illuminate: Carol Shields on Writing* (2016), edited by her daughter Anne Giardini and grandson Nicholas Giardini. The chapters are eclectic, both intimate and academic in tone, as they reflect different relationships with this beloved writer within our Can Lit circle—and beyond."

—Laurie Kruk, Professor in English Studies, *Nipissing University, Canada*

Nora Foster Stovel
Editor

Relating Carol Shields's Essays and Fiction

Crossing Borders

Editor
Nora Foster Stovel
Department of English and Film Studies
University of Alberta
Edmonton, AB, Canada

ISBN 978-3-031-11479-3   ISBN 978-3-031-11480-9   (eBook)
https://doi.org/10.1007/978-3-031-11480-9

This Palgrave Macmillan imprint is published by the registered company Springer Nature
Switzerland AG.
The registered company address is: Gewerbestrasse 11, 6330 Cham, Switzerland

For Carol Shields and her readers

Acknowledgments

I wish to acknowledge, first and foremost, Carol Shields's family, especially Don Shields, Anne and Nicholas Giardini, and Sara Cassidy, as well as Karen McDiarmaid and the Carol Shields Estate and the Carol Shields Literary Trust. I also wish to thank the Canada Council for the Social Sciences and Humanities Council of Canada Strategic Grant that enabled me to research the Shields Archives at the National Library and the Insight Grant that has enabled me to pursue this research. I also wish to thank the University of Alberta Faculty of Arts for the McCalla Professorship that allowed me to pursue my study of Shields's writing and to edit this collection of essays, as well as an edition of her complete poetry published in 2021. I wish to thank Mark Abley, Philip Cercone, and Molly Beck for their valuable advice and guidance.

I want to thank the contributors who helped make this edition an interesting and illuminating collection. I also wish to thank Christl Verduyn, Coral Ann Howells, Cynthia Sugars, and Warren Cariou for allowing me to republish their substantially revised essays in this collection. I also wish to thank Marta Dvořák and Manina Jones for permission to reprint Christl Verduyn's essay, originally published in *Carol Shields and the Extra-Ordinary*, Neil Besner and *Prairie Fire* for permission to reprint Warren Cariou's substantially revised essay, originally published in *Carol Shields: The Arts of a Writing Life*, and the University of Ottawa Press for permission to publish a revised version of Cynthia Sugars's essay, originally published in *The Worlds of Carol Shields*. I also want to thank Anne Giardini for her engaging preface and Alex Ramon for his interesting Afterword and Christl Verduyn and Aritha van Herk for their insightful prologue and epilogue that frame these essays.

BOOKS BY CAROL SHIELDS

NOVELS

Small Ceremonies
The Box Garden
Happenstance
A Fairly Conventional Woman
Swann: A Mystery
A Celibate Season (with Blanche Howard)
The Republic of Love
The Stone Diaries
Larry's Party
Unless

SHORT STORIES

Various Miracles
The Orange Fish
Dressing Up for the Carnival
Collected Stories

POETRY

Others
Intersect
Coming to Canada
The Collected Poetry of Carol Shields

PLAYS

Departures and Arrivals
Thirteen Hands
Fashion Power Guilt and the Charity of Families (with Catherine Shields)
Anniversary: A Comedy (with Dave Williamson)
Women Waiting
Unless
Larry's Party—the Musical (adapted by Richard Ouzounian with music by Marek Norman)
Thirteen Hands and Other Plays

CRITICISM

Susanna Moodie: Voice and Vision

BIOGRAPHY

Jane Austen: A Life

ANTHOLOGIES

Dropped Threads: What We Aren't Told (edited with Marjorie Anderson)
Dropped Threads 2: More of What We Aren't Told (edited with Marjorie Anderson)

ESSAYS

Startle and Illuminate: Carol Shields on Writing

CONTENTS

NOTES ON CONTRIBUTORS

Brenda Beckman-Long is Associate Professor of English at Briercrest College, which is affiliated to the University of Saskatchewan. She is the author of *Carol Shields and the Writer-Critic* (2015), a reappraisal of Shields's innovative work in relation to women's activism, life writing, and feminist and critical theory. She has a doctorate from the University of Alberta and a postdoctorate from McMaster University, and she teaches and publishes in the areas of Canadian literature, Canadian women's writing, trauma, and autobiography studies.

Neil Besner was born in Montreal and grew up in Brazil, where he has taught and lectured widely, mainly on Canadian literature. He taught Canadian literature at the University of Winnipeg from 1987 until his retirement in 2017. He served in several senior administrative roles, as Dean of Humanities (2002–2004), Dean of Arts (2005–2007), Associate Vice President, International (2008–2009), Vice President, Students (2009–2010), and Vice President, Research and International (2010–2012); his last post was as Provost and Vice-President, Academic (2012–2017). He writes mainly on Canadian literature, the short story, and the poet Elizabeth Bishop, with books on Mavis Gallant (1988), Alice Munro (1990), an edited collection on Carol Shields (1995), and numerous articles, as well as co-edited books on the short story in English (1991) and on poetry in English (1997). His prize-winning translation from Portuguese into English of a Brazilian biography of Elizabeth Bishop (2002) was a major source for the 2013 feature film *Reaching for the Moon*. In 2001–2002 he was the Seagram's Chair at the McGill Institute for the Study of Canada, and from 2002 to 2004 he served as President of ACCUTE (Association of Canadian College and University Teachers of English). From 2004 to 2020 he was the general editor of the Laurier Poetry Series (LPS), a contemporary Canadian poetry series with Wilfrid Laurier University Press, with 30 volumes published to date. His first memoir and most recent book, *Fishing with Tardelli: A Memoir of Family in Time Lost*, was published in 2022.

Warren Cariou was born into a family of Métis and European ancestry in Meadow Lake, Saskatchewan. He has published works of fiction and memoir, as well as critical writing about Indigenous storytelling, literature, and environmental philosophy. He is the General Editor of the First Voices, First Texts series of critical editions at the University of Manitoba Press, and he has edited numerous collections of Indigenous literature, including, most recently, a special issue of *Prairie Fire* and *CV2* magazines co-edited with Katherena Vermette, entitled *ndncountry*. He has also edited books by Marvin Francis, Lisa Bird-Wilson, David Alexander Robertson, and other celebrated Indigenous writers. He has created two films about Indigenous communities in western Canada's tar sands region, and he has written numerous articles, stories, and poems about Indigeneity and petroleum. He is Professor of English at the University of Manitoba, where he directs the Centre for Creative Writing and Oral Culture.

Marta Dvořák, who was born in Budapest and raised in Canada, became Professor of Canadian and World Literatures at the Sorbonne. The book she has recently authored, *Mavis Gallant: The Eye & the Ear*, published in 2019, sets up a connection between the Paris-based Gallant's writing and the whole spectrum of the arts. Her interest in late modernists was already behind her first monograph, *Ernest Buckler: Rediscovery and Reassessment*, listed by the ICCS among the 30 most important books in the last 25 years of Canadian Studies. Arguing a global circulation of influence via rhetoric and narratology, Dvořák has written and edited books on (post)modern writers from Margaret Atwood to Nancy Huston. Recent books include *Carol Shields and the Extra-Ordinary* (edited with Manina Jones) and *Tropes and Territories* (with W.H. New), both 2007; *Crosstalk* (with Diana Brydon, 2012); and *Translocated Modernisms* (with Dean Irvine, 2016). Dvořák has also published on short story writers ranging from Katherine Mansfield and Janet Frame to Alice Munro. She has contributed chapters to Cambridge UP's *Literary History of Canada* (2009) and

Companion series, notably *The Cambridge Companion to Margaret Atwood* (2006/second edition in press) and *The Cambridge Companion to Canadian Literature* (2016, second edition), as well as to *The History of Canadian Literature* (2008).

Anne Giardini (Carol Shields's daughter) an executive, director, and writer, has served on several boards, including CMHC, TransLink, HydroOne, WWF-Canada and Pembina Institute, among others. She is the author of two novels and co-editor of *Startle and Illuminate: Carol Shields on Writing* (2016), a collection of essays by Carol Shields on her own writing and advice to aspiring writers. Anne has been Chair of the Vancouver Writers Festival, a board member of the Writers Trust of Canada, and Chancellor of Simon Fraser University. In 2009, she was appointed Queen's Council and received a Queen Elizabeth II Diamond Jubilee Medal in 2013. Anne was appointed Officer of the Order of Canada for her contributions to the forestry sector, higher education, and the literary community in 2016, and appointed to the Order of British Columbia in 2018.

Coral Ann Howells is Professor Emerita, University of Reading and Senior Research Fellow, Institute of English Studies, University of London. She has published widely on contemporary Canadian fiction, especially writing by women. Her publications include *Private and Fictional Words: Canadian Women Novelists of the 1970s and 80s* ((1987), *Margaret Atwood* (1996, 2005), *Alice Munro* (1998), and *Contemporary Canadian Women's Fiction: Refiguring Identities* (2003). She edited the *Cambridge Companion to Margaret Atwood* (2006), co-edited with Eva-Marie Kroller the *Cambridge History of Canadian Literature* (2009) and is co-editor of the final volume of the *Oxford History of the Novel in English* (2017). Her revised edition of the *Cambridge Companion to Margaret Atwood* was published early 2020. She is a fellow of the Royal Society of Canada.

Smaro Kamboureli is the Avie Bennett Chair in Canadian Literature at the University of Toronto. Her most recent publications include *Land/Relations: Possibilities of Justice in Canadian Literatures*, edited with Larissa Lai; "Literary Solidarities/Critical Accountability: *A* Mikinaakominis/TransCanadas Special Issue," *University of Toronto Quarterly* (co-edited with Tania Aguila-Way); "Diaspora," *Oxford Research Encyclopedia of Literature*; and a bilingual English/Italian edition of her poetry book, *in the second person, in seconda persona.* Other publications include *Scandalous*

Bodies: Diasporic Literature in English Canada and *On the Edge of Genre: The Contemporary Canadian Long Poem*. She has also edited many books, including Lee Maracle's *Memory Serves: Oratories* and Barbara Godard's *Canadian Literature at the Crossroads of Language and Culture*, and co-edited (with Christl Verduyn) *Critical Collaborations: Indigeneity, Diaspora and Ecology in Canadian Literary Studies*, (with Dean Irvine) *Editing as Cultural Practice in Canada*, and (with Kit Dobson) *Producing Canadian Literature: Authors Speak on the Literary Marketplace*.

Alex Ramon is a British critic and academic currently based in Łódź, Poland. He holds a PhD from the University of Reading, UK, and is the author of the book *Liminal Spaces: The Double Art of Carol Shields* (2008). His work on Shields has also been published in the edited collections *Carol Shields: Evocation and Echo* (eds. Aritha van Herk and Conny Steenman-Marcusse, 2009) and *The Worlds of Carol Shields* (ed. David Staines, 2014). His most recent article, "Mordecai and Him: Canadian-Jewish Identity and Yanofsky's 'Really, Really, Really Unauthorised' Biography," was published in *Kanade, di Goldene Medine?—Perspectives on Canadian-Jewish Literature and Culture* (eds. Majer, Fruzinska, Kwaterko, Ravvin; 2018). Ramon's research interests include British and Canadian fiction and film, gender theory, and adaptation. He is currently working on a study of novel-to-film adaptations and a collection of critical pieces and interviews.

Christian Riegel is Professor of English at Campion College, University of Regina. He has published *Writing Grief: Margaret Laurence and the Work of Mourning* and *Twenty-First Century Canadian Writers* and the essays "Mourning, Memorial, and the Yizkor Books in Eli Mandel's Out of Place," "Writing Grief: The Fraught Work of Mourning in Fiction," and "Robert Kroetsch's *Stone Hammer Poem*: Elegy and Memorial." He is Director of the IMPACT (Interactive Media, Poetics, Aesthetics, Cognition, and Technology) Lab at the University Regina where he pursues interdisciplinary collaborative research that bridges digital humanities, cognitive science, new media art, software systems engineering, and disability studies. His research team has created digital tools for individuals with severe mobility challenges that enable them to create art with their eye only, using advanced eye tracking devices.

Wendy Roy is Professor of Canadian Literature at the University of Saskatchewan. She has published several articles on Carol Shields's writings, as well as on fiction by other Canadian authors, including Margaret Atwood and Margaret Laurence. Her monograph *The Next Instalment: Serials, Sequels, and Adaptations of Nellie L. McClung, L.M. Montgomery, and Mazo de la Roche* was released in fall 2019. She is the co-editor (with Susan Gingell) of the collection *Listening Up, Writing Down, and Looking Beyond: Interfaces of the Oral, Written, and Visual* (2012), and she is author of *Maps of Difference: Canada, Women, and Travel* (2005). Her current SSHRC-supported research project on apocalyptic and dystopian fiction by Canadian women writers includes an analysis of Shields's story "Words."

Nora Foster Stovel is Professor Emerita at the University of Alberta. She has published on Jane Austen, D.H. Lawrence, Margaret Drabble, Carol Shields, and Margaret Laurence, including *Divining Margaret Laurence: A Study of Her Complete Writings* (2008). She has edited Margaret Laurence's *Heart of a Stranger* (2003) and *Long Drums and Cannons: Nigerian Dramatists and Novelists* (2001), plus *Jane Austen Sings the Blues* (2009) and *Jane Austen and Company* (2011). She is composing *"Sparkling Subversion": Carol Shields's Vision and Voice* and *Women with Wings: The Romantic and Classical Ballerinas*. She has edited *The Creation of iGiselle: 19ᵗʰ-Century Ballet Meets 21st-Century Video Games* (2019); *"Recognition and Revelation": Margaret Laurence's Non-Fiction Writings* (2020); *Early Writings by Margaret Atwood* (2020); *The Collected Poetry of Carol Shields* (2021); and *Relating Carol Shields's Essays and Fiction: Crossing Borders* (2022).

Cynthia Sugars is Professor of English at the University of Ottawa. She is the author of *Canadian Gothic: Literature, History, and the Spectre of Self-Invention* (2014) and editor of *The Oxford Handbook of Canadian Literature* (2015). She is also the co-editor of several book collections, including *Canadian Literature and Cultural Memory* (2014) and *Unsettled Remains: Canadian Literature and the Postcolonial Gothic* (2009). She is currently the editor of the scholarly journal *Studies in Canadian Literature*.

Aritha van Herk is the author of five novels, *Judith, The Tent Peg, No Fixed Address, Places Far from Ellesmere*, and *Restlessness*. Her irreverent but relevant history of Alberta, *Mavericks: An Incorrigible History of Alberta*, frames the exhibition on Alberta history at the Glenbow Museum in Calgary. With George Webber she has published *In This Place: Calgary*

2004–2011 and *Prairie Gothic* (Photographs by George Webber, Words by Aritha van Herk), both books that develop the idea of geographical and historical temperament as tonal accompaniment to landscape. Most recently, she has published a work of prose poetry, *Stampede and the Westness of West*. She is a member of the Order of Canada, a member of the Alberta Order of Excellence, a fellow of the Royal Society of Canada, and a recipient of the Lorne Pierce Medal, awarded to recognize achievement in imaginative or critical literature in Canada, and of the Lt. Governor of Alberta Arts Award. She has published hundreds of articles, reviews, and essays on Canadian culture. She teaches literature and creative writing in the Department of English at the University of Calgary in Alberta.

Christl Verduyn is Professor Emerita of English and Canadian Studies at Mount Allison University, Canada. Her research and teaching areas span the fields of Canadian and Québécois literatures, women's writing and criticism, multiculturalism and minority writing, life writing and Canadian studies, and she is the author, editor, or co-editor of over a dozen books in these areas. Before joining the faculty at Mount Allison, Christl Verduyn taught at Wilfrid Laurier University (2000–2006), where she chaired the Canadian Studies Program, and at Trent University (1980–2000), where she was Chair of Women's Studies (1987–1990), and Chair of Canadian Studies (1993–1999). A past editor of the *Journal of Canadian Studies*, recipient of the Governor General's International Award for Canadian Studies and of the Order of Canada (CM), she is a fellow of the Royal Society of Canada (FRSC) and a 3M National Teaching Fellow.

Foreword: "Both Feet off the Ground"

Anne Giardini

"A narrative is, well, a story, and a story is—a narrative, of course."
—Carol Shields

It might be said that essays are concerned with facts, and novels with imagination, but I do not believe that my mother, the late writer Carol Shields, would have acceded to these categorizations. Her own essays were highly imaginative—as became clear to me when my son Nicholas Giardini and I edited her essays for *Startle and Illuminate: Carol Shields on Writing* (2016)—and her novels filled with real-world subjects that attracted her lively, deliberative mind.

Her novels were intelligently and playfully self-aware, often breaking any "fourth wall" between the imaginative and the actual, between the invented and the nature of invention. Her books included a fictional biography of a writer, a sustaining friendship between a writer and her translator, and, notably, in *The Stone Diaries*, photographs of real people, including relatives and strangers, who stood up for the book's characters. Her short stories subverted established forms, including the stories she called "little weirdies." She understood that fiction could be at least as complicated and indefinite as actual life. More than once, she told of the freedom she found in the realization that the narrative arc, as taught to students of literature and writing, was as absurd as a spatula. She explains her views in her essay "Boxcars, Coat Hangers and Other Devices":

It wasn't until I had been teaching literature for several years and passing on these inscribed truths to others that I started to lose faith. The diagram, which I had by then drawn on the blackboard perhaps fifty or sixty times, began one day to look like nothing so much as a bent spatula, and yet my students, hunched over the seminar table, were dutifully copying this absurd image into their notes.

Suddenly, I wasn't interested in the problem-solution story I had grown up with. The form seemed crafted out of the old quest myth in which obstacles were overcome and victories realized. None of this seemed applicable to the lives of women, nor to most of the men I knew, whose stories had more to do with the texture of daily life and the spirit of community than with personal battles, goals, mountaintops, and prizes. (*Startle* 27)

Shields opens her essay titled "The Short Story (and Women Writers)" with these words:

When Robert Callasso's book *The Marriage of Cadmus and Harmony* came out, it was interesting to watch editors squirm as they tried to figure out which list to put it on. Fiction or non-fiction, this mix of folklore, history, poetry, narrative, commentary. Which was it? All the above? Or none of the above? (*Startle* 97)

In a 1970s university paper titled "Boundaries: The Writer's Second Self," she wrote that critics and academics who interpreted fiction as autobiography suffered from "an oversimplified view of literature, from a compulsion [...] to categorize the forms of writing and a desire to impose on literature definable and teachable genres." She explained:

If one subscribes to the theory that it is not a writer's self which is revealed in his writing, but a sort of second self, then the onus upon him to distinguish between the separate spheres of fiction and autobiography will all but disappear. At the very least the boundaries will soften to a less arbitrary and more flexible interpretation.

Insight into the inherent flexibility of fiction, a determination to push the spatula to the back of the drawer, and books, including Betty Friedan's *The Feminine Mystique* (1963) and Simone de Beauvoir's *The Second Sex* (1949), alerted Shields to vital material that had been overlooked, minimized, and marginalized. With Marjorie Anderson, she called for women across Canada to write essays for a book that would address, as the publisher's blurb for the first collection of *Dropped Threads* promised, "the holes in the fabric of women's talk of the last thirty or forty years, [the] defining moments in their lives rarely aired in common discourse: truths they had never shared, subjects they hadn't written about before or otherwise found a place for" (n.p.).[1] *Dropped Threads* became a bestseller, and a second collection was published. "Our feeling was that women are so busy protecting themselves and other people that they still feel they have to keep quiet about some subjects," she told Marsha Lederman of *The Globe and Mail* on February 7, 2002.

Everywhere, Shields saw subjects worthy of exploring. She loved to discuss her research and discoveries with friends and her family. In her final weeks, for example, she was reading and thinking about apples, beekeeping, and sonnets—which compared to cutlery drawers, the words lined up in rows. "Think of that rectangle, perfect in its proportions, that plastic cutlery tray in your kitchen drawer, with its sharp divisions for forks, knives, and spoons," she wrote in "Segue," her final, unfinished work of fiction.[2] She was also reading about Iceland, where her mother-in-law had been born, and the Swedish Chicago neighborhood of her own childhood.

My mother's avid interest in the things of the world is evident in the opening pages of "Segue," where her protagonist lists what a sonnet might be about, a list that exemplifies what Marta Dvořák in this volume terms an "amplifying device of chaotic enumeration":

> new and possible subjects: the smell of taxis, the texture of bread, sleep, chewing gum, Picasso, flints and arrowheads, the cello, the shape of coastal islands and the children who are born on islands, cabbage, shingle beaches, feet, Styrofoam, photographs of the newborn as they appear in the newspaper (with sleek seal baby faces stroked in stone). Or a medieval wooden Christ image that Max happened upon at the Art Institute, brooms and brushes and dustpans and the concept of debris (how we half treasure what we can't wait to throw away), a table set for eight (and its companion sestet "Table Set for Seven"), the beauty of coinage when neatly stacked on a counter, urban alleys after dark, and—a mere jump away—the commingling of hollyhocks and overhead wire, and then human faces and their afterimage—an afterimage not being anything like an aura, but possessing a different kind of density altogether. ("Segue" 5)

Granite in *The Stone Diaries*, homelessness in *Unless*, labyrinths in *Larry's Party*, mermaids in *The Republic of Love*—any of these subjects could have been turned by her hand into extended essays. In her novels, in her stories, and in her plays, poetry and essays, she wrote around and under and through her interests, making them deserving of notice, revealing her characters' curiosity, and encouraging our own.

Shields often spoke of a novel's capaciousness. Though she remembered and quoted the warning by, I think, John Updike, that novelists should not allow themselves to be distracted by too much research, that they should be selective, should drop facts into their fiction, as if using tweezers or an eye-dropper, she adored mini-essays in literature, Philip Roth's extended passages on glove making, for example, in his novel *American Pastoral*. Roth had visited Gloversville, New York, once the center of American glove manufacturing, to ensure that his fictional depiction of how gloves were made was accurate. A considerable amount of his research made it into the novel, which some reviewers found excessive, but which Shields applauded and emulated. For *Segue*, she planned to visit Sweden Town in Chicago. Here is a pertinent passage from a 2003 interview with *The Chicago Tribune*:

> Carol Shields wants to see Chicago, the great geographical grab bag of it, the city and its ever-spreading nimbus, from Old Town to Oak Park to Andersonville to Winnetka. As much as she can pack into four days, with dwindling stores of energy.
>
> It is research for her 11th book—a book she never thought she'd live to write—and it is something else as well: a quiet and reflective homecoming for the Pulitzer Prize-winning author who, at sixty-seven, is dying of breast cancer.
>
> "Things do come back to me," Shields says of the Chicago area, which has lived vividly in her memory since she left in 1957, with occasional trips back to visit friends and family members. She hears a certain sound—the clack and roar of an "L" train, for instance, shouldering its way through the city as if it owned the place—or sees a particular image and it all comes back, all of it, the private library of memories that furnishes her mind.

I worked with my mother on a few projects. During a one-week visit in, I believe, the summer of 1984, we wrote a short story together, published as "A Wood" in the collection *Various Miracles* (1985). She set some guidelines before we started. We would each write a page and pass it to the other. The recipient had full editing freedom, and then wrote the next page, and so on back and forth. (She later remembered it slightly differently, that we were limited to making "two or three small changes to each other's pages.") My mother referred to "A Wood" in her essay "The Short

Story (and Women Writers)" as "an odd and slippery story [that] has something of the linguistic roughness you see in translations" (*Startle* 100).

This model of structure and openness is one of the hallmarks of my mother's writing. When we pitched, wrote, and delivered an address together at the Annual General Meeting of the Jane Austen Society of North America held in Richmond, Virginia, in October, 1996, the theme of which was Jane Austen and her Men, John Gray's 1992 book *Men Are from Mars, Women Are from Venus* was still in general currency. We decided to write on whether Gray's Martian archetypes of both men and women could be found in Jane Austen's novels, and we returned to the edit, write, one-page-at-a-time model. As it developed, I remember our delight as we both warmed to and expanded the theme. The talk became a close parsing of how the Austenian women employed the permitted strategies of the time to guide, shape, and interpret relationships.

What I remember from both projects is the almost gleeful shared sense of reaching from time to time a jumping-off point, when we blurred structure or convention, or made a small leap into illogic. There was an unstated agreement to bend the rules, including how we worked together, whenever we wished. I have written previously, in "Reading My Mother," "my mother takes one foot off the ground, rarely both"; these projects represented a chance to step off the earth together.

That image of one foot or both came up in my mother's life in interesting ways. In interviews, my mother spoke of writing while raising children as having one foot in one world and another in the real world.[3] She remembered (and told my father) that the rule in her sorority house when she was an undergraduate was that male visitors had to have one foot on the floor at all times (attesting to a lack of imagination on the part of the rule-makers). She described being both American and Canadian as having a foot on each side of the border.[4] She told Ruth Thomas in an interview, "I felt more playful writing stories. I can do all sorts of things with them, whereas with a novel I'm committing myself to a particular tone or voice or direction—a certain architecture anyway. With stories you can have an idea and spin it around for as long as it will stay aloft. I feel that I am tap-dancing when I write stories. I can get both feet off the ground."[5]

NOTES

1. Publisher's blurb for *Dropped Threads: What We Aren't Told*. Ed. Carol Shields and Marjorie Anderson. Toronto: Vintage 2001, https://www.penguinrandomhouse.ca/books/166009/dropped-threads-by-carol-shields-and-marjorie-anderson/9780679310716
2. For a fuller discussion of Shields's final, unfinished novel *Segue*, see Nora Foster Stovel's essay "'Fragments on My Apple': Carol Shields's Unfinished Novel."
3. *Independent*, July 18, 2003.
4. Mel Gussow, "Artisan of Quiet Crises and the Little Things."
5. Ruth Thomas, *Scottish Book Collector*.

WORKS CITED

Giardini, Anne. "Reading My Mother." *Prairie Fire: a Canadian Magazine of New Writing: Carol Shields*. Ed. Neil Besner and G.N.L. Jonasson. Winnipeg: Prairie Fire Press, vol. 16, no.1 (Spring, 1995): 6–11. Print.

Giardini, Anne, and Nicholas Giardini, Eds. *Startle and Illuminate: Carol Shields on Writing*. Toronto: Random House Canada, 2016. Print.

Gussow, Mel. "Artisan of Quiet Crises and the Little Things." *The New York Times, Books*. May 10, 1995. Print.

Shields, Carol, and Anne Giardini. "Martians in Jane Austen?" Journal of the Jane Austen Society of North America, Persuasions No. 18, 1996. Print. http://www.jasna.org/assets/Persuasions/No-18/3872eb924b/shields-giardini.pdf

Shields, Carol. "Afterword." *Dropped Threads*. Toronto: Vintage Canada, 2001. Print.

———. "Segue." *The Collected Stories*. Toronto: Random House Canada, 2004. 1–20. Print.

———. "The Short Story (and Women Writers)." *Startle and Illuminate: Carol Shields on Writing* (97). Ed. Anne Giardini and Nicholas Giardini. Toronto: Random House Canada, 2016. 97–107. Print.

———. 2003 interview with *The Chicago Tribune*. April 6, 2003 https://www.chicagotribune.com/news/ct-xpm-2003-04-06-0304060497-story.html *Tribune*

Stovel, Nora Foster. "'Fragments on My Apple': Carol Shields's Unfinished Novel." *Canadian Literature* 217 (Summer 2013): 186–96. Print.

Thomas, Ruth. *Scottish Book Collector*, 2000. Print.

Introduction: *Relating Carol Shields's Essays and Fiction: Crossing Borders*

Nora Foster Stovel

Imagine the rejoicing that would ensue if another novel by Jane Austen were discovered. So it is when previously unpublished writing by any beloved author is released. Carol Shields's daughter, novelist Anne Giardini, and grandson, Nicholas Giardini, edited *Startle and Illuminate: Carol Shields on Writing* (2016), with an appropriate quotation by Carol Shields as epigraph: "*I've always believed fiction to be about redemption, about trying to see why people are the way they are.*" It contains essays that chronicle Shields's writerly experience and the advice she gives to aspiring writers, offering them "a handrail to creation," as Aritha van Herk visualizes it.[1] Alex Ramon states, "a study which reads [Shields's] essays and literary criticism *against* rather than *through* her fiction would be especially welcome at this stage [...] since her work anticipates current re-evaluations of postmodernist thought by over twenty years." He claims that Shields produced "a significant body of criticism in which [she] rigorously developed and revised her ideas regarding the function of literary

N. F. Stovel (✉)
University of Alberta, Edmonton, AB, Canada

1

fiction" (Ramon 2008, 178, 176). Although her essays are lesser known than her fiction, Shields's accomplishments in that genre are considerable and offer insights into her objectives as a writer and the innovative ways in which she accomplished them. Thus, Shields's essays can throw valuable light on her fiction, as fourteen distinguished scholars argue in the essays included in this collection.

Part I: Carol Shields's Nonfiction

Carol Shields is most famous as a novelist, and rightly so, but admirers of her fiction may not be aware that she was also a poet, playwright, editor, critic, and biographer. Not only did she compose poems, plays, stories, novels, and biographies, but she also wrote numerous essays, a genre traditionally dominated by male authors, beginning with the sixteenth-century French writer Michel de Montaigne, whose personal and informal French style has been interpreted as "feminine," and late-sixteenth-century English author Sir Francis Bacon, whose more empirical, pragmatic style has been perceived as "masculine," as Christl Verduyn explains in her germinal essay "(Es)saying It Her Way: Carol Shields as Essayist"[2] included in this collection. Verduyn asserts, "Her particular style of essay-writing represents a kind of symbiosis between the broad essay genre and her personal artistic vision," as "Shields moved easily between the Montaigne and Bacon forms of essaying—combining or synthesizing the two traditions" (68). These two forms are inextricably interconnected, especially in Shields's practice, and demand comparison.

In the twentieth century, starting with Virginia Woolf, women writers adopted the essay genre, traditionally employed by male writers, and adapted it for their own purposes. The essay form enabled Canadian women writers—including Margaret Atwood, Margaret Laurence, and Carol Shields—to advocate for issues about which they cared profoundly in a persuasive manner inappropriate, they believed, for fiction, as their essay-writing style is more explicitly political than their fiction.[3] Verduyn claims, "the essay form lends itself to the discourse and practice of feminist writers" (66), as some critics "locate the essay within the poetics of French feminist practice" (64). She argues, "Canadian women's essay-writing deserves as much critical attention as their texts of fiction and poetry," adding, "This is certainly the case for Carol Shields" (61, 67). She concludes, "Shields's accomplishments as an essayist are considerable, though generally under-acknowledged" (75). *Relating Carol Shields's Essays and*

Fiction: Crossing Borders, it is hoped, will help to rectify that neglect and demonstrate the value of Shields's nonfiction in illuminating her fiction, as it reveals her priorities and techniques.

Just as Margaret Laurence began writing essays—such as "Time and the Narrative Voice," "Gadgetry or Growing: Form and Voice in the Novel," and "Ivory Tower or Grass Roots?: The Novelist as Socio-Political Being," collected in *"Recognition and Revelation": Margaret Laurence's Short Nonfiction Writings* (2020)—in order to explain the innovative narrative techniques that she employed in her novels, which proved too experimental for many (mostly male) reviewers—so Carol Shields began writing essays—such as "Writers are Readers First," "Myths That Keep You from Writing," and "The Short Story and Women Writers," collected in *Startle and Illuminate: Carol Shields on Writing*—to explain her rejection of the traditional rules for writing fiction and quest for new forms to trace the "arc of a human life," especially the experience of women. As Shields claims that her aim is to redeem women and their unrecorded lives, so she also aims to create feminine structures to convey that experience. Shields's essays clarify her iconoclastic approach to rules of narrative and illuminate her revisionist policies, elucidating the development of her fiction, both novels and short stories, as her writing gradually becomes more explicitly feminist, as well as more daringly postmodernist.

The term "essay" derives from the French verb *essayer*, meaning to "try" or "attempt," suggesting a form that allows for experimentation, improvisation, and spontaneity, as opposed to strictly regulated literary genres, such as the sonnet, which Shields also revered and practiced.[4] The lack of rigid definitions and clear characteristics for the genre allowed practitioners greater opportunities for experimentation. Verduyn labels the essay an "anti-genre, defying rules and regulations," claiming, "the essay is the most adaptable of all forms" (38). Moreover, "[a] central reason why [Shields] was attracted to the essay genre," Verduyn argues, was that "it allowed her greater freedom, particularly to explore the nature of writing itself." Indeed, the essay form enabled Shields to emphasize the self-reflexive, metafictional nature of writing, to characterize writing as performance, as Marta Dvořák argues in her essay "'Controlled Chaos' and Carol Shields's 'A View from the Edge of the Edge,'" which is included in this collection.

Shields, who began as a child by writing poems and stories, came to the essay genre comparatively late in her writing career. She mentions in a 1997 interview with Eleanor Wachtel about *Larry's Party* that she now plans a new direction for her writing: "I'm interested in other forms of writing now. I'm very interested in *essays, writing about writing, writing about literature.* I hope to write another novel and would like to see that happen, but I am also open to new things now" (*RI* 80, emphasis added). Always interested in "crossing borders"[5]—not only between Canada and the United States, as she herself did and as her characters Daisy Goodwill and Larry Weller do, but also between genres, she challenged tradition. The scholar-critics included in this volume also cross borders between genres, she challenged tradition exploring Shields's nonfiction to discover her views on fiction. Certain of Shields's essays are particularly valuable for this purpose.

Shields was especially creative in adapting the essay genre, as her nonfiction writing ranges from traditional essays for scholarly conferences, through oral addresses, to more personal, creative pieces, often composed for travel or women's magazines, blurring the borders between fiction and nonfiction. As Verduyn argues, "Her essays move fluidly into the realm of fiction, and she makes ready use of the tools and techniques of fiction writing, including characters, dilemmas, metaphor, the narrative pause, exaggeration, word-work or language, and imagination." She concludes, "There is no irreconcilable difference between fact and fiction, between the observable and the speculative in Shields's essays" (74). Indeed, the parallels between Shields's fiction and nonfiction are emphasized by the quotations from her novels that the Giardinis embed in her essays included in *Startle and Illuminate: Carol Shields on Writing.*

In her foreword to *Relating Carol Shields's Essays and Fiction: Crossing Borders,* Anne Giardini addresses the similarities and differences between her mother's writerly practices in her short stories and essays. Carol Shields enjoyed collaborating, perhaps resulting from her experience in theatre, and she collaborated with friends and family members on stories, essays, and plays. Giardini is well positioned to draw such a comparison, as she collaborated with her mother on the story "A Wood" in the 1985 collection *Various Miracles* (109–22)[6] and the essay "Martians in Jane Austen," which they presented dialogically at the 1996 Jane Austen Society of North America annual general meeting and published in *Persuasions,* as she recalls how these two genres overlapped in her mother's writerly practice.

Shields was particularly concerned with the structure of fiction. She begins by viewing the novel in a conventional manner as "a boxed kit" (244), as she recalls in "Arriving Late: Starting Over," but ends by "blurting it all out," like Reta Winters in *Unless* (*Unless* 270), deciding to "Be bold *all the way through*" (*Startle* 146), as she advises students to be.[7]

Shields's journey from boxed kit to brave blurting is a fascinating one. In the following essays fourteen scholars explain, by drawing on the Giardini collection *Startle and Illuminate: Carol Shields on Writing*, as well as previously published essays, how Shields's essays illuminate the revisionist policies of her fiction. She begins by challenging the rules, as her essays reveal.

In "A View from the Edge of the Edge" she celebrates the success of "marginal" writing, as Canadians, Westerners, and women write from the edge, sending "reports from the frontier" of fiction—"fresh news from another country" (*Startle* 35).[8] In "Narrative Hunger and the Overflowing Cupboard," she rails against the regulations regarding the unities and authoritarian restrictions of political correctness, that she calls "relics from the patriarchy" (*Startle* 98), that have governed literary creation for generations and suppressed whole areas of society, including female experience.[9]

Shields's essays reveal her rebellion against the "orgasmic pattern" (*Startle* 99) of the conventional rising and falling line of action, which she compares to a "bent spatula" or perhaps a spent phallus, in favour of the innovative structures she employs in her own novels. She claims that "Women's writing has already begun to dismantle the rigidities of genre [...] and to replace that oppressive narrative arc we've lived with so long, the line of rising action—tumescence, detumescence—what some feminists call the ejaculatory mode of storytelling" (*Startle* 35). She rejects traditional plot: "Resolution in itself began to feel false, the Grail, the Goal (with capital Gs), large noble gestures, sudden blinding insight, an exaggeration and level of heat that is the equivalent of hurled crockery or a burst of sunlight" (*Startle* 98).

In "The New New New Fiction" she addresses the rumored death of the novel and the future of fiction. She believes the novel is alive and well and is in the process of transforming from traditional realism and recent postmodernism into new forms that convey the subjective consciousness—that which cannot be conveyed on the film or television screen:[10] "Diurnal surfaces could be observed by a fiction writer with a kind of deliberate squint that distorts but also sharpens beyond ordinary vision, bringing forward what might be called the subjunctive mode of one's self or others, a world of dreams, possibilities, and parallel realities" (*Startle* 29).

Shields believes that new structures are necessary for the survival of the novel. She explains how she conjured up a visual image or metaphor to provide the structure for her early novels. In "Boxcars, Coat Hangers and Other Devices" (*Startle* 23–30), she explains how she employed the concept of boxcars to organize the nine-month narrative of her first novel *Small Ceremonies* (1976), mirroring the human gestation period, coat hangers to demarcate the week-long action of her second novel, *The Box Garden* (1977), and nesting boxes to visualize the complex narrative method of *The Stone Diaries* (1993)—a technique that contributed to her winning the Governor General's Award for Fiction in Canada and the Pulitzer Prize in the United States for the same novel, namely *The Stone Diaries*, thanks to her dual citizenship.

In "The Love Story" (*Startle* 93–6), Shields advocates for the possibility of romantic love in the contemporary world and stable marriages based on gender equity. This relates to Shields's courtship novel *The Republic of Love* (1987), as Brenda Beckman-Long argues in "Transforming Love: Critical and Religious Discourses in Carol Shields's *The Republic of Love*."

"Where Curiosity Leads" (*Startle* 83–92), drawn from two papers entitled "Others" and "Gender Crossing," relates to Shields's fascination with mazes and her incorporation of them in her popular novel *Larry's Party* (1997), as Warren Cariou's essay "*Larry's Party*: Man in the Maze and 'Where Curiosity Leads'" illustrates. In both "Where Curiosity Leads" and "Narrative Hunger and the Overflowing Cupboard," Shields addresses the relationship between fiction and biography and voices her fascination with the unknowability of others. Indeed, a fixation on the "otherness" of others constitutes the core of *Swann* (1987), as Cynthia Sugars argues in her essay "'The Alchemy of Re-Imagined Reality': Biographical Gothicism in Carol Shields's *Swann: A Mystery*" and as Smaro Kamboureli argues in her essay "In/visibility, Race-Baiting, and the Author Function in Carol Shields's *Unless*," where she addresses the mystery of otherness, realized in the figure of the Muslim woman. *Unless* (2001), Shields's last novel, parallels her essays, as her advice to writers in *Startle and Illuminate* is reflected in her narrator/protagonist Reta Winters's creative writing experience, as Wendy Roy demonstrates in her essay, "Advice to Writers in Carol Shields's *Unless*."

Shields declares, "As a woman who has elected a writing life, I am interested in writing away the invisibility of women's lives, looking at writing as an act of redemption" (*Startle* 105–6), a claim that echoes the epigraph for *Startle and Illuminate*. She redeems those lost, *ordinary* women, whose lives failed to make the public record, in her portrayal of Daisy Goodwill in *The Stone Diaries*, as Christian Riegel demonstrates in his essay on "Shields's Theory of Fiction Writing: Grief and Memorial in *The Stone Diaries.*" In "Reading My Mother" Anne Giardini affirms, "I like to think that, in her books, my mother is providing proof, not only of her lost heroines, but of their importance" (12).

Verduyn's germinal essay, "(Es)saying It Her Way: Carol Shields as Essayist," opens the collection, providing the prologue, as she establishes the background to Shields's own essays so eloquently by explaining the origins of the genre in the writings of seventeenth-century French author Michel de Montaigne, whose creative practice contrasts with sixteenth-century English author Sir Francis Bacon's structured practice, arguing that Shields combines their disparate approaches in her own practice. She summarizes the development of the genre by subsequent writers and analyzes Shields's use of the form, focusing on several texts, including her *Penguin Life of Jane Austen* (2003), which she labels "an extended biographical essay" (71).

PART II: CAROL SHIELDS'S SHORT FICTION

Carol Shields, most famous for her ten novels, published fifty-six stories in three collections—*Various Miracles* (1985), *The Orange Fish* (1989), and *Dressing Up for the Carnival* (2000)—all republished after her death in *The Collected Stories* (2004). Shields's short fiction—beginning with her first collection, *Various Miracles*, which Coral Ann Howells terms, in her essay "Space for Strangeness: Carol Shields's Short Stories" in this collection, "[t]he most experimental of all her writings"—was critical to her development as a novelist because the short form provided her with the freedom for innovation and experimentation that revolutionized her subsequent novels, beginning with her watershed novel *Swann* (1987).

In her essay "The Short Story (and Women Writers)" in *Startle and Illuminate: Carol Shields on Writing* (97–108), Shields recalls her revolution in writing that began with her short stories and defends her innovative, experimental approach to the story genre in *Various Miracles* (1985): "I began in the early eighties, while writing a series of short stories called *Various Miracles*, to swerve away from the easy comfort zone of so-called epiphanies that accounted for the traditional rondure of short stories, those abrupt but carefully prepared-for lurches toward awareness, the manipulative wrap-up that arrived like a hug in the final paragraph"

(*Startle* 98). She describes the variety of denouements with which she experimented:

> I wanted stories that soared off into mystery and disruption, not mere flat openness but a spiraling into space or a melting into another narrative as happens at the end of a story I wrote titled "Home." Or I would fast-forward the final paragraph into the future, something that occurs in another story called "Flitting Behaviour." Or dive with it into the past, which is the kind of ending that occurs in a piece called "Scenes." I wanted these endings to hold an aesthetic surprise that spun *off* the narrative, but wasn't necessarily generated *out* of it. (*Startle* 99)

As Anne Giardini recalls in her engaging Foreword to this edition, Shields told Ruth Thomas in an interview, "I felt more playful writing stories. I can do all sorts of things with them, whereas with a novel I'm committing myself to a particular tone or voice or direction—a certain architecture anyway. With stories you can have an idea and spin it around for as long as it will stay aloft. I feel that I am tap-dancing when I write stories. I can get both feet off the ground."

She discusses the manner in which she deviated from the story's conventional structure: "I tried in the short story 'Scenes' to dislocate the spine of a traditional story, that holy line of rising action that is supposed to lead somewhere important, somewhere inevitable, modelled perhaps on the orgasmic pattern of tumescence followed by detumescence, an endless predictable circle of desire, fulfillment, and quiescence" (*Startle* 99). She comments in her essay "The Short Story (and Women Writers)" in *Startle and Illuminate: Carol Shields on Writing*, "I was for some reason drawn to randomness and disorder, not circularity or narrative cohesion. In fact, I had observed how the human longing for disruption was swamped in fiction by an almost mechanical model of aesthetic safety" (*Startle* 99). Marta Dvořák addresses Shields's predilection for randomness and disorder effectively in her essay included in this collection.

Focus on female experience requires feminine structures. Shields explains the influence of female discourse on the structure of her stories: "I had started in the early 80s to pay attention to the way in which women, sitting around a table for instance, tell each other stories. I noticed that they dealt in the episodic, and tended to suppress what was smoothly linear, to set up digressions, little side stories, often of a genealogical nature, which were not really digressions at all but integral parts of the story, to throw into the kitty" (*Startle* 99–100). Shields adopts that digressive structure in her stories very successfully.

This edition of essays by distinguished Shields scholars pays tribute to what Shields terms "the collective nature of stories" (*Startle* 100). It includes essays by Neil Besner on the sense of playfulness evinced in her stories from "Various Miracles" in her first collection to "Absence" in her last; by Coral Ann Howells on transcendence in stories from *Various Miracles* and *The Orange Fish*; by Nora Foster Stovel on Shields's improvisational, "What-if" stories in *Dressing Up for the Carnival*; and by Marta Dvořák on Shields's love of randomness in her short fiction, also progressing from "Various Miracles" in her first collection to "Absence" in her last. Each critic applies the principles expressed in various Shields essays to illumine her short fiction.

In his essay, "The Short of It: Carol Shields's Stories," Neil Besner claims Shields's stories demonstrate experimentation, playfulness, and performativity. In her essay "Space for Strangeness: Carol Shields's Short Stories," Coral Ann Howells explains how Shields's stories in both *Various Miracles* and *The Orange Fish* allow us to enter "a world of dreams and possibilities and parallel realities." In "'Be a Little Crazy; Astonish Me': Carol Shields's Improvisational Flair in *Dressing Up for the* Carnival" Nora Foster Stovel suggests that the improvisational techniques in Shields's stories are inspired by her experience of teaching creative writing, as recorded in her essay "Be a Little Crazy; Astonish Me" (*Startle* 37–48) and as illustrated by her several "what-if" stories in her last collection, *Dressing Up for the Carnival* (2000). In "'Controlled Chaos' and Carol Shields's 'A View from the Edge of the Edge,'" Marta Dvořák focuses on certain features of chaotics that she argues are operative in Shields's oeuvre, questioning why a writer who likes to investigate connections and correspondences should cultivate randomness, if not the better to flaunt her control. Drawing on "A View," Dvořák applies Shields's love of the random to stories from "Various Miracles" in her first collection to "Absence" in her last.

In describing the author as "Shields Ludens" and exploring the performative elements of her stories in his essay, "The Short of It: Carol Shields's Stories," Besner asserts, "I am not aware of a contemporary writer of stories who more cheerfully, coyly, cunningly and slyly has had such serious and continuing fun with the form." He shows "how, throughout her career, she deployed the story form and its resources for important ends: first, experiment and serious play; and second, the crafted revelation, often surprising, of isolated characters in isolated moments." He argues that her stories form a distinctive constituent of her fictional idiom and resonate with her novels in form, style, and substance. He concludes that "renewed and more careful attention to Shields's short stories—which she wrote throughout her long career—can bring new light, an enlarged understanding of all of Shields's work" (49–50).

In her essay "Space for Strangeness: Carol Shields's Short Stories"[11] Coral Ann Howells argues that, for Shields, the value of stories is that they widen our angle of imaginative vision, allowing us to move beyond the limits of dailiness into "a world of dreams and possibilities and parallel realities." Shields's essay "Narrative Hunger" offers a metafictional commentary on the human desire for stories and the role of the storyteller, who, through narrative artifice, offers a glimpse of the extraordinary within the ordinary. In her short story experiments Shields plays across the boundaries between realism, fantasy, and myth, refocusing realism to accommodate epiphanic moments of imaginative transcendence of ordinariness. Howells shows how two stories—"Home" from *Various Miracles* and "Hinterland" from *The Orange Fish*—illustrate how Shields constructs these spaces for strangeness within her narrative frame as she meshes mythic patterns into a network of contemporary human relationships. In "Home," she uses the Ulysses myth and Langland's *Piers Plowman* as her intertexts, while "Hinterland" figures the Christian mythology around the Virgin Mary—one featuring the "miracle" of a translucent aeroplane and the other a little golden statue of a "*Vierge Ouvrante*" in a Paris museum. These apparently fragmented narratives, with their shadowy mythic parallels and shifting angles of subjective vision, manage to relocate everyday experience in a different dimension through their self-conscious revisioning of myths in a postmodern secular age.

In "'Be a Little Crazy; Astonish Me': Carol Shields's Improvisational Flair in *Dressing Up for the* Carnival," Nora Foster Stovel argues that improvisational techniques in Shields's stories are inspired by her experience of teaching creative writing, as expressed in her essay titled "Be a Little Crazy; Astonish Me" in *Startle and Illuminate* (37–46). Shields's last collection of short stories, *Dressing Up for the Carnival*, includes several "what-if" stories—including "Weather," "Windows," "Reportage," "Stop!," and "Absence"—that read like improvisations. For example, what if there were a tax on windows or what if all the meteorologists went on strike and there were no weather? This improvisational quality reflects Shields's role as a teacher of creative writing courses—an experience reflected in "Chemistry," wherein Shields transforms her creative writing course into a recorder course.[12] Her students recall that Shields assigned improvisations, such as "'Write an entire story in a single sentence,'" in her creative writing courses, as she confirms in "Be a Little Crazy; Astonish Me" and as her creative writing teaching notes in the National Library confirm, as she lists topics, such as a missing letter on a typewriter, that correspond to stories in *Dressing Up For the Carnival.* This "what-if" world opens up alternative dimensions—the "subjunctive" mode that Shields terms "a world of dreams, possibilities, and parallel realities" (*Startle* 29)—worlds that she creates in her stories.

In her essay "'Controlled Chaos' and Carol Shields's 'A View from the Edge of the Edge,'" Marta Dvořák argues that Shields provides valuable perceptions on marginalization in multiple fields, from place and gender to language and (national) literature. Questioning the limits of our conceptual frameworks of reference, she dwells on notions whose interconnections roil beneath the surface: freedom and control, constraint and invention, reading and writing, the "cross-network of influences," and metafiction. Her essay investigates to what extent Shields's reflections, suffused with colliding centripetal and centrifugal tensions, are operative in her fiction with its rhetorical and aesthetic agendas. Through multiple micro-analyses, the discussion engages with certain features of chaotics and illuminates the way they inform her textual process. The rhetorical devices Shields artfully deploys are shown to range from chaotic enumeration and vertical pile-ups of repetition and variation to embedded perspectives and even the disruptive parenthesis and the odd man out.

PART III: CAROL SHIELDS'S LATER NOVELS

Relating Carol Shields's Essays and Fiction: Crossing Borders includes several essays on Shields's novels, wherein authors Cynthia Sugars, Christian Riegel, Warren Cariou, Wendy Roy, and Smaro Kamboureli read her novels through the lens of her nonfiction. It contains six essays on Shields's most highly regarded novels, including, in chronological order of their publication, *Swann: A Mystery, The Republic of Love, The Stone Diaries, Larry's Party,* and *Unless.*

In her essay "Open Every Question, Every Possibility," Shields attempted to define the novel in response to current arguments about the death of the novel, a form that she argued was alive and well: "We may not know exactly what a novel is, but there are certain characteristics of the novel as we know it and write it—that is, the novel that went off like a firecracker in 1740 and that continues to be, in our society anyway, the literary form of choice." She identifies some of the characteristics, such as "a texture that approximates the world as we know it," "Characters who in their struggles with the world resemble ourselves," "Dilemmas that remind us of our own predicaments," "Scenes that trigger our memories or tap into our yearnings," and "Conclusions that shorten the distance between what is privately felt and universally known, so that we look up from the printed page and say, 'Ahah!'" (*Startle* 118–9).

In *Northanger Abbey,* Jane Austen, about whom Shields published a literary biography, *Jane Austen: A Life,* defends the novel, still a relatively new form in her era, against the defamations of its critics, as "some work in which the greatest powers of the mind are displayed, in which the most thorough knowledge of human nature, the happiest delineation of its varieties, the liveliest effusions of wit and humour are conveyed to the world in the best chosen language" (*NA* 38). In her last novel, *Unless* (2001), Shields offers her own definition of the novel, as her heroine writer Reta Winters reflects:

> I thought I understood something of a novel's architecture, the lovely slope of predicament, the tendrils of surface detail, the calculated curving upward into inevitability, yet allowing spells of incorrigibility, and then the ending, a corruption of cause and effect and the gathering together of all the characters into a framed operatic circle of consolation and ecstasy, backlit with fibre-optic gold, just for a moment on the second-to-last page, just for an atomic particle of time. (*Unless* 13)

We can observe the new freedom to experiment with innovative structures that Shields learned by composing her short stories for *Various Miracles* in her subsequent novel, *Swann.* In "'The Alchemy of Re-Imagined Reality': Biographical Gothicism in Carol Shields's *Swann: A Mystery,*"[13] Cynthia Sugars argues, drawing on Shields's essay "To Write Is to Raid" (*Startle* 34–35), that Shields's 1987 novel *Swann: A Mystery* offers a parodic take on the interrelations of biography and fiction, a topic central to many of Shields's published meditations on the art of writing. This self-reflexive interest in biographers and writers informed her fascination with the sheer unknowability of others. Indeed, a fixation on the "otherness" of others constitutes the core of *Swann: A Mystery.* Here, academics and biographers gather to discuss the life and oeuvre of another "othered" and fictionally disguised figure—that of Mary Swann herself.

This elusiveness of the fictional biographical subject is echoed, Sugars argues, on a metatextual level, as the novel plays with two Canadian literary intertexts: the fictional poetess of Paul Hiebert's 1947 novel, Sarah Binks, and the real-life poet of the 1970s, Pat Lowther. In its portrayal of the academics and biographers who grapple over the reputation of Mary Swann, the novel offers a satirical reworking, 40 years later, of the early Canadian literary satire by Hiebert, *Sarah Binks*, about the fictional and dubiously talented "songstress of Saskatchewan." Shields's Mary Swann also conjures elements of the real-life poet Pat Lowther, she argues, who, like Swann, was violently murdered by her husband in 1975. The multiple levels of biographical disguise in *Swann* are tantalizing, as Shields tackles questions of literary influence and biographical fictionalization, particularly as she conjures the ghosts of Canadian literary predecessors through her presentation of the uncanny bio-critical afterlife of Mary Swann.

Drawing on Shields's essay "The Love Story," Brenda Beckman-Long argues, in "Transforming Love: Critical and Religious Discourses in Carol Shields's *The Republic of Love*," that Shields parodies the romance novel to explore embodied language and evolving feminisms. She claims that Shields also participates in both a critical turn and a religious turn in literature. In "The Love Story," Shields traces an enlarged vision of love to the Venerable Bede, and, in her novel, she interrogates autonomous selfhood by exposing what René Girard calls the imitative nature of desire. In a feminist double strategy, she undermines individual autonomy and original desire as symptomatic of middle-class romanticism. In a collage of religious and secular discourses, the novel troubles binary oppositions of the sacred and profane, masculine and feminine, language and the body. Beckman-Long sees Shields as a writer-critic, who enacts a renewal of the love story and an ethical call for love in action.

In his essay on "Shields's Theory of Fiction Writing: Grief and Memorial in *The Stone Diaries*" Christian Riegel considers Shields's theories of fiction writing, as expressed in her essays, especially "Open Every Question, Every Possibility," in relation to the ways that she articulates grieving and memorializing in *The Stone Diaries*. Shields is interested in engaging the complex possibilities of fiction to underscore the notion of the transformative female imagination as it relates to details of the quotidian lives of her characters and emphasizes the metafictional, postmodern, and female, in particular. Shields suggests a theory of how fiction writing might extend beyond her theories of fictionality, the postmodern, and the feminine, as conveyed in her essays. Just as she resituates ideas about how women's fictional autobiography functions, she also transfigures conventional ele-giac writing to define the fraught nature of the way women deal with death in the mid-to-late twentieth century. She thus engages the funda-mental nature of what happens when grief is experienced, when the dead are remembered, and what role language plays in these events.

Warren Cariou, in "Man in the Maze: 'Where Curiosity Leads' and *Larry's Party*" engages with the symbolic resonances of the maze motif in Carol Shields's penultimate novel, arguing that Shields's implicit compari-son of maze-maker and novelist presents a compelling statement of post-modern aesthetics and gender politics. Inspired by Shields's experiments in bio-fiction, Cariou takes an autobiographical approach to the reading of this text, exploring its relationship to his own life and writing. He argues that Larry's dinner party at the end of the novel is a playful thought exper-iment in gender roles, presenting a male character who gradually takes on a persona reminiscent of Virginia Woolf's Mrs. Dalloway. Larry's (stereo) typical maleness, which is on display in many other parts of the book, is rendered unstable by his hosting of the eponymous party. However, other aspects of the novel's ending—especially the reunion of Larry and Dorrie at the conclusion of the party—raise the spectre of contrivance and autho-rial intrusion. Nonetheless, what may seem to be an aesthetic flaw of the book (a sentiment that Shields herself later expressed) is also a valuable opportunity to explore the meaning of contrivance within a postmodern view of the subject. The essay concludes with an examination of the inter-connectedness of contrivance and happenstance: two poles of readerly engagement with the themes of fate and embodied identity that resonate throughout *Larry's Party*.

Wendy Roy argues in her "Advice to Writers in Carol Shields's *Unless*," that, while Shields's advice to writers is most clearly articulated in *Startle and Illuminate: Carol Shields on Writing* (2016), she has a long history of writing and speaking about what it means to be a writer, in interviews and speeches, and also in her fiction. One of Shields's most sustained discus-sions of writing is in her final novel, *Unless* (2002). *Unless* incorporates evocative descriptions of the techniques and importance of writing, includ-ing narrator Reta Winters's opening disquisition on "a novel's architec-ture" (13) and her conclusion that "[t]his matters, the remaking of an untenable world through the nib of a pen" (208). Much of the latter half of *Unless* focuses on Reta's construction of characters and plot lines for her new novel, including guidance on how to construct a sequel.[14] It also explores how *not* to give advice, through the character of her new editor,

Arthur Springer. Reta's advice to herself in *Unless*, and her repudiation of the misguided recommendations of her editor, together constitute Shields's own best guidance to writers. Her final novel is a polemic that can be read in conjunction with her essays as a nurturance of the craft and politics of writing both for writers of fiction and for academics who study Shields's fiction. Roy argues, "*Unless* can be read in conjunction with her essays, interviews, and letters, and with some of her previous works of fiction, as encouragement in the craft and politics of writing. This encouragement is of value both to writers of fiction and to writers of academic studies" (189).

In "In/visibility, Race-Baiting, and the Author Function in Carol Shields's *Unless*," Smaro Kamboureli, drawing on Shields's essay "Writing from the Edge," reads *Unless* as a text that constructs the Muslim woman as an authorial ruse in order to both raise and problematize matters of "race." Keeping in mind Shields's views about writing, and distinguishing between the novel's historical author and the author as inscribed in the text, Kamboureli focuses on the technologies of visuality and control that comprise the protagonist's first-person narrative, but also on the ways in which they are ironically inversed by the author function. It is this reversal, she argues, that both questions and upholds the narrator's representations of otherness. With particular emphasis on how the narrator visualizes her household, as well as Toronto's urban imaginary (where her daughter and the Muslim woman are situated), as panoptical and circumscribed constructs, she reads the Muslim woman's minimalist representation as a calculated manifestation of authorial agency designed at once to lure critical attention and to put Canadian civility to the test.

Shields emphasizes the inextricable connection between reading and writing in her essay "Writers Are Readers First" (*Startle* 1–14), while Beckman-Long portrays her as a writer-critic.[15] Inevitably, Shields's writing was greatly influenced by her reading. In her essay "The Writing Life" she reveals the writer's vulnerability to harsh reviews and declines to reveal "a glint of the fang" in her reviews of other writers' books. In his Afterword, "'Little Shocks of Recognition': Carol Shields's Book Reviews," Alex Ramon addresses a thus-far neglected aspect of Shields's non-fiction writing: the book reviews that she produced between the late 1970s and early 2000s. Published initially in academic journals and then in national and international periodicals, as her own literary fame grew, Shields's reviews constitute a significant part of her non-fiction output, offering a valuable insight into her engagement with the work of her contemporaries, and often illuminating the concerns of her own fiction. Opening with an overview of Shields's reviewing, including her evolving methodology, Ramon's essay then focuses on Shields's critiques of three non-fiction texts by American women writers: Annie Dillard's *An American Childhood* (1987), Erica Jong's *Fear of Fifty: A Midlife Memoir* (1994), and Ruby Side Thompson's diaries, edited and published as *Ruby: An Ordinary Woman* (1995). Ramon illustrates how Shields's contrasting responses to these texts illuminate the concerns with the genre of life-writing and the trope of "ordinariness" that permeate her own fiction.

In her interview with Harvey De Roo, Shields declares, "I especially love rewriting" (54). She affirms in a July 13, 1996 letter to Blanche Howard about revising *Larry's Party* (1997), "This tinkering/polishing/pressing period is something I look forward to enormously" (*MF* 335). She figures "mending" her portrait of Jack Bowman in *Happenstance* (1980) as going over her text with a darning needle (Wachtel 33), polishing her portrayal of Larry Weller in *Larry's Party* (1997) as smoothing it with "a small piece of sandpaper" (*Startle* 89), and revising *Unless* (2001) as picking it apart with a small pair of gold tweezers—all gender-specific metaphors of revision. Aritha van Herk's epilogue, "Etching on Glass: Carol Shields's Re-Vision," addresses Shields as a writer, reader, revisionist, and creative writing teacher in terms of the metaphor of "etching." Through an exploratory close reading and ficto-critical response to Anne and Nicolas Giardini's 2016 edition of Shields's comments on writing gathered in *Startle and Illuminate: Carol Shields on Writing,* she explores how to implement the wisdom and experience of this dexterous writer.

Although these scholars of Canadian literature hail from many centres in Canada and indeed the world, they all have one thing in common: their admiration for the writing of Carol Shields. All their essays throw fresh light on Shields's work, inviting us to read it with new eyes.

The perceptive papers of these fourteen contributors explore Shields's own nonfiction writings to reveal how they reflect and illuminate the brilliance of her fiction.

NOTES

1. In her story "Dying for Love" in *Dressing Up for the Carnival* (2000) Shields's suicidal heroine clings to a "slender handrail of hope" (48). In her "Introduction: Potluck" to *Carol Shields: Evocation and Echo,* van Herk coins the phrase "a handrail to creation" (4).

2. This essay was first published in *Carol Shields and the Extra-Ordinary* edited by Marta Dvořák and Manina Jones for McGill-Queen's U P in 2007 on pages 59–79.

3. The essays of Margaret Atwood, including those in her collection *Negotiating with the Dead: A Writer on Writing*, exemplify the range of her non-fiction, as it applies to her own fiction.

4. See *The Collected Poetry of Carol Shields* (2021) edited by Nora Foster Stovel.

5. Shields employs this phrase in her essay "The Short Story (and Women Writers)" (*Startle* 103). Please see Nora Foster Stovel's essay, "'American or Canadian': Carol Shields's Border Crossings" in *A Review of Canadian Studies in the United States* 40. 4 (December 2010): 517–29. Print.

6. Anne Giardini composed "A Wood" as a sequel to the original story for *Carol Shields: Evocation and Echo.*

7. The narrator in *Unless* echoes these sentiments: "I am willing to blurt it all out, if only to myself. Blurting is a form of bravery. I'm just catching on to that fact. Arriving late, as always" (270). "Be bold all the way through" is the title of a chapter in *Startle and Illuminate: Carol Shields on Writing* (141–8) and echoes the advice she gave to her writing students.

8. "A View from the Edge" was delivered as an address at Harvard University in 1997 and published in *Carol Shields and the Extra-Ordinary*, edited by Marta Dvořák and Manina Jones in 2007. It is partially included in "Writers Are Readers First" in *Startle and Illuminate: Carol Shields on Writing* (1–14).

9. "Narrative Hunger and the Overflowing Cupboard" was previously published in *Carol Shields, Narrative Hunger, and the Possibilities of Fiction*, edited by Edward Eden and Dee Goertz. In the Giardini edition, previously published essays are often given new names that lead us to read familiar essays with new eyes. For example, "Open Every Question, Every Possibility" (*Startle* 115–30) is a retitling of "Narrative Hunger and the Overflowing Cupboard"; "Writing from the Edge" (*Startle* 131–40) is a retitling of "A View from the Edge of the Edge," and "Writing What We've Discovered—So Far" (*Startle* 109–14) was originally titled "The New New New Fiction."

10. In "'Controlled Chaos' and Carol Shields's 'A View from the Edge of the Edge'" Marta Dvořák refers to "the modernist and postmodern break with realism and its rule of plausibility."

11. Howell's essay was first published under the title "Space for Strangeness: Carol Shields's Short Stories" in *Open Letter* 13.2 (Spring 2007): 40–51. It has been substantially revised.

12. In my May 2003 interview with Shields, she told me that, in her first class at the University of Ottawa, a night course in creative writing, she had a class of "mature" women and "puerile" men—so different that she thought

the room would overbalance. She said she was rather "school-marmish" at first. Her story "Chemistry" was inspired by this class, although she altered the course subject matter from a creative writing class to a class in playing the recorder. She remained friends with some of the women who kept in touch with her and also kept on writing. Later, she taught creative writing for one year at the University of British Columbia.

13. Sugars's chapter is a substantially revised reprint of an essay first published in *The Worlds of Carol Shields*, edited by David Staines (2014).

    Cariou's chapter is a substantially revised reprint of "Larry's Party: Man in the Maze" published in *Carol Shields: The Arts of a Writing Life*.

14. See Wendy Roy's "Revisiting the Sequel: Carol Shields's Companion Novels."

15. Beckman-Long is the author of *Carol Shields and the Writer-Critic* (2015).

Works Cited

Atwood, Margaret. "*Orientation*: Who do you think you are?" *Negotiating with the Dead: A Writer on Writing*. Cambridge: Cambridge UP, 2011. 1–28. Print.

Austen, Jane. *Northanger Abbey* in *The Novels of Jane Austen*, ed. R. W. Chapman. 3rd ed., rpt., 5 vols. London: Oxford UP, 1933, rpt. 1965. Print.

Beckman-Long, Brenda. *Carol Shields and the Writer-Critic*. Toronto: University of Toronto Press, 2015. Print.

De Roo, Harvey. "A Little Like Flying: An Interview with Carol Shields." *West Coast Review*, vol. 23, no. 3 (winter, 1988): 21–56. Print.

Giardini, Anne, and Nicholas. *Startle and Illuminate: Carol Shields on Writing*. Toronto: Random House Canada, 2016. Print.

Giardini, Anne. "Reading My Mother." *Prairie Fire: a Canadian Magazine of New Writing: Carol Shields*. Ed. Neil Besner and G.N.L. Jonasson. Winnipeg: Prairie Fire Press, vol. 16, no.1 (Spring, 1995): 6–11. Print.

Howard, Blanche, and Allison Howard. *A Memoir of Friendship: The Letters between Carol Shields and Blanche Howard*. Toronto: Viking Canada, 2007. Print.

Howells, Coral Ann. "In the Subjunctive Mood: Carol Shields's *Dressing Up for the Carnival*." *Yearbook of English Studies* 31 (2001): 144–54.

Laurence, Margaret. "'Recognition and Revelation': Margaret Laurence's Short Nonfiction Writings*. Ed. Nora Foster Stovel. Montreal: McGill-Queen's UP, 2020. Print.

Roy, Wendy. "Revisiting the Sequel: Carol Shields's Companion Novels." *The Worlds of Carol Shields*. Ed. David Staines, Ottawa, ON: Ottawa UP, 2014. 63–79. Print.

Shields, Carol, and Anne Giardini. "Martians in Jane Austen?" *Persuasions: Journal of the Jane Austen Society of North America* 18 (1996): 191–203. Print.

Shields, Carol. "Afterword" to *Dropped Threads: What We're Not Told*. Ed. Carol Shields and Marjorie May Anderson. Toronto: Vintage Canada, 2001a. Print.

———. "Arriving Late: Starting Over." *How Stories Mean*. Ed. John Metcalf and J. R. Struthers. Erin: Porcupine's Quill, 1993. 87–90 and 244–51. Print.

———. "Carol Shields: About Writing." *The Arts of a Writing Life*. Ed. Neil K. Besner. Winnipeg: Prairie Fire Press, 1995, 261–2. Print.

———. "Be bold *all the way through*" (*Startle* 146). Print.

———. "Chemistry." *The Orange Fish: The Collected Stories*. Toronto: Random House Canada, 2004a. 228–247. Print.

———. "Coming to Canada—Age Twenty-Two" in *Coming to Canada: Poems*. Ottawa, Canada: Carleton University Press, 1992: 27. Print.

———. "Dying for Love." *Dressing Up for the Carnival: The Collected Stories*. Toronto: Random House Canada, 2004b. 431–439. Print.

———. *Jane Austen: A Life*. New York: Viking, 2001b. Print.

———. "Narrative Hunger and the Overflowing Cupboard" in *Carol Shields, Narrative Hunger, and the Possibilities of Fiction*. Ed. Edward Eden and Dee Goertz. Toronto, ON: U of Toronto P, 2003. 19–36. Print.

———. "The Short Story (and Women Writers)." *Startle and Illuminate: Carol Shields on Writing*. Ed. Anne Giardini and Nicholas Giardini. Toronto: Random House Canada, 2016. (97–107). Print.

———. *Unless*. London; New York: Fourth Estate, 2002. Print.

———. "A View from the Edge of the Edge." *Carol Shields and the Extra-Ordinary*. Ed. Marta Dvořák and Manina Jones. Montreal, QC: McGill-Queen's UP, 2007. 17–29. Print.

Van Herk, Aritha. "Introduction: Potluck." *Carol Shields: Evocation and Echo*. Ed. Aritha van Herk and Connie Marcuse. Groningen: Barkhuis, 2009. 1–5, Print.

Stovel, Nora Foster. "'American or Canadian': Carol Shields's Border Crossings." *A Review of Canadian Studies in the United States* 40. 4 (December 2010): 517–29. Print.

———. *The Collected Poetry of Carol Shields*. Ed. Nora Foster Stovel. Montreal: McGill-Queen's University Press, 2021. Print.

———. *"Recognition and Revelations": Margaret Laurence's Essays*. Ed. Nora Foster Stovel. Montreal: McGill-Queen's U P, 2020. Print.

———. *Relating Carol Shields Essays and Fiction: Crossing Borders*. Ed. Nora Foster Stovel. London: Palgrave Macmillan, 2022. Print.

Verduyn, Christl, "(Es)saying It Her Way: Carol Shields as Essayist." *Carol Shields and the Extra-Ordinary*. Ed Marta Dvořák and Manina Jones. Montreal and Kingston: McGill-Queen's U P, 2007. 59–79. Reprinted in *Relating Carol Shields's Essays and Fiction: Crossing Borders*. Edited by Nora Foster Stovel. Print.

Wachtel, Eleanor. *Random Illuminations: Conversations with Carol Shields*. Fredericton, N.B.: Goose Lane Editions, 2007. Print.

Prologue: (Es)Saying It Her Way: Carol Shields as Essayist

Christl Verduyn

Carol Shields was widely recognized as a talented, imaginative, and accomplished novelist, playwright, and poet. It is not as well appreciated, however, that she was also an extremely competent and proficient essayist. What attracted her to this form of writing? What was she trying to accomplish in her essays such that she added the genre to her literary repertoire? What was the relationship between her essay-writing and the other genres she practiced with so much success?

One of Shields's last and most substantial writing accomplishments was a Penguin Life of Jane Austen. Her decision to take on this project was somewhat surprising, given her views on the limits of the biographical form. Indeed, Shields was asked about this issue directly in a BBC radio interview in 2001. Her reply offers an insight into what attracted her to the essay form. "I thought of it as an essay," Shields explained, "with a biographical spine, and along the way I would talk about novels in general, novels of [Austen's] time, the writer's dilemma, particularly their day to day problems as fiction makers."[1]

C. Verduyn (✉)
Mount Allison University, Sackville, NB, Canada

© The Author(s), under exclusive license to Springer Nature
Switzerland AG 2023
N. F. Stovel (ed.), *Relating Carol Shields's Essays and Fiction*,
https://doi.org/10.1007/978-3-031-11480-9_2

This reply points us very much to "Shields territory"—the demands of writing, the details of writers' everyday lives, the exploration of the ordinary and the quotidian. Shields's genius and success lay in her exceptional capacity to synthesize the mundane with the profound and the ordinary with the extraordinary, in compelling, insightful, and satisfying ways. She used the essay form in a unique and expansionary manner. It offered her another highly flexible mode of writing to reflect on and explore connections and contradictions in human experience. Her particular style of essay-writing represents a kind of symbiosis between the broad essay genre and her personal artistic vision. The essay form lent itself extremely well to her writing skills and, in particular, to her belief in the centrality of story or narrative to life and to its artistic representation. Shields's essays are convincing examples of Graham Good's sense of the essay as a sort of "non-fictional cognate of certain kinds of fiction."[2]

In this chapter I will consider and assess Shields's work as an essayist by focusing on four of her publications: "Eros" in the collection *Desire in Seven Voices* (1999), edited by Lorna Crozier; Shields's "Afterword" in both volumes of *Dropped Threads: What We Aren't Told* (2001, 2003), which she co-edited with Marjorie Anderson; her award-winning biographical essay *Jane Austen* (2001); and "Narrative Hunger and the Overflowing Cupboard" (2003).[3] I will begin by sketching out a theoretical and intellectual context for the consideration and assessment of Shields's work as an essayist. Even a brief exploration of the essay as genre will reveal why, like many writers, Carol Shields was drawn to the form. This introductory framework will allow us to consider her work as an essayist from gender and political perspectives. Shields's use of the essay deftly combines or synthesizes what have historically been two competing historical traditions in essay writing.

THE ESSAY: CONCEPTUAL AND HISTORICAL FRAMEWORK

Assessments of the essay form have been infused with controversy, contradiction, and condescension. Indeed, one of the great ironies of considering the genre is this: while it is widely regarded as inferior in status to the novel, poetry, drama, and other literary forms, its practitioners have included some of the most influential thinkers of all time. Until recently, these practitioners have appeared to be predominantly men. This phenomenon has conferred a particular political resonance upon the essay in some quarters. What is generally accepted, though, is that in its history, evolution, and form, the essay has suffered from a kind of shapelessness. This negative impression—unfair, in many ways—has historical as well as conceptual roots.

The essay as genre has twin origins and adherents, one stemming from a personal and informal French tradition and the other from a more formal and empiricist English tradition. The interplay of these two traditions has generated a dynamic or dialectic, which mirrors the tension between Continental and Anglo-American empirical philosophy, with both negative and positive effects. On the one hand, the tension between the traditions has generated the impression of the essay's shapelessness, alluded to earlier. On the other hand, it has also created tremendous opportunities—political and otherwise—for experimentation and innovation in writing.

The origins of the essay lie in France, and first its practitioner was the sixteenth-century French writer Michel de Montaigne. Indeed, the very word itself—essay—is derived from the French. The verb *essayer* means to try or to attempt something. In 1580, Montaigne published a collection of writings entitled *Essais* in which he "tried" to express in prose his thoughts and feelings on a variety of different subjects. These writings or essays very much comprised an exercise in "giving it a try" or "having a say" on a number of subjects, which gave them a distinctly exploratory feel, form, and character. This style of writing was not unrelated to the substance of the issues or matters being discussed. Indeed, the latter more or less demanded the former. As in other transformative historical epochs, changed circumstances demanded changed modes of analysis and articulation if the new world was to be penetrated with any insight. Montaigne was a writer shaped by the Renaissance and the society in which he lived. His writings examined and interrogated the various political, religious, and scientific paradigm shifts of that era. The essay form allowed him the space and freedom to do so, unconstrained by traditional rules and expectations of writing. Montaigne adopted a highly personal and informal approach, infusing his writing about the era with his own experiences of the changing times. In this way, life and writing, content and form, converged in the new activity of "essaying." Graham Good's characterization effectively evokes this accomplishment: the Montaigne essay comprised "testing and tasting one's own life while experiencing it"; thus, "the essay [w]as a sample of the self" (Good 32).

Montaigne's essays were very much an exercise in "having a try." They were personal and informal in style. In this, his essays marked a radical departure from the prescribed forms of classical rhetoric of his day. What made the essays compelling and convincing—what gave them their "authority"—was the very experience upon which the text was based, which in turn encouraged a certain kind of format. The essays had a more "natural" form. This defied the limiting demands and constraints of traditional writing, such as unity in format, consistency in presentation and argumentation, and even relevance to the moment. The new form of writing was decidedly experimental for the times. It submitted to the essayist's flow of thought at the moment. Thus, it embraced spontaneity in expression and in formulation. The essay offered liberation from a linear format and argumentation and provided a more free-form presentation that allowed unconventional connections of facts, arguments, and speculations. Indeed, the essay's speculative character was a substantive feature in itself. The essay did not have to bring "closure" to a subject. The exploration itself could be the substance of the essay. The emphasis was squarely on process and exploration, rather than a necessary conclusion.

Montaigne's essay style has come into and gone out of favor over the years. That it has done so is not surprising for such a radical and personal approach. On the one hand, critics have offered both formal and political objections. Many have complained that the Montaigne essay is self-indulgent—overly focused on the personal and under-concerned about facts. Others have seen the personal essay as being essentially apolitical and insufficiently attentive to the larger social, economic, and political forces that should inform any argument or assessment if it is to have any relevance or use. On the other hand, many have championed and supported the Montaigne essay form as an essentially radical form of writing. French feminists of the twentieth century, for example, such as Hélène Cixous and Luce Irigaray, practiced a Montaigne-style essay. Germany's T.W. Adorno saw "the essay's freedom from specialization and genre boundaries as one way to destabilize [these] hierarchical divisions" (Kirklighter 3). Thus, Montaigne set the stage for the personal, polemical form of essay, as practiced by Continental thinkers and activists to the present day.

Toward the end of the sixteenth century, England's Sir Francis Bacon tried his hand at the new essay form in a very different manner. His *Essays* (1597) were constructed in a diametrically opposite way to those of Montaigne. Instead of starting from personal reaction to changed or new circumstances, Bacon focused on the observable facts that made up these situations. His essays comprised sets of empirical observations that described with ostensible scientific accuracy the unfolding new world.

These essays were to be offered to readers to help them understand their environment before reacting to it and making consequential decisions. Thus, the Bacon essay comprised advice and counsel to his contemporaries. This approach was in stark contrast to Montaigne's personal, open-ended speculations. A Montaigne essay might or might not have been "useful" to the reader, given its speculative nature, which typically drew no conclusions or calls to action. In contrast, Bacon's essays were essentially utilitarian exercises with a motive: to take the facts of the situation and draw a definitive, defensible conclusion. This conclusion would in turn delineate a line of action. The Bacon essay, then, aimed to provide guidance to improve individuals' conditions and attain their rational ends. The content or purpose of the essay demanded a different style. Where Montaigne's essays were personal and spontaneous, Bacon's took a more "detached" and scientific approach that required a degree of discipline and rigor to lead to a sought-for conclusion.

Ultimately, the two essay forms had very different purposes or strategies. The Montaigne essay was personally motivated, while the Bacon essay had a utilitarian public purpose. As Kirklighter suggests, "The didactic nature of [Bacon's] essays moves away from the inconclusive skepticism that pervades Montaigne's form. Bacon's essays were meant to reach a public audience that would act on his word" (Kirklighter 10). In this sense, Bacon's essays had a more direct political intent than Montaigne's essays of "self-revelation."

To sum up, by the end of the sixteenth century, there were two contrasting or competing ways of "trying to say" something in a new writing format, two ways of using the essay form to assess and evaluate new circumstances and prepare a call to action. The French-style essay can be characterized as personal, intimate, informal, or conversational. The English essay can be described as impersonal, objective, methodical, rational, and pedagogic. These are, of course, ideal types, and even Montaigne and Bacon themselves did not remain completely bound by their features. For example, Montaigne drew on empirical evidence and observation to argue the merits of experience. Similarly, Bacon resisted oppressive literary traditions; his essays were based on objective study and not the religious authority that formed the foundation for claims about moral conduct in earlier eras (Good 46). At bottom, both essayists were motivated by and interested in the same thing: how to generate knowledge that was derived from experience and observation, rather than from preordained doctrine.

THE ESSAY: EVOLVING CHARACTER AND PRACTICE

Four centuries later, both the Montaigne and the Bacon essay traditions retain their modern adherents and practitioners. Over the years, intellectuals and activists around the world and across social circumstances have embraced the essay form to articulate personal response and advance personal insight or to assess circumstances and issue calls to action. How might this extensive, rich, and varied essay-writing experience be summarized?

A good starting point is to assess the critical issue of the essay's ostensible "shapelessness." Indeed, one can point to an almost universal observation consistent across the vast body of literature about the essay. Most observers agree that the essay is a very difficult genre to define. McCarthy characterizes it as an "enigmatic and elusive genre which seems to defy definition" (McCarthy ix). How can one make sense of something that is simultaneously associated with "the facetious, the trivial, and the anecdotal on the one hand and with the learned treatise and useful, effective expository writing on the other" (Butrym 4)?

Some analysts have attempted to construct a typology or analytical framework for situating and analyzing the essay form. These attempts have had mixed and varying results. Some work has been done to create a continuum of genres that stretches from the essay to the novel, the play, and the poem.[4] Others have attempted to locate the essay within the poetics of French feminist practice, understood as "a movement of interweaving concepts that demand neither origin nor end, completeness nor continuity. The essay recognizes that there is no single reality, but rather realities that are discontinuous and brittle, and that people are not 'lords and masters' of creation" (Brugmann 75).

It might be fair to conclude that the essay can be considered a non-genre, or a "non-generic" genre—in essence, an anti-genre. This characterization attributes to the essay form a powerful dialectical possibility. On the one hand, the essay is seen or depicted as a "lesser" genre because it cannot easily be marketed or branded as a specific form, with qualities, rules, and so on that highlight and confer authority upon mainstream genres. On the other hand, the absence of generic rules or qualities offers limitless possibilities and freedoms; providing the essay form with opportunities for innovation and transcendence.

The essay, then, encompasses numerous and different kinds of writing. Succinctly put, "the essay is the most adaptable of all forms" (Dobree 47).

This attribute in turn makes the form far more accessible than other literary genres. Indeed, many have characterized the essay as potentially the most democratic form of writing, because the genre lends itself to variation on all levels, including form, content, and purpose. First, the essay form is open to consideration of different kinds of material or substance, either in the subject matter being addressed or in the facts/evidence/observations/experiences used as the content of the essay. Second, it is open to different styles or modes of expression, as well as different kinds of argumentation and reasoning. Third, the essay is allowed to have different functions or to pursue different purposes. It can aim to persuade and convince or to present a story or history, real or imagined. It can take the form of a play or that of dialogue, poetry, or meditation. The essay can be dramatic, ironic, even "essayistic" (Scholes and Klaus). Good has commented that the initial thrust of the essay was "in the direction of formlessness" (Good 1). Butrym, too, has remarked on the essay's ability to "draw us by indirection out of ourselves." The "formlessness" of the essay form is arguably one of its strengths, permitting individuals to "speak to each other across the boundaries of our narrower selves" (Butrym 1).

The essay lends itself to a range of opportunities, from intellectual practice of the highest formal discipline and elegance to the most personal, soulful articulation in an open-ended and spontaneous manner. Good thus concludes that "the essay is neither an élite form nor a mass form … it is a democratic form, open to anyone" (Good 186). Kirklighter takes this point a step further. She extends her evaluation of the essay form across the traditional western European and American "borders" of the genre to evaluate and explore Latin American essay practice. "The leaders in Latin American essay scholarship consider the essay whether it be personal or not as paramount to understanding the historical, cultural, and political complexities of these nations" Kirklighter reports (Kirklighter 4). In Latin America the essay has comprised a form of political and social writing that aims to further democratic changes.

The democratic character of the essay form is not to be confused with the particular substance or practice of the essay. The genre has been used for reactionary as well as for progressive purposes and by elitists as well as democrats. In *The Politics of the Essay: Feminist Perspectives*, editors Ruth-Ellen Boetcher Joeres and Elizabeth Mittman challenge the exuberantly over-ambitious claim that the essay is non-elite. The essay has been marked by elitism, they argue, not only of social class but also of gender. In this regard, where gender and class are considered, the essay has had no different historical track record than other genres. For the first 300 years of its existence as a genre, Joeres and Mittman assert, the essay lay firmly outside the domain of the woman writer and her concerns. That said, they note that the genre has been malleable, accessible, and open enough to ultimately allow non-traditional writers, such as women and minorities, to use the essay's form. In their practice, these essayists have contributed to the transformation or extension of the genre to meet their personal and political needs (Joeres and Mittman 2–3).

Over the past century in particular, women essayists and women's essays have begun to be acknowledged. What is particularly intriguing is the extent to which the essay form has provided a good "fit" or practice for gendered writing. In simple terms, the more personal, informal style of the Montaigne essay has been characterized as "feminine," while the rational, objective Baconian essay has been aligned with the masculine. In this manner, notwithstanding their historical exclusion from essay practice, the essay form lends itself to the discourse and practice of feminist writers. As Joeres observes:

> Whereas essayists, the actors and agents, are almost always defined very clearly as "masculine," the essay itself is placed over and over again into a space that is uncannily feminine, at least as the qualities adhering to the "feminine" have been defined since the eighteenth century. Essays are called a mixture of anecdote, description, and opinion. Essays are said to focus on a little world, on details. Essays seem, according to Theodor Adorno, to form patterns of relationships "rather than a straight line of necessary consequences ..." Essays stress process rather than product. (Joeres and Mittman 19–20)

The essay sits on a seam between acculturated assumptions and social constructs about women and women's writing and what seems actually to characterize women's essays in general. The latter is not easily pin-pointed or proved, as Joeres and Mittman point out (Joeres and Mittman 16). Thus, for example, such a well-known essayist as Virginia Woolf may be considered to "essay" in the Montaigne mode. But women write many different styles of essays. The Latin American tradition of essay-writing by women understands the form as primarily a political instrument.[5] This is a far cry from the view of the "feminine" essay that is highly introspective or deeply removed from the hard edges of daily reality.

To sum up, the essay form has become a kind of anti-genre, defying rules and regulations. This space allows freedom to "try things out" in terms of the form of writing, the subject matter addressed, and the purpose of the writing. The essay form's accessibility has created a space to investigate and interrogate changing conditions and circumstances, where new content requires new form and purpose in writing. This accessibility has offered productive opportunities for "non-traditional" writers such as women to explore and address their condition and to propose change and action.

Within the Canadian context, women writers have taken up this opportunity to great effect. The Canadian literary scene boasts a rich and lengthy female tradition of essay-writing. This extends from the writings of Emily Carr, Nellie McClung, Margaret Laurence, Adele Wiseman, Jane Rule, and Miriam Waddington to more recent collections by women such as Dionne Brand, Di Brandt, Nicole Brossard, Elly Danica, Smaro Kamboureli, Lee Maracle, Daphne Marlatt, Nourbese Philip, Gail Scott, Lola Lemire Tostevin, Aritha van Herk, Bronwen Wallace, and Phyllis Webb. Recently, two of Canada's foremost women writers added major essay publications to their oeuvres, both in 2001: Margaret Atwood's *Negotiating with the Dead: A Writer on Writing* and Carol Shields's *Jane Austen*. Essay-writing by Canadian women writers has been and continues to be integral to their work. This dimension of their writing comprises an ongoing challenge to literary traditions and to the societal status quo alike. Indeed, Canadian women's essay-writing deserves as much critical attention as their texts of fiction and poetry.[6] This is certainly the case for Carol Shields.

CAROL SHIELDS AS ESSAYIST

Where does Carol Shields fit in this long tradition of "essaying"? To what extent did she take advantage of the opportunities provided by the essay form? And how did she make use of the genre, in terms of form, content, and purpose?

The second of these questions is fairly straightforward, although readers may be surprised by the extent of Shields's use of the essay form. A search of the Shields fonds at Library and Archives Canada reveals that the author "essayed" extensively.[7] Not surprisingly, given their form and the continuing low authority of the essay, most of Shields's essays did not appear in academic journals or in "serious" publication outlets. Many of her essays were presented as conference papers or public talks, and they remain unpublished (and ready for an edited collection!). Others were published, albeit in popular and mainstream venues such as magazines and newspapers. Altogether, Shields's essays provide excellent, evocative examples of the author as essayist, "having a try" or "a say" on a variety of topics.

The four texts selected for consideration here—"Eros" in *Desire* (1999); Shields's "Afterword" in both volumes of *Dropped Threads: What We Aren't Told* (2001, 2003); *Jane Austen* (2001); and "Narrative Hunger and the Overflowing Cupboard" (2003)—illustrate how she used the essay form on a variety of topics, in various ways, and for multiple purposes. By way of foreshadowing and illustration of the cross-bordering involved in the essays, this section begins with an analysis of Shields's piece entitled "Eros." First published in the collection *Desire in Seven Voices*, edited by Lorna Crozier, "Eros" was subsequently included in Shields's collection of short stories *Dressing Up for the Carnival* (2000). This publication history reveals how the author made use of the essay form in a "de-regulated" way, drawing as readily on fiction as on fact. Shields moved easily between the Montaigne and Bacon forms of essaying—indeed, combining or synthesizing the two traditions.

"Eros"

The first example of Shields's work as an essayist is her contribution to a collection of works exploring the topic of desire. The collection includes essays by Susan Musgrave, Evelyn Lau, Lorna Crozier herself, Bonnie Burnard, Shani Mootoo, Dionne Brand, and finally Carol Shields. Shields contributes what editor Crozier terms a "fictionalized essay" (Crozier 27). She chooses an imaginary situation to address the theme of desire, which presents a variety of analytical and methodological challenges. The purpose of "Eros" is to explore desire in more than a bloodless or analytical way, drawing on real-life details and experiences to make a transcendental point. In the process, "Eros" transforms the ordinary into the extraordinary and the fictional into reality.

In the essay, Ann and Benjamin have come to Paris to rescue what has become a passionless marriage. Like others in the hotel where they are staying, their window opens onto an inner courtyard. Their time in Paris is disappointingly sedate until the last day. Through the open windows, they hear a woman cry out in orgasm. A "half-singing, half-weeping, wordless release" (Shields, "Eros," 164) seems to block out all of the competing and distracting mundane sounds of the hotel, of Paris, and indeed of France. Like a call to action, it triggers the reawakening of Ann's and Benjamin's desire for each other. Shields writes: "This must be it, this force that funnelled through the open air, travelling through the porous masonry and entering her [Ann's] veins ... She imagined that each room on the air shaft was similarly transformed, that men and women were coming together ecstatically as she and Benjamin were doing" (165).

Even a brief excerpt from "Eros" illustrates how Shields makes use of the transformative work of imagination. She regularly calls on the imagination to harness the observable and mundane facts of everyday life to the cause of action and explanation. She is Baconian, in that she uses observation and the real to draw a conclusion and to offer a utilitarian call to action. At the same time Shields follows Montaigne, for she uses language and personal imagination to transform the ordinary facts of life into something extraordinary—a speculative and open-ended vision. "The combined sounds they made," she writes, "formed an erotic random choir, whose luminous, unmoored music was spreading skyward over the city. This was all they ever needed for such perfect happiness, this exquisite permission, a stranger's morning cry" (165).

Of course, writers typically draw upon their imagination and command of language to transform reality for some purpose. This is a writer's stock and trade, practiced to differing degrees of skill and success. What is remarkable in Shields's writing is how this strategy of transformation is as characteristic of her essays as of her fiction. "Eros" is a powerful and evocative example. Recalling that long-ago morning in Paris, Ann is seated at a friend's dinner table. Her hand extends beneath the table to rest in the crotch of the guest beside her, a man she scarcely knows. Earlier in the evening, Ann had taken issue with the man's Baconian position that the sexual act required an authoritative verbal gloss in today's world. "These days explication is required," the man had insisted, "in order to sanction the commands of the blood" (146). For Ann, this is an old-fashioned and retrograde position, and yet she finds herself connected to the man and "part of the blissful and awakened world" (166).

"Eros" contains all the elements of the essay from both Bacon and Montaigne and beyond, as characterized above. In the first instance, its purpose is to address new territory or circumstances that have not typically been addressed so openly, in particular women's erotic desire. Its mode of operation combines the objective or descriptive—the facts of everyday life—with feelings and imagination—the personal. And it addresses the topic in a speculative way while drawing a conclusion and prescription. The notion of being awake to the world is a theme that recurs in Shields's writing.[8] It complements her determination "to say what had once been unsayable" (*Dropped Threads* 347). This was the project of the enormously successful two-volume *Dropped Threads: What We Aren't Told*. With this project, Shields the essayist expanded her practice to editing the essays of other women.

DROPPED THREADS: WHAT WE AREN'T TOLD

Shields edited *Dropped Threads* (2001 and 2003) with her friend Marjorie Anderson with a view to exploring new territory—the "what" in life that we are not told. Their focus was women's experience of reality, articulated in an open and collective way. The ultimate aim of the collection was to open up and understand the world as "told" by women.

For Shields, this project required a different form if the new territory was to be explored to effect. She wanted women's experiences and lives to be presented in a fluid shape, which itself would say something about women's lives. A collection of short essays was the ideal solution. *Dropped Threads* afforded "the apprehension of a structure," Shields wrote in her "Afterword" to the 2001 collection (*Dropped Threads* 347), a shape with enough fluidity and form to (es)say something about women's lives. In effect, the volume is an example of the strategy adopted by Montaigne, to use the essay form in a highly personal and "feeling" manner as a way of breaking through into understanding and (self) discovery. "There were the things our mothers hadn't voiced," Shields wrote, "the subjects our teachers had neglected, the false prophetic warnings (tempus fugit, for example) we had been given and the fatal silence surrounding particular areas of anxiety or happiness. Why weren't we told?" (1246). Replies poured in. "The essays expressed perplexity at life's offerings: injury and outrage that could not be voiced (*Woman, hold thy tongue*), expectations that could not be met, fulfillment arriving in unexpected places, the need for touchness, the beginning of understanding, the beginning of being able to say what had once been unsayable. Or, in my case, the apprehension of a structure that gave fluidity and ease" (1346–7).

The short essay allowed women, many of them first-time essayists, to "try out" writing, to use the open-ended, fluid form to break through and explore, analyze, and critique their world. This is the achievement of the essays in *Dropped Threads*. Women from a variety of walks of life contributed to the volume.[9] Their varied experiences constitute the empirical (Baconian) facts of the subject matter. Their essays embrace a wide variety of themes, issues, and (Baconian) conclusions, as the essayists express the surprise of self-discovery, insights, and truths, or as Shields put it, "the beginning of being able to say" (1347). For these writers, this is also the beginning of the essay.

Dropped Threads, then, combines elements of both the Bacon and the Montaigne essay strategies. This experiment in essaying recalls Butrym's observation about the genre's ability to "draw us by indirection out of ourselves ... [to] speak to each other across the boundaries of our narrower selves" (Butrym 1). The very form of the collection allows a substantive exploration and far-reaching readership.

JANE AUSTEN

Shields's award-winning *Jane Austen* is an extended biographical essay that employs the same empirical evidence used by the biographer, but in a different way. Shields starts with the facts—dates, situations, events, and so on—and transforms them into an imaginative narrative and speculative form. This process allows her to draw a conclusion and to bring resolution, meaning, and insight to the substance of everyday life. In this way, she combines Baconian empiricism with the speculation of the Montaigne method. She transforms the personal and empirical into the collective and moves from the speculative to a conclusion. This study of the writer Jane Austen adopts the fluid form noted by Shields in *Dropped Threads* and allows a remarkable and innovative interplay between imagination and facts.

Shields begins her essay on Jane Austen's life and literary work with an account of a paper that she and her daughter Anne Giardini delivered at a conference in 1996. The paper focused on "the politics of a glance."[10] The authors argued that, through the "glance" of her characters, Austen was able to inscribe the political and historical background of her times, which some Austen critics claimed was lacking in her work. For Shields and Giardini, Austen was clearly and deeply engaged with her time and place, her eyes wide open on the world.[11] The glance serves as a double metaphor and framework. On the one hand, it demonstrated the fact that women lived—and still live—constrained lives in the world. On the other hand, this reality does not imply that they were unaware of their circumstances. The glance is the medium through which this awareness is conveyed.

In her subsequent long essay about Jane Austen for the Penguin Lives series, Shields departs from traditional biographical practice. Austen biographers typically have read the facts of her life (birth, travels, death, and so on) into the substance of her novels. "In so doing," Shields comments, "the assumption is made that fiction flows directly from a novelist's experience rather than from her imagination" (11). Shields proposes instead to "read *into* [her] own resistance, instead of seeking a confirmation or denial embedded in the fiction" (11). The resistance she has in mind is not entirely clear to the reader early on in her analysis. It soon becomes apparent, however, that the imagination plays a key role. As noted above, Shields has been celebrated for the way in which she uses and transforms the ordinary and everyday in her fiction. In her essay on Jane Austen's life, she builds substantially on the imagined and imaginative to transform the facts into something greater. This process can be seen in the very language of the essay.

An early historical fact or event in Austen's life will illustrate Shields's technique. In the context of presenting some basic information about Austen's date and place of birth, physical appearance, and so on, Shields turns to two topics that she favors in her own writing: family and home life. Austen's childhood spurs Shields's imagination. Jane's mother, Cassandra Austen, placed her babies with a local family until they could walk and talk. For Shields, this fact has meaning beyond the empirical reality:

> It can be *imagined* that the abrupt shift from mother's breast to alien household made a profound emotional impact on the child. This early expulsion from home was the first of many, and it is *doubtful* whether she had much to say about such later separations, just as she had little power over her other domestic arrangements... Her fictional expression can be *imagined* as a smooth flow of narrative deriving from her confined reality, but a flow that is interrupted by jets of alternate possibility, the moment observed and then repositioned and recharged. (13, emphases added)

This passage parallels the excerpt from "Eros" discussed above. It replicates the textual movement from factual reality (babies fostered out; the limited power of women of Jane Austen's class, time, and place) to imagined and imaginative thought. From the constraining confines of reality,

Shields produces a smooth narrative flow. From a moment observed—a glance—the world is repositioned and recharged. This is the pattern and technique that she uses to create textual movement and to generate insight. Upholding the pattern is the author's transformative prose. *Jane Austen* abounds in phrases that hold facts at arm's length and transforms them in the process: "it can be imagined" (13); "it is doubtful" (13); "it can be thought" (14); "May or may not have" (18); "on the whole it can be said that" (21): "we can only guess" (29); "[it] can be assumed" (29); "[it] may be imagined" (32); "must have" (34); "may have" (34); "it cannot have been a surprise" (38); "it must have offered" (38); "must at times have imagined and projected"(39); "it is commonly believed" (82); "there can be little question" (99); "it might be thought" (102); "everything we know of her during this period [the middle of her life] is a guessing game, a question that leads around and around [to an even greater silence]" (110).

This is not to suggest that Shields's biographical essay on Austen is short on facts or information. Indeed, it still carries a full factual load. The concrete, empirical reality of Austen's situation in life is clearly delineated and firmly established. Like other women of her circumstances, Austen was dependent on the goodwill of family and friends for life's needs. Her writing depicts women trapped by social barriers and barred from active lives. Shields's essay shows that such conditions applied in Jane Austen's own life as well. Thus, there is considerable biographical substance as traditionally understood. But there is something more substantial and consequential as well: the way in which Shields uses the interplay of fact and imagination to push the study into deeper waters.

Like the two volumes of *Dropped Threads*, Shields's *Jane Austen* sold extremely well. It met with the favor of critics (e.g., jurors of the 2002 Charles Taylor Prize for Literary Non-Fiction, which it won) as well as mainstream readers. Readers everywhere seem to find a great deal of satisfaction in what Shields's writing often offers, including her essay on Jane Austen: a resolution of the day-to-day, with all its petty demands and details, and the world of the imagination, with its promise and pleasure. There is comfort and reassurance in such resolutions—for readers as for characters: Ann and Benjamin resolving to revive their relationship in a Paris hotel; Jane Austen pole-vaulting class prejudice through reading and writing. Like Shields and through her writing, the reader resists dissolution and the defeats incumbent on the acceptance of dichotomy. In her essays as in her fiction, Shields resolves dichotomy by transforming the ordinary into the extraordinary.

"NARRATIVE HUNGER AND THE OVERFLOWING CUPBOARD"

The final essay under consideration here, "Narrative Hunger and the Overflowing Cupboard,"[12] offers an exceptional insight into the purpose of Shields's writing and how and why she used the essay form. This essay also suggests why writing is itself the subject of so much of her work, a theme that lends itself particularly well to the essay form. Finally, "Narrative Hunger and the Overflowing Cupboard" very clearly inverts the typical fictional narrative, turning facts in on themselves to form a speculative narrative. In raw form, this process illustrates how Shields uses the essay genre to take empirical facts and transform them through speculation into wide-reaching conclusions.

Her point of departure in "Narrative Hunger and the Overflowing Cupboard" is the sight of a street person in Paris. A man sits on the city sidewalk with a sign around his neck that reads, "*J'ai faim*" (I am hungry). An hour later, the essayist sees the man eating a large sandwich. She reacts first as a writer and lover of language and remarks that the sign should be corrected to "*J'ai eu faim*" (I was hungry). On second thought, though, it occurs to her that she is seeing something else altogether. What she sees is "a man momentarily satisfied but conscious of further hunger to come, and gesturing also, perhaps, toward an enlarged or existential hunger, toward a coded message, a threaded notation, an orderly account or story that would serve as a witness to his place in the world" (19). This passage evokes the strategic purpose and character of the essay genre as Shields practiced it: an account or story that serves as witness to the world. Like the preceding examples, "Narrative Hunger and the Overflowing Cupboard" privileges the narrative component of the account as Shields reflects on the human need for story. People have a natural, healthy longing for story, she maintains, from letters to Ann Landers to obituaries in the newspaper, from primary school texts to civilization's most prized pieces of writing.

For Shields, narrative is all-important. It is the necessary ingredient both of life and of writing—essays included. Form and matter in Shields's essay-writing are not limited to empirical description or the manipulation of observable facts. Her essays move fluidly into the realm of fiction, and she makes ready use of the tools and techniques of fiction-writing, including characters, dilemmas, metaphor, the narrative pause, exaggeration, word-work or language, and imagination. There is no irreconcilable difference between fact and fiction, between the observable and the speculative in Shields's essays. Hunger here is both "real" and the substance of the narrative, in a manner akin to how hunger exists even when cupboards overflow with food. In her essays Shields discounts and discourages the acceptance of conventional wisdom and the received notion of the dichotomy between reality and fiction. She perceives instead that fiction is not strictly mimetic. In "Narrative Hunger and the Overflowing Cupboard," she declares that fiction springs out of and illuminates the world, rather than mirroring it back to us. Narrative, she asserts, "questions experience, repositions experience, expands or contracts experience, rearranges experience, dramatizes experience, [and] brings, without apology, colour, interpretation and political selection" (24). This is a compelling description not only of narrative but also of Shields's conception of the essay. Narrative, she declares in this essay, gets *"inside reality rather than getting reality right"* (35).

For Shields, then, an essay may draw as comfortably and usefully on fiction as it does on fact, whether the subject matter is Jane Austen or desire or narrativity. This feature of her essay-writing allows her to pursue her fascination and faith in writing itself. It accounts for the fact that so many of her essays have writing as their main focus. Shields's essays regularly provide her with opportunities to (es)say something about writing and writers and the details of their own daily lives. In this way, they assert a wholehearted affirmation of—indeed, insistence upon—the centrality of narrative in life and in writing. This affirmation extends to her essay-writing as well. For Shields, this exercise and articulation takes full advantage of the freedom and opportunity provided by the essay form.

CONCLUSION

Shields's accomplishments as an essayist are considerable, though generally under-acknowledged. On the one hand, they offer a number of transparent insights into what she was trying to do as a writer and how she accomplished her objectives. On the other hand, the substance and strategies of her essays are as compelling and, in many ways, as satisfying as her fiction.

The essay form offers writers freedom and opportunity—in how they write, in the subjects they choose and observe, and in the purpose of their writing. The realm of the essay can reach from the world of Montaigne to the world of Bacon, from feelings to facts, from the subjective to the objective, from spontaneity to discipline, from speculation to science, from dreaming to action. Carol Shields's essays comprise all of the above. They synthesize the approaches set out by Montaigne and Bacon in intriguing and innovative ways, typically using fiction to illustrate facts in the aim of finding resolution. A central reason why she was attracted to the essay genre was that it allowed her greater freedom, particularly to explore the nature of writing itself.

NOTES

1. Mark Lawson, "Interview with Carol Shields." *Front Row*, BBC Radio 4, 6 March 2001, 7:15 p.m., quoted in Faye Hammill, "My Own Life Will Never Be Enough for Me: Carol Shields as Biographer [Jane Austen]." *American Review of Canadian Studies*, 32, no. 1 (spring 2002), 143–148.

2. Early in his study of the genre, *The Observing Self,* Good discusses the essay as "a sort of fiction, in the context of the novel" (12), "a non-fictional cognate of certain kinds of fiction" (13).

3. Archival copy, dated 15 March 1995, later revised 31 August 1995 and delivered as an address at Hanover College, 26 September 1996. I heard a version of the essay as a keynote speech at the Nordic Association for Canadian Studies conference in Reykjavik, Iceland, in August 1999. A final version of the essay is featured in Eden and Goertz, *Carol Shields, Narrative Hunger, and the Possibilities of Fiction.*

4. See Scholes and Klaus, *Elements of the Essay.*

5. See Kirklighter, *Traversing the Democratic Borders of the Essay.*

6. When, in April 1997, Toronto Star literary reviewer Bert Archer complained that he could not remember the last time he had read a good essay published in Canada, he apparently had not been reading the essays of the country's women writers. See Bert Archer, "The Art of the Essay," *Toronto Star,* 5 April 1997, M16. "Essay writing is an art and a skill," Archer stated, lamenting what he saw as a lack of good essayists in Canada.

7. Shields, "Giving Your Literary Papers Away;" "Framing the Structure of a Novel;" "Making Words/Finding Stories;" "What's in a Picture;" "The Personal Library;" "Leaving the Brick House Behind;" "Jane Austen: Images of the Body;" "Creative Writing Courses;" "'Thinking Back through Our Mothers';" "Marian Engel Award Acceptance Speech 1990;" "News from Another Country;" "A View from the Edge of the Edge."

8. This is a topic worth exploring further. Speaking with Ann Dowsett Johnston about writing *Unless* (*Maclean's* 115, no. 15 [15 April 2002]:

48–51), Shields remarked how she was "more at ease with writing this novel than with others. Cancer makes one serious, and awake." Speaking earlier with Jennifer Jackson ("'Soft-spoken Subversive' Doing What She Loves," *Kingston-Whig Standard*, 13 March 2001), Shields observed that "this state of being awake [following the birth of her first child, at the age of twenty-two, which snapped her out of a 'rather sleepy girlhood'] spread to the rest of my life and, I believe, made me more alert, more perceptive, more aware of the shades of feeling, of the large and small collisions of personality." Earlier still, "in her 1996 address at the graduation ceremonies for the Balmoral Hall School for Girls in Winnipeg, Shields, as Lesley Hughes recounted in *Chatelaine*, stated ... 'Just wake up and be yourself'" (quoted in *Contemporary Canadian Biographies*, August 1997).

9. The contributors include writers, academics, ranchers, politicians, homemakers, journalists, and lawyers.

10. See Shields's 15 March 1995 draft of "Narrative Hunger and the Overflowing Cupboard" (lac, Carol Shields fonds) for more on "the glance": "Such a wealth of material to draw on, but never ... quite ... enough. And never quite accurate either, glancing off the epic of human experience rather than reflecting it back to us" (4). The opening image of this essay—a Parisian street person with a sign that reads "J'ai faim" around his neck—seems to anticipate the narrator's daughter in *Unless*.

11. Shields, 15 March 1995 draft of "Narrative Hunger and the Overflowing Cupboard," 4.

12. In Eden and Goertz, *Carol Shields, Narrative Hunger, and the Possibilities of Fiction*, 19–36.

Works Cited

Brugmann, Margaret. "Between the Lines: On the Essayistic Experiments of Hélène Cixous in 'The Laugh of the Medusa.'" *The Politics of the Essay: Feminist Perspectives*, edited by Joeres Ruth-Ellen Boetcher and Elizabeth Mittman, Bloomington and Indianapolis, Indiana University Press, 1993. 73–84.

Butrym, Alexander J., editor. *Essays on the Essay: Redefining the Genre*. Athens and London, The University of Georgia Press, 1989.

Crozier, Lorna, editor. *Desire in Seven Voices*. Vancouver, Douglas & McIntyre, 1999.

Dobrée, Bonamy. *English Essayists*. London, Collins [n.d.].

Eden, Edward, and Dee Goertz, editors. *Carol Shields, Narrative Hunger, and the Possibilities of Fiction*. Toronto, University of Toronto Press, 2003.

Good, Graham. *The Observing Self: Rediscovering the Essay*. London and New York, Routledge, 1988.

Joeres, Ruth-Ellen Boetcher, and Elizabeth Mittman, editors. *The Politics of the Essay: Feminist Perspectives*. Bloomington and Indianapolis, Indiana University Press, 1993.

Kirklighter, Cristina. *Traversing the Democratic Borders of the Essay*. New York State, University of New York Press, 2002.

Lynch, Gerald, and David Rampton, editors. *The Canadian Essay*. Ottawa, University of Ottawa Press, 1991.

McCarthy, John A. *Crossing Boundaries: A Theory and History of Essay Writing in German 1680–1815*. Philadelphia, University of Pennsylvania Press, 1989.

Scholes, Robert, and Carl H. Klaus. *Elements of the Essay*. New York: Oxford University Press, 1969.

Shields, Carol. "Art of Darkness, World of Wealth" Rev. of *When the Sons of Heaven Meet the Daughters of the Earth* by Fernanda Eberstadt. *Globe and Mail*, 15 March 1997, D14.

———. "Creative Writing Courses: A Lecture Given in Trier, April 1990a." (LAC, Carol Shields fonds, first accession, B. 63 f.12 p.87).

———. "Eros." In Crozier, *Desire in Seven Voices*.

———. "Fiction or Autobiography," *Atlantis*, vol. 4, no. 1, 1978. 49–54.

———. "Framing the Structure of a Novel." *The Writer*, vol. 111, no. 7, 1998a. 3–6.

———. "Giving Your Literary Papers Away." *Quill & Quire*, vol. 64, no. 11, 1998b. 43.

———. "Harvard Seminar: A View from the Edge of the Edge." (LAC, Carol Shields fonds, second accession f–8 p. 90).

———. *Jane Austen*. Penguin Lives series. New York, Viking, 2001a.

———. "Jane Austen: Images of the Body: No Fingers, No Toes." (1991a) (LAC, Carol Shields fonds, first accession B. 63 f.16 p.87); later *in Persuasions: Journal of the Jane Austen Society of North American*, vol. 13, 16 Dec. 1991. 132–7.

———. and Marjorie Anderson, editors. *Dropped Threads: What We Aren't Told*. Toronto, Vintage Canada, 2001b.

———. *Dropped Threads 2: More of What We Aren't Told*. Toronto, Vintage Canada, 2003a.

———. "Leaving the Brick House Behind: Margaret Laurence and the Loop of Memory" (26 September 1991) (LAC, Carol Shields fonds, first accession f.24 p.84); later in *Ranam: Recherches anglaises et nord-américaines*, vol. 24, 1991b. 75–7.

———. "Making Words/Finding Stories." *Journal of Business Administration*, vol. 24, 1996a–98. 36–52.

———. "Marian Engel Award Acceptance Speech 1990b." (LAC, Carol Shields fonds, first accession f–13 p.87).

————. "Narrative Hunger and the Overflowing Cupboard." In *Carol Shields, Narrative Hunger, and the Possibilities of Fiction*, edited by Edward Eden and Dee Goertz. Toronto, University of Toronto Press, 2003b. 19–36.

————. "News from Another Country." In *The Second Macmillan Anthology* (Toronto: Macmillan); reprinted in *How Stories Mean*, edited by John Metcalf and J.R. Struthers, 91–3. Erin, ON, The Porcupine's Quill, 1993.

————. "The Personal Library." *Globe and Mail*, October 1992. (LAC, Carol Shields fonds, first accession B 62 f.34 p.85).

————. "'Thinking Back through Our Mothers': Tradition in Canadian Women's Writing." With Clara Thomas and Donna Smyth. In *Re(dis)covering Our Foremothers: Nineteenth-Century Canadian Women Writers*, edited by Lorraine McMullen. Ottawa, University of Ottawa Press, 1990c. 9–13.

————. "What's in a Picture," *Civilization*, vol. 3, no. 5, 1996b. 112.

PART I

Essays on Carol Shields's Short Stories

The Short of It: Carol Shields's Stories

Neil Besner

I wanted stories that soar[ed] off into mystery and disruption.
—Carol Shields

It's not surprising that, when we think of Carol Shields, we think first of the novelist rather than of the poet, playwright, critic, editor, biographer, or writer of short stories. I don't intend to try to sway you; to convince you of the error of your ways; to mount an impassioned plea to consider more closely or carefully Shields's stories—to argue, say, that in our age of such commendably short new forms of discourse, of discourse at lightning speed—an age of new forms as yet only dimly apprehended, such as the tweet, the (new meaning of) text, the Instagram, and the twitter, of emails punctuated by omg and lol and btw and ttyl (and, in this fearful moment of the Coronavirus, by new abbreviations like WFH)—as if among these forms the short story were finding newly naturalized, if virtual, allies, all insisting on less and less, and less and faster.

N. Besner (✉)
University of Winnipeg, Winnipeg, MB, Canada

N. F. Stovel (ed.), *Relating Carol Shields's Essays and Fiction*,
https://doi.org/10.1007/978-3-031-11480-9_3

None of that constitutes my intention. Nor do I want to declare some sort of false war between the novel and the short story. These never were opposed forms; nor do they really sit comfortably in a hierarchy of forms. Under Shields's pen as under many others', the short story is not a kind of shorthand, and it never was. Nor is this the place to advocate for the venerable and demonstrably longer tradition of the story as distinct from that of the novel (although that is true; the short story *is* more venerable and has a longer history): to remind of the roots of story in fable or joke, in orality and recitation and in living memory, in what in many ways preceded and prefigured print and (our older sense of) text and of extension. All of that is a story for another day.

No, my aims here are more modest. In short, I want to propose our giving more time and attention—as she did herself—to Carol Shields's stories for other, more particular and more telling reasons. I would like to argue that renewed and more careful attention to Shields's short stories—and she wrote stories throughout her long career—can bring new light, an enlarged understanding of all of Shields's work.

But first, a last disclaimer: I don't believe that Shields wrote stories at any point in her career as preparations, or ground-clearing exercises, or a form of note-taking for her novels, where, allegedly, the real action was. This is a common, if enduring, misconception about the form—that it is a training ground, an apprenticeship for novelists. Not so. Not for Mavis Gallant or Alice Munro on one hand; or Joyce or Chekhov on another; nor for Mansfield; not for Hemingway or Faulkner or Fitzgerald in another register, or Bellow or Roth or Malamud or Updike in another, or Ray Carver in one ethos and era, Jorge Luis Borges in another. (Or, for that matter, and closer to home, for Atwood, or Szusi Gartner, Jennifer Duncan, Elyse Gasco, Clark Blaise, David Bergen, Matt Cohen, or Guy Vanderhaeghe, among many others.) What is more useful to consider, I think, is to discuss to what particular ends contemporary writers are shaping the story form. In Shields's case, I would like to show how, throughout her career, she deployed the story form and its resources to several related ends—among them two that are vital to all of her writing: first, experiment and serious play; and second, the crafted revelation, often surprising, of isolated characters in isolated moments (I'll explain that more fully shortly). Finally, I'm going to try to show that the elements of experiment and serious play are related to the kind of revelation of character I'm referring to here that is embedded in these elements' common performative context.

Of course, none of this is to say that there are no other forces afoot in her stories; it is only to say that these important aspects recur, and that they invite our further attention and engagement. They resonate.

But let Carol Shields speak for herself for a moment; and consider the tone, the quiet eyebrow-arched irony of one of her opening observations about the short story in her essay "The Short Story (and Women Writers)" in the collection co-edited by her daughter Anne and grandson Nicholas, *Startle and Illuminate: Carol Shields on Writing:*

> A short story as everyone knows is a prose narrative that can be read in a single sitting, never mind what that quaint abstraction, a single sitting, means. A novel is the same thing except longer, like several sittings presumably. How long is a novel or a story? About as long as a piece of string. A narrative is, well, a story, and a story is—a narrative, of course. (97)

This quiet demolition of shibboleths, *pace* Poe, continues throughout Shields's essay as she cheerily, airily names and then discards hoary theory upon age-old Terse Truths about the form: early on, she gently reminds us: "Every detail in a short story must contribute to its total effect. Chekhov and Hemingway said so, so it had to be true" (*Startle,* 97–8). Again, the disarming but telling tactic: merely by naming the practice, debunk it; merely by invoking the Past Masters' confident claims, dismiss them. And then, Shields the surgeon arrives, with skillful scalpel cutting deftly through the newly exposed skin to lay bare those old integuments, discard them, and lead us away from these numbing norms to move toward her own poetics: "A story had to have conflict, that old word. It took some time to understand just what a setup the ascending storyline was, and how little of the texture and boldness of life, of women's lives in particular, could be shaped to fit its contours" (*Startle,* 98).

In Christl Verduyn's germinal essay in this collection, "(Es)Saying It Her Way: Carol Shields as Essayist," Verduyn begins to frame her discussion with a general inquiry: "What was the relationship between her [Shields's] essay-writing and the other genres she practiced with so much success?" Verduyn addresses this issue in an admirably wide-ranging treatment of both the history of the essay as a form and its relevance to all of Shields's work. Here, I am confining my reading of Shields's essays to their relevance and relation to her stories; but Verduyn makes a compelling case for understanding Shields's essays as fundamental rather than incidental to all of her writing. Similarly, in her introduction,

"Relating Carol Shields's Essays and Fiction: Crossing Borders," Nora Foster Stovel argues persuasively that "Shields's essays can throw valuable light on her fiction, particularly as many of her essays, especially those collected in the Giardini edition, focus on her own fictional writing techniques, as she offers advice to aspiring authors" (2).

The long story of how during Shields's entire career she conjured with "women's lives in particular," and not only, of course, in her short stories, is a very big subject for another day; but here it is helpful to see just how strongly she felt about the old (and principally male) strictures in relation to the short story, and to begin to think about how *all* of Shields's stories might reflect, as if prismatically, as if radiantly, her commitment to trying something other, something less formulaic, something more playful in her stories than these quoted dicta might allow; as she puts it, she "wanted stories that soared off into mystery and disruption, not mere flat openness but a spiraling into space or a melting into another narrative ...." (*Startle*, 99).

First, then, Shields, experiment, and play: I'm not aware of a contemporary writer of stories who more cheerfully, coyly and cunningly and slyly has had such serious and continuing fun with the form. (This, from the writer accused and condemned in some quarters of celebrating quiet middle-class lowbrow female domesticity, stodgy kitchen kitsch.) This aspect of her stories reveals to us a figure I like to think of as Shields Ludens. In her scintillating essay in this collection, Marta Dvořák astutely and elegantly describes this aspect of Shields's writing as a "more impressionistic, elliptical aesthetic of indeterminacy whose repeated leitmotifs leave a wake of meaning that gently fades, rather than clinching the circumference and significance of the whole story" (Dvorak, 6–7). Dvorak goes on to argue convincingly that "Shields's outlook and (as a corollary) her fictional production are quite naturally informed by the theory of chaotics, which postulates a paradoxical system in which the only phenomenal determinacy lies in the certainty of unpredictability" (Dvorak, 7).

To begin contemplating this facet, think of "Various Miracles"—the title story of her first book of stories, published in 1985—with its synchronous circumstances, and tell me that Shields didn't read Borges, that erudite master of cosmic (and, often, comic) happenstance shaped into telling circumstance; what moves and delights us in this story, I think, is its bright, casual, and airy descent and incarnation of the "miraculous" to settle at street-level, where it lingers, half luminous, half gritty, as a kind of counterpoint to, as well as a sanctification of, both the banality and the half-felt meaning of everyday living. And that, too, is one of the marks of Shields's stories. Or, toward the other end of her career, think of Shields's three-and-a-half-page amusement, "Flatties," from her last collection of stories, *Dressing Up for the Carnival* (2000), with its peculiar, if distinctive, recipes, its quaintnesses and drolleries, its customs and geography. It is entirely plausible to believe that "Flatties" are as real as their recipes would indicate—maybe one could have a go at a Flattie in one's own kitchen—and set them beside a box of Matzoh—and that they are, in turn, as plausible as the people who make them and as plausible as the places these people live. "Flatties" are made, not in a galaxy far far away, but in a nearby, next-door world—as if Shields wished to explore, to play with, to experiment with evoking the history of small everyday customs such as diet. To amuse to an end: to suppose with her readers, that *this* is how a small, commonplace tradition looks, *these* are its origins. Think of "Weather" from the same last collection, with its climate cancelling ethos, its weatherless ambience. What could be more everyday and more pervasive than the weather? What if there were no weather? This, at play, is the work of the so-called novelist of ideas writ differently. Not condensed; not trivial; not whimsical; and not simply "what if?", which would take us into another mode. Shields is intent on making small plausible worlds with one element gone missing, or gone awry, or recurring variously, miraculously—calling into question our more common understanding of sequence, of causality, of narrative chains, of plot.

Notice, too, that in the story "Various Miracles"—indeed in most of what I am calling these seriously playful stories—one wouldn't say that readers are arrested first, if at all, by character. It isn't the nature of the woman in the street, her manuscript pages dispersed in the wind, that we contemplate; it is, rather, the strangely synchronous arrangement of events that the story is built upon. Now turn to consider the serious play of Shields's story, "Absence," also from *Dressing Up for the Carnival*, in which, tellingly, both the letter and the pronoun "I" have been excluded, producing a selfless, if wholly self-conscious meditation on a woman writing without or beyond or outside of a self. She is in a Room of her Own Making and Writing; but the voice, the writer, is without an I. Here is a meaningful play and experiment at the level of language and of diction and of vowels: remove the first person, and who is speaking, who is writing? What self, what voice obtains, and how, to what end? Of course, this serious play with conceptions of absent writing or speaking or remembering selves doesn't arise only in Shields's stories; it recurs throughout her work, emerging in another related, more complex and expanded form in *The Stone Diaries* in Daisy Goodwill's impossibly variegated voices and selves, just as Shields's fascination with parts of speech plays such an important role in *Unless*.

I don't want to claim for a moment that experiment and play, and their particular forms, are confined to Shields's stories. But I do think it's true that in her stories, experiment and play become more prominent, more visible as foreground, as in "Various Miracles." Further, I would say that one could compile a very long list of Shields stories in which experiment, in which serious play are likewise prominent; these are not occasional or idiosyncratic elements, one-offs. And—as in "Absence"—this play often leads to or is inextricably bound up with language (as in another early story, collected in *Various Miracles*, "The Metaphor is Dead—Pass It On," with its thunderingly pedantic Professor and his ballooning figures of speech; and, as in this story, the play with language often leads to or is already bound up with a favorite Shields target, the pretentious academic—like so many of us). Of course, the pretentious ones reappear in her novels, to different effect, and we can all name them there; but, in these more confined and precise precincts, they disport themselves, not more briefly, but more typically; you would not want to think at length about the character of the Professor in "The Metaphor is Dead," although you would and should want to think carefully about the complexities of the characters of the various academic players in *Swann*, as elsewhere in her novels. But, in Shields's stories, one is more apt to encounter, and to think first, of a turn of phrase, a twist of plot, a miraculous synchronicity, an absurdity—and not as miniatures or prototypes. In short, these elements are more simply performative in this form: this is play and experiment *shown* as such, performing as such; or, in other words, these instances signify, they mean, as enactment, demonstration, performance. They do a turn; they are small-staged; they call attention to themselves in ways and in modes not as well suited to the longer fictional forms. This is not a case of precious miniaturism; rather, it is one of the distinctive marks of a different form, the story, in Shields's hands. And these elements are not available in her novels in the same way. Coral Ann Howells makes a persuasive claim for what she describes as Shields's "subtle formal experimentalism" in her stories: "The most experimental of all her writings, these stories are the products of her disillusion with the conventions of literary realism in the early 1980s, combined with her negotiations with postmodernist theory" (Howells, 2).

Let me move on to character and to what I referred to, clumsily, in my opening as "the crafted revelation of isolated characters in isolated moments." Critics have commented on character development and its relation to the short story genre for a very long time, and what I'm about to suggest in closing by considering two of Shields's stories, one very well known, the other less so, is partly indebted first to Frank O'Connor's fundamental book on the short story, first published in 1963, *The Lonely Voice*, in which he famously advises that all modern short stories came out from under Gogol's "Overcoat," and somewhat less famously alludes to the story's predilection for lonely characters on the margins of society. (Interestingly, the book has been considered current enough to have been republished over 40 years later, in 2004, with an introduction by Russell Banks.) I'm also indebted to the widely shared traditional view of the epiphany as it applies to short fiction. But these are points of departure, as I hope you'll see.

Most readers of Shields's short stories will remember "Mrs. Turner Cutting the Grass," the second story in *Various Miracles*; perhaps many will also remember Clara Hughes's fine essay on the story. Please forgive the quick and bald plot summary: Mrs. Turner is a widow, presented both at the very beginning and at the end of the story in a moment as she cuts the grass on the lawn of her River Heights home in Winnipeg, ten years after her husband Gord has died. Between this fixed portrait, beginning and end, the story opens out like an accordion to fill in the years between "Girlie" at 17 and the widow of the present. She'd left small-town Manitoba, shamed by her father's discovery of her in a hotel room with a married man; fled by bus in 1930 to New York, where she'd worked in a movie house, lived with a man who abandoned her when her baby was born, abandoned her baby herself, and returned to Manitoba, to be taken in by her family anew. In recent years, following Gord's death, she's travelled widely with her two sisters.

The story turns on two perceptions of Mrs. Turner. One is most notoriously represented by a poet-professor travelling in Japan with the three sisters on a tour bus; he enshrines her in a poem as the incarnation of ignorant and tasteless and dowdy and culturally illiterate North American middle-aged women on tour, spoiling the view wherever they go. That view is widely shared by his audiences, as his book of poems becomes a hit, and his reputation soars. Here are the story's opening and closing paragraphs:

> Oh, Mrs. Turner is a sight cutting the grass on a hot afternoon in June! She climbs into an ancient pair of shorts and ties on her halter top and wedges her feet into crepe-soled sandals and covers her red-gray frizz with Gord's old golf cap—Gord is dead now, ten years ago, a seizure on a Saturday night while winding the mantel clock. (7)

Now the closing:

> In the summer, as she cuts the grass, to and fro, to and fro, she waves to everyone she sees. She waves to the high school girls who timidly wave back. She hollers hello to Sally and Roy Sascher and asks them how their garden is coming on. She cannot imagine that anyone would wish her harm. All she's done is live her life. The green grass flies up in the air, a buoyant cloud swirling about her head. Oh, what a sight is Mrs. Turner cutting her grass, and how, like an ornament, she shines. (18)

I'm going to assume that most of us remember this story well enough that I don't need to say more about what happens between the two portraits. What I'm interested in considering is not the implied judgments of all the representations of and comments, explicit or implicit, on Mrs. Turner, although there's plenty to think about on that score. What I'm more interested in are the twinned and opposed and staged portraits—the performances of Mrs. Turner Cutting the Grass. By this I mean that meaning and significance in the story are secondary, and interpretation might be seen to begin with Mrs. Turner's twinned and opposed appearances (in both senses of the term). Yes, readers are alternately instructed, chided, directed by that narrative voice and gaze that dissects the neurasthenic and preening poet-professor; the callow schoolgirls; the self-righteously green eco-neighbors. But consider, first, the performance of Mrs. Turner, cutting the grass. There she is: isn't there something luminous and shining about her at story's end?

Yes, there is, but how and why? Not only, I'd suggest, because of everything we've just learned, leading to this new understanding of the opening portrait; but also because Mrs. Turner, as if she were a restricted Mrs. Dalloway, appears, performs (again). I know: why refer to a figure in a novel—doesn't that undercut my own argument about the distinctiveness of the story form? Yes and no, and more no: what Mrs. Dalloway and Mrs. Turner share—and there they are—is a mode, an appearance, a radiance: a performance. (There is also to my ear a fainter resonance with Molly

Bloom's Yes!—but that's about the erotic in Shields's fiction—and in this story—and a vital subject for another day.) Mrs. Turner performs: and the form of epiphany available—this is another Shields hallmark, I'd argue—is ironic, a moment of simultaneous diminishment and exaltation, an ornamental moment that fixes Mrs. Turner. Yes; all she's done is live her life. And been judged by minor poets, readers, high school girls, gardeners; by all her various audiences, including, most vitally, her readers. She appears, and shines like an ornament, enhaloed by clouds of grass. She simply is. Full stop. Interpretation of character, it might be argued, invites if not demands narrative or logical or psychological extension. Performance demands or invites spectators. Character in Shields's short stories invites less of the former and more of the latter.

A last and related example from later in Shields's career, from the title story of her third book of stories, *Dressing Up for the Carnival*. Approximately 15 years later (we don't know when either the earlier or the later story was written, but let's assume that the dates of publication at least signal, probably, the order in which they were composed), the second story is more explicit than the first about masks, dress, appearances, and carnivals. This story makes it clear that everyone dresses up for the carnival, and that's fine; the first sentence advises us: "All over town people are putting on their costumes" (1), but we quickly discern that the performance they are all dressing for, dressing up for, is simply everyday life.

In Nora Foster Stovel's view, *Dressing Up For The Carnival* is distinct among Shields's books of stories, in that it "employs a framework": "beginning with the title story, 'Dressing Up for the Carnival,' and concluding with the final story, 'Dressing Down,' suggesting preparation for life and then for death" (Stovel, "Be A Little Crazy: Astonish Me," 74). I agree with Stovel: this book of stories in its entirety is more shaped, more formed, than her earlier books of stories. At this level, the story amuses and entertains with its sequence of portraits: Tamara, the clerk-receptionist for the Youth Employment Bureau, becomes no longer just that, but "a woman in a yellow skirt" (*Dressing*, 2); Roger, 30, divorced, burly, holding a mango, has been likewise transformed; the Bordon sisters, back from a ski trip, still wear and bear all the markers of that elation; Wanda, on an errand for her bank manager, picks up a new pram for him and is thereby transformed herself into a joyfully wishful mother; Mr. Gilman, at eighty a prim bachelor, has been transformed simply by buying a blaze of daffodils to take to his daughter-in-law's for his ritual dinner; high school football hero Ralph's sister Mandy, sent home to retrieve his forgotten helmet, is transformed into someone who for the first time can see—and see so intimately as to become—her brother, that "deep-voiced stranger" (*Dressing*, 7). So far, so good: in six pages, we have been given five cameos. Now the story accelerates to its conclusion, with five more cameos presented in less than one page, leading to the final paragraph:

> We cannot live without our illusions, thinks X, an anonymous middle-age citizen who, sometimes, in the privacy of his own bedroom, in the embrace of happiness, waltzes about in his wife's lace-trimmed nightgown. His wife is at bingo, not expected home for an hour. He lifts the blind an inch and sees the sun setting boldly behind his pear tree, its mingled coarseness and refinement giving an air of confusion. Everywhere he looks he observes cycles of consolation and enhancement, and now it seems as though the evening itself is about to alter its dimensions, becoming more (and also less) than what it really is. (*Dressing*, 8)

I can never read this closing without William Carlos Williams's great poem "Danse Russe" coming to mind, with its self-proclaimed "happy genius of my household" dancing in front of the window, singing to himself, "I am lonely, lonely./ I was born to be lonely./ I am best so!"

But set Williams's poem aside, although the parallels, and there are more, are striking. There is lots more to say here. And leave aside the radiant Mrs. Dalloway, and Molly Bloom as well. What's left is X, the "anonymous, middle-aged citizen," dancing in his wife's nightgown in the bedroom, at sunset; and Mrs. Turner, cutting the grass. In the end, these short but memorable performances cannot be said to exemplify; illustrate; illuminate; or demonstrate my argument about character, and revelation, and performance in Shields's stories, any more than the examples of experiment and serious play can finally stand for very much more than themselves. But, in short, there they are.

WORKS CITED

Borges, Jorge Luis. *Labyrinths: Selected Stories and Other Writings*. New York: New Directions, 1962. Print.

Giardini, Anne and Nicholas Giardini, Eds. *Startle and Illuminate: Carol Shields on Writing*. Toronto: Random House Canada, 2016. Print.

O'Connor, Frank. *The Lonely Voice: A Study of the Short Story*. New York: Harper and Row, 1963. Print.

Shields, Carol. *Dressing Up for the Carnival*. Toronto: Random House Canada, 2000. Print.

———. *Various Miracles*. Toronto: Vintage/Random House Canada, 1985. Print.

———. *Swann: A Mystery*. Toronto: Stoddart, 1987. Print.

———. *The Stone Diaries*. Toronto: Random House Canada, 1993. Print.

———. *Unless*. Toronto: Random House Canada, 2002. Print.

———. "The Short Story (and Women Writers)." Giardini, Anne and Nicholas Giardini, Eds. *Startle and Illuminate: Carol Shields on Writing*. Toronto: Random House Canada, 2016. 97–107. Print.

Williams, William Carlos. "Danse Russe." In *The Complete Collected Poems of William Carlos Williams, 1906–1938*. New York: New Directions, 1938. Print.

"Space for Strangeness": Carol Shields's Short Stories

Coral Ann Howells

"All writers know about the magic of opening sentences, the golden door that takes you into the story, pushes at the future and nudges your expectations,"[1] and taking my cue from Carol Shields's gleaming metaphor, I shall begin this essay with two quotations—one from Lewis Carroll's *Through the Looking Glass* and one from her last unfinished work "Segue," from which I've taken my title. Both may be usefully brought together as twinned reflections on Shields's writing process, for one is about narrative desire and the other is about narrative craft. In the first passage, Alice is talking to her cat, holding it up to the mirror above the mantelpiece in the drawing room and describing how her familiar domestic world is reversed on the other side of the mirror:

> Now, if you'll only attend Kitty, and not talk so much I'll tell you all my ideas about Looking-glass House. First, there's the room you can see through the glass—that's just the same as our drawing-room, only the

C. A. Howells (✉)
University of Reading, Reading, UK

Institute of English Studies, University of London, London, UK

N. F. Stovel (ed.), *Relating Carol Shields's Essays and Fiction*, https://doi.org/10.1007/978-3-031-11480-9_4

things go the other way. I can see all of it when I get upon a chair—all but the bit just behind the fire-place. Oh! I do so wish I could see *that* bit![2]

Alice's avid desire to see that invisible bit of the room outside the frame finds a parallel in Shields's concept of "Narrative Hunger," which she believes is an indelible part of the human personality. "There is so much that lies out of reach, so much that touches only tangentially on our lives," so that we have an insatiable curiosity for the "inaccessible stories of others," and she goes on to argue that we need a new angle of vision that "renews our image of where *we* are in the world" (*Startle* 118). This alternative way of seeing might be achieved via what Nora Foster Stovel in her Introduction calls "the Shields squint," which, Shields explains, "distorts but also sharpens beyond ordinary vision" in order to represent through narrative artifice the bit we cannot see: "a world of dreams and possibilities and parallel realities" ("Boxcars, Coat Hangers and Other Devices," *Startle* 29).

In the passage from "Segue," a woman sonnet writer is thinking about her craft: "I want space for strangeness to enter—not obscurities or avoidances, but idiosyncrasies of grammar or lexicon, so that the sound is harsh, even hurtful."[3] We hear that same preoccupation with "skills of language (attention to rhythm, extension of vocabulary and distortion of syntax)" in "Myths That Keep You from Writing" (*Startle* 19) and in Reta Winters's obsession with the "little chips of grammar" highlighted by Wendy Roy in "Advice to Writers in Carol Shields's *Unless*" (183). With her efforts to bring what is outside to inside the frame of the sonnet, the emphasis here is on subtle formal experimentalism—even a discreet iconoclasm—which goes beyond readers' expectations, and, though the sonnet is a far more prescriptive form than the short story, I believe we might use this crafty meditation as an emblem for Shields's narrative art in her short stories.

The most experimental of all her writings, these stories are the products of her disillusion with the conventions of literary realism in the early 1980s, combined with her negotiations with postmodernist theory. As she wrote to Blanche Howard in 1988, "I have tried reading critical theory, but it leaks out of my head as fast as I pour it in, and besides, I distrust a great deal of it."[4] Despite her skepticism , Shields acknowledged that postmodernism gave her "that precious oxygen of permission" to go beyond the limits of realism, which, as she had discovered, "was, perhaps, not real enough," because it left out too much—and, like Alice, she uses the image of the mirror with its limitations to make her point ("Narrative Hunger"

34). Her response was to refocus realistic fiction with a deliberate squint, telling her stories through a series of shifting perspectives or different angles of vision: "Instead I wanted stories that soared off into mystery and disruption, not mere flat openness but a spiralling into space or a melting into another narrative as happens at the end of a story I wrote called 'Home'" (*Startle* 99). As Neil Besner remarks in his essay "The Short of It: Carol Shields's Stories" included in this collection, quoting this passage, Shields treated the short story as an experimental space for serious play.

From "Home" in her first short story collection *Various Miracles* (1985) to *Unless* (2001) and "Segue," right across the arc of her career, Shields carried on conversations with herself and her readers that are echoed in women's voices in her novels about the craft and purpose of writing. As she declared, "I wanted to create new structures that would give stability to the less stable material of my books and help me stay on course … I use my structure as narrative bones, and partially to replace plot" ("Boxcars," *Startle* 29). She is preoccupied with the question of how to create "the feeling of completion …when we feel something being satisfied or reconciled or surrendered or earned" ("Myths That Keep You from Writing," *Startle* 19), always leaving other hinted-at narrative possibilities still in circulation in a gesture beyond closure—"the way in which the story is unrolled for the reader, the manner in which we move from revelation to revelation" ("Pacing," *Startle* 69). Shields learned a great deal from Alice Munro, as she advised other writers to do: "Learn from her. Reading her is as good as taking a creative writing course."[5] For both these women the meaning of a story emerges from its "complex patterning rather than from the tidiness of a problem/solution set-up."[6]

Those narrative bones may be provided by visual images or metaphors, that "complex microcircuitry" which Simone Vauthier analyzed, or by a myth patterning that introduces a discourse at odds with quotidian events, exceeding the individual apprehensions of the characters in the stories. Myth patterns are what Shields refers to as "deep structures" in narrative, as is suggested by her comments on *Ulysses* as a tale of the wanderer, the outsider, when she remarks on the long history of storytelling and on the way that stories out of different cultures and periods maintain remarkably persistent patterns ("Open Every Question," *Startle* 125). For Shields, myth remains important in her contemporary narratives, though she uses myths in a very postmodern manner. She is not, like T.S. Eliot, using myth to castigate the modern world for its degeneration from an ancient holistic world view, but more in the manner of Joyce's *Ulysses*, as a kind of shadowy blueprint that opens up spaces for imaginative transcendence of ordinariness by intimating connections between present and past experience, while also marking differences and dislocations. Shields's method reveals a very critical relation to myths both Greek and Christian; she recognizes the need for recurrent narrative patterns, but in no sense is this a nostalgia for a lost order. Her stories are both a celebration and a subversion of myth in a self-conscious revisioning process, as she enmeshes mythic patterns in a network of contemporary human relations.

As will be evident in the two stories through which I have chosen to explore some of the ways Shields constructs spaces for strangeness to enter her narrative framework, allusions to Greek and Christian mythology are important components. They enrich "the natural gas of the quotidian" with their intimation of wider imaginative dimensions beyond the limits of present time or individual identity, shaping "a sense of wholeness that lifts fragmentariness and disconnectedness into some precarious unity by having each story rest on its own complex microcircuitry."[7] In the story "Home" (*Various Miracles*, 1985), Shields uses the Ulysses myth, as well as another medieval Christian intertext, while a second story, "Hinterland" (*The Orange Fish*, 1989),[8] features a medieval Shrine Madonna through which Shields considers the Christian mythology around the Virgin Mary—a figure about whom, as Marina Warner noted, "the amount of historical information...is negligible".[9] Yet the cult of the Virgin Mary, Mother of God, has persisted in Western society over the centuries, elaborated in religious iconography and story, to become an emblem "rooted in the culture," as the folklorist Fay McLeod describes mermaid legends and their intersection with the Virgin cult in her lecture "Mermaids and the Mythic Imagination".[10] Though mythical and mystical beliefs have no resonance for Shields's contemporary characters, her story subtly twists together the sacred and the profane through the figures of the little wooden sculpture of the Virgin and the American tourists.

"Home" is one of Shields's "hymns to the provisional" (as Margaret Atwood described *Unless* in her obituary to Shields)[11] and one of the stories that Shields comments on herself:

In this story each of a hundred passengers on a transatlantic flight experiences a simultaneous moment of happiness, and the energy generated by their accumulated euphoria causes the walls of the aircraft to become, for a moment, translucent. (I confess I was a little surprised by what was rolling out onto my clean white paper: translucent aeroplanes? Wait a minute—wasn't that the stuff of science fiction? Wasn't this out of my territory?"[12]

Defending her choice, Shields also asks: "Who makes the rules? ... Do we accept the fact that fiction is not strictly mimetic, that we want to it to spring *out* of the world, *illuminate* the world, not mirror it back to us?" ("Open Every Question," *Startle* 122). That translucent aeroplane, a radiant metaphor for human interconnectedness, may be one of the "various miracles" in this collection, balanced by another possible "miracle" at the end of the story, but the title suggests that the story is about *something else*—"Home"—even though it turns out to be about travel and unhomeliness for the most part. Though presented as a continuous narrative on the page, it is a story that displays "an ostensible shapelessness" (Verduyn 26), with its changes of geographical and temporal location, shifts in angles of vision, patterns of coincidence, and its switches between realism and the one magic realist moment with the translucent aeroplane—all of which contrives to disorient the reader slightly, disturbing our sense of "reality."

What is so strange about this story is its organization of fictional space—shifts from one country to another, alternations of open and closed spaces, images of ascent and descent, and Shields's representation of imaginative subjective space. In the first section about travelers on the plane from Toronto, Shields moves between omniscient narrative and indirect interior monologue as she describes the unspoken feelings of six passengers and the pilot, tracing how they all shift from negative conditions of homesickness, dyspepsia, and anguish of one kind or another, to a state of perfect balance and reconciliation. This condition of rare happiness shared by every one of the hundred passengers is recorded by the narrator—though it remains unaccounted for—as the effect of "some extraordinary coincidence (or cosmic dispensation or whatever)" (182). As Marta Dvořák remarks, "Shields flaunts randomness as system" (106). Possibly it is a physiological condition induced by the air of the cabin, or the dinner of duckling with orange sauce, or more surrealistically, "some random thought dredged out of the darkness of the aircraft" (182)—enough to cause "a slant" (182) in the collective angle of perception. This heady combination of elusive causes results in the inexplicable circumstance that so dazzles a lonely boy standing on a beach in Greenland as the plane flies across the skies one midsummer night:

It must have been that the intensity and heat of this gathered happiness produced a sort of gas or ether or alchemic reaction—it's difficult to be precise—but for a moment, perhaps two, the wall of the aircraft, the entire fuselage and wings and tail section became translucent. The layers of steel, the rivets and bracing and ribwork turned first purple, then a pearly pink, and finally metamorphosed to the incandescence of pure light. (183)

The story now shifts in focus to the boy on the ground, and it becomes his story, but, before we leave that magic realist moment, the narrator notes that this extraordinary image is a communal phenomenon, the product of a shared human feeling, though invisible to the passengers themselves, all of whom are sealed in their own private fantasy worlds. We return to the boy named Piers, who is left wondering what he has seen in the sky. As the son of a Danish Lutheran pastor, he does not read science fiction; nor does he know about miracles, for his church "strictly eschewed angelic hosts" (184), but as he grows up, Piers searches for words to fit what he saw. As an adolescent, he finds the word "phenomenon," which nicely blurs the boundaries between science, philosophy, and the inexplicable; later, when he goes away to New York as a theology student, he invests the image with spiritual significance as evidence of the hand of God: "All his life seemed to him to have been a centrifugal voyage around that remembered vision—the only sign of mystery he had ever received" (185).

It is doubly interesting that his name is Piers, not only because it is a version of Peter ("Thou are Peter, and upon this rock I will build my Church," Matthew 16:18; Christ's words ring ironically when we consider that Piers in this story has lost his belief in the Trinity), but also interesting because it reminds us of the hero of William Langland's Middle English poem, *Piers Plowman*, which is a Christian visionary poem wherein Piers sees a vision of the Tower of Truth and the Dungeon of Wrong, with the earth in between, "a fair field of folk." That poem is as filled with visions as it is with satirical barbs again contemporary labor conditions and the corruption of the Church, but Langland's Piers becomes a Christian guide, whereas Shields's Piers even begins to doubt that he has seen a vision at all after his lover, a medieval historian (in a neat allusion to the *Piers Plowman* connection), debunks his story and suggests that he consult a psychiatrist. As Shields has commented, "I'm told by my linguistic friends that English is poor in words that describe mystical or transcendental experiences" ("Open Every Question," *Startle* 126). Always an outsider and a wanderer, Piers goes as a tourist to Mexico. He is a modern Ulysses figure who is

> Often orphaned spiritually or else psychologically, and often wounded, maimed in some way, either metaphorically or otherwise...[often] in transit, in a state of what George Steiner calls in-betweenness, and further confused by disappearing landmarks or by the absence of shared events or ceremonies. ("Narrative Hunger" 29; shorter version in *Startle* 125)

It is at Acapulco airport that the second "miracle" occurs, and once more Piers is involved—though unaware of it. The angle of vision shifts to that of a young baggage checker called Josephe, who observes first with fright, then amusement, and finally awe, that every single one of the passengers on the New York flight is wearing blue jeans! Marta Dvořák's close textual analysis of this passage highlights the incongruities and playful ironies of these visible connections, and irony is further strengthened by this incident as Piers's childhood visionary experience is replayed in what looks like a complete reversal. Whereas for him versimilitude had been dismantled in a moment of magic realism, now the miraculous is nothing more than Josephe's recognition of coincidence. Emptied of any possible theological resonance, her "miracle" is oddly allied with the uncanny and with consumerism. Perhaps all this conforms to the rather shocking atmosphere of "raw duplicity" which hangs over the Acapulco airport terminal. It is Piers who unknowingly confirms this "miracle" as he quickly passes into and then out of Josephe's frame of vision. The young woman is left like Alice, wishing she "could see *that* bit," but she cannot:

> She tries hard to get a good look at the last passenger's face, the one who sealed the effect of unreality, but the other passengers crowd around her desk, momentarily threatened by her small discoveries and queries, her transitory power. (186)

Different in quality as they are, the narrative manages to bring the two extraordinary occurrences together by holding them in a common frame of reference, which is only explained in the final paragraph:

> In no time it's over; the tourists, duly processed, hurry out into the sun. They feel lighter than air, they claim, freer than birds, drifting off into their various inventions of paradise as though oblivious to the million invisible

filaments of connection, trivial or profound, that bind them to one another
and to the small planet they call home. (186)

Those "various inventions of paradise" echo "his or her private visions
of transcendence" on the plane, where shared states of feeling are juxtaposed with the same dispersal of a sense of community when everybody is
isolated, locked into their own little fantasy worlds. Even the concept of
paradise has become privatized and commodified. Yet it is this vision of an
unacknowledged common humanity which finally transcends irony as the
final "miracle" is revealed by the narrator through the language—those
"million invisible filaments of connection" (186) that are part of the
"complex microcircuitry" weaving back through images of light and glass
and transparency to the "little lights" all going on to produce the luminous aeroplane. When that imagery is balanced against the "small planet
they call home," we can see how this story might be read as a parable of
"Homo Viator," a secular version of man searching for his heavenly home
(Vauthier 129). However, I prefer to see Piers as both like and unlike Piers
Plowman, a failed visionary in a post-Christian world, helplessly adrift in a
"fair field of folk," just as he is like and unlike Ulysses, a wanderer who
does not recognize his homecoming when he lands because he is unaware
of the web of interconnections that the narrator's deliberately squint-eyed
view has revealed. From that other angle of vision, the shadows of myth
are reflected inside the story frame in a narrative which allows the reader
to see "the randomness of a human life, its arbitrary and fractured experiences, that nevertheless strain towards a kind of wholeness" ("Arriving
Late" 249).

"Hinterland," with its suggestive title, uses Christian iconography even
more explicitly than "Home" to open a "space for strangeness to enter"
her contemporary narrative frame. This time the central image is a little
golden statue of the Virgin Mary in the Musée de Cluny, and again the
world that Shields represents is a secular consumerist one—this time a
world of American tourists in Paris, a world where religion has become a
kind of "cultural haunting,"[13] and where religious icons are drained of
sacred significance and housed in museums. It is the variety of forms that
this "cultural haunting" assumes that I wish to trace in Shields's post-
Christian story, where the characters' values are entirely humanist.

This is the story of a middle-aged Midwestern couple from Milwaukee,
Meg and Roy Sloan, who come to Paris for three weeks in September
1986—"an uneasy, untrustful time in the world's history" (278) during

the swathe of terrorist bombings by Arab extremists in Paris, which, between September 1985 and September 1986, killed thirteen people and injured fifty-five others. (These bombings were instigated by the Committee of Solidarity with Arab and Middle East Political Prisoners, based in Beirut, a ghostly premonition of 9/11 and subsequent terrorist threats.) Indefatigable travelers, the Sloans defy their American friends' suspicions of foreign places "full of people who were rude and unprincipled" (279) and of foreign dangers ("It seemed that Americans were singled out by terrorists, regardless of their background" 278). However, Paris is both an escape from domestic problems and also a site of potential violence and unlocated death threats, from which, as tourists, they believe they are exempt: "We're fatalists" (279), as Meg has told their friends. Once in Paris and settled into their small hotel, they studiously maintain an appearance of normalcy, going about their sightseeing while ignoring the fact that bombings are occurring with frightening regularity on the streets of Paris. They even smile with gratitude at the security guards when they are body-searched on their visit to the Musée de Cluny, which is where the main action of the narrative is focused. It is there that Meg sees a statue of the Virgin Mary, which she tells her husband about over lunch.

> "I loved her," says Meg, returning to the Virgin. "I *loved* her. Not that she was beautiful, she was more odd than beautiful. Her face, I mean. It was sort of frozen and pious, and she had these young eyes."
> "How young?"
> "Very. Like a teenager's eyes. They bulged. But the main thing was her stomach. Or her chest rather. It opened up, two little golden doors on hinges, beautiful, and inside was this tiny shelf. It was amazing, like a toy cupboard."
> "And?"
> "Inside her body, on this shelf—now this is pretty strange—was a whole crucifixion scene, all carved with little figures, tiny little things like dolls. I'm not describing it very well, but—" ...
> "That's all," Meg says. "There she was, this little golden teenager, and inside her she was carrying a scene from the future. Like a video or a time bomb or something. It's the one thing "I'll remember out of all that stuff we saw this morning. Just her." (285–6)

Meg is describing a "*Vierge Ouvrante*,"[14] a medieval devotional sculpture where the painted wooden body of the Madonna is hinged from the neck down to open out, revealing scenes from the life and sacrificial death of Christ. Inside the central womb space is the figure of God supporting a cross on which Christ's body is hanging, flanked by two painted panels in the manner of a triptych; the whole constitutes a theatrical representation that makes visible the mystery of God's divine plan for mankind's salvation. These statues were popular from the twelfth to the fifteenth centuries in Germany, France, and Spain, though they are now quite rare. There are only about forty in the world, as they were condemned at the time of the Reformation as indecent in their representations of a pregnant Virgin or a breastfeeding mother, and most were destroyed. The best-known one is a fourteenthcentury gold-painted Madonna from Cologne, now in the Metropolitan Museum of Art in New York, and there is also a very attractive early fifteenth-century polychrome example from Prussia in the Musée de Cluny.[15] However, neither is quite the same as the one Shields describes, for they are both Nativity statues, whereas what Meg sees is an Annunciation statue which makes visible the miraculous moment when God enters the human time frame. The Virgin's body is the place of intersection where the Word becomes Flesh and the whole process of salvation is set in motion. Christ's destiny is figured long before his birth ("The Lamb of God that was slain before the creation of the world," Revelation 13:9), and the *Vierge Ouvrante* allows viewers to see the encrypted future with its revelation of God's promise to redeem mankind. As Marina Warner remarks, "Popular sentiment recognizes that Jesus could not have been born a man without a mother and without life could not have accomplished his destiny, and it therefore accords Mary a crucial place in the economy of salvation" (Warner 221).

Life, death, and redemption are closely linked through the figure of Mary, though in Shields's story, Meg's response is not to the sacred but to the strange: "She was more odd than beautiful," and Meg seems to make no connection between what that figure represents and what is happening in the world around her (although as if subconsciously aware, she uses the image of a "time bomb.") The notion of mortality is heightened by the terrorist threat on the streets of Paris and later inside the museum itself, but what becomes of the concept of redemption in the modern secular world? That question is answered not by the characters but through the narrative structure and language, where curious doubling effects mesh together the Virgin's statue, the American tourists, and the terrorist bombs, so that boundaries between medieval belief and contemporary experience become destabilized, though not eradicated, in this realistic fiction. As Brenda Beckman-Long suggests in her study of *The Republic of*

Love and the continuing significance of mermaid (and sacred) myths, included in this collection, Shields participates in both the critical and religious turns in literary history in her "narrative collage of religious and civil discourses," which "troubles binary divisions, such as the sacred and profane" (139).

Roy returns to the museum that afternoon on his own when Meg goes to visit a fashion warehouse, and his reactions to the statue are entirely different from hers, though no less secularized. As the head of a technical college in downtown Milwaukee, he is less interested in the theatricality of medieval art, which he finds "luridly dramatic," than in the mechanical construction of the "ingenious little casket" (289) of the Virgin's body. In fact, he is so interested that, in a moment of strangeness when "the density of the room seems to have shifted" (290), this law-abiding citizen does a forbidden thing: "he reaches out and pushes one of the little doors" (290). (Such changes of density or atmospheric pressure always signal moments of apperception, as in "Home" or the moment of radiant understanding at the dinner party in *Larry's Party*.) Immediately a museum guard appears and announces in English that Roy "must leave the museum." Is Shields invoking the shade of the angel Gabriel with his tremendous announcement of the Annunciation, translating it into parodic form with the stout old attendant ordering Roy out or is this attendant a stand-in for the archangel Michael expelling Adam and Eve from the Garden of Eden? However, this is merely intertextual teasing, for it turns out that the guard's words have nothing to do with Roy's transgression. There is a bomb scare inside the museum, and Roy is herded toward the exit with all the other visitors, experiencing in that moment of panic a rift of consciousness when his whole life, with all its accumulated memories, frustrations, and disappointments, drains away from the intensely focused present moment. But nothing has happened really; it is only a false alarm, and, as he walks back to his hotel, Roy feels that he has been pushed "as close to the edge of his life as he's ever likely to be" (293), and then reprieved. Is this a miracle or is it a postmodern deferral of epiphany?

The narrative assiduously leaves open both possibilities, but, as it modulates back into the rhythms of the everyday, Roy's response encourages the reader to see his experience as a kind of redemption, although one that is registered as intensely private, subjective. Shields does not use the theological vocabulary of deliverance from sin, but Roy certainly undergoes a purgation in his moment of terror when he is freed from the burden of his own past, leaving him "emptied out, light-headed, agonizingly alert"

(293) for the first time in years. That entirely human dimension of his experience is confirmed by Meg's wifely commiseration later that evening when they are having dinner: "Of course you ran ... there's nothing shameful about wanting to save your own life. I mean, there's nothing selfish about it or cowardly" (294). The instinct for survival is implicitly set against the statue's emblematic representation of Christ's sacrificial death for the redemption of humanity, spelling out the gap between human and divine.

In a pattern of doubling and almost-repetition so characteristic of many Shields's stories (including "Home" and her novel *Happenstance*) Roy's experience is replayed in a different key by his wife's moment of strangeness in the fashion warehouse. Hers, however, is more like Alice going through the looking-glass, "as though she had stepped into a room where the air was thinned and, at the same time, more tremblingly present" (295). Disappointed and faintly ashamed at her own vanity, she had fled the warehouse and, on impulse, had phoned their daughter back in Milwaukee, whose return to the family home with her children when her marriage broke up had been the main reason why Meg and Roy had decided to escape to Paris. Much to her surprise, Meg hears that the marriage has been patched up and their daughter is about to leave their house. Meg's unspoken relief at this news leaves her feeling dizzy, as if—like Roy in the museum—she had stumbled into a different dimension of reality. Here is a second small redemption, though for Shields's characters redemption is possible only in the here and now and in human terms.

There would seem to be a complete separation between the figure of the Virgin as the vessel for redemption in traditional Christian terms and what the Sloans have experienced. But that is not quite so. In the final paragraph, as the perspective shifts back to that of the omniscient narrator, the multiple strands of the story are deftly interwoven around the themes of mortality, predestination, and redemption. With one of her characteristic imaginative squints, the narrator does what the Sloans themselves resist doing as she glances into the future lives of this ageing couple. After all, the pattern is so predictable that it can be figured in miniature "in a space the size of this small table" in Paris (295), where they are having dinner. They will grow old and die, for every human life ends in death, and, like the statue of the Virgin, they too carry the future inside their own bodies. The difference is that the statue can be opened to reveal what is in the hinterland, whereas Meg's suit jacket remains neatly buttoned up. There is one other important difference: the "*Vierge Ouvrante*" figures the

Christian belief that mortality and redemption go together as part of God's plan for mankind, whereas, for the modern secular consciousness, that link has been broken. Disturbingly, the only time the word "redemption" occurs here is in relation to the terrorist attacks, but its use is oblique and adjectival, and it has been transposed from its Christian context to one of threat from Islamic extremists. Terror is described as having a "redemptive power," which recalls Roy's sudden sense of release in his moment of panic at the museum. As the narrator opines, even that will be forgotten when he is on his deathbed in favor of more sentimentalized memories of marital intimacy at a Paris dinner table:

> The memory will divide and shrink like a bodily protein, and terror, with all its freshness and redemptive power, will give way, easily, easily, to the small rosy singularity of this shaded lamp, and the arc of light that cuts their faces precisely in half. (296)

With its images of singularity and division, as the illusion of containment in the present is shattered by the implications carried in the future tense, this ending allows the reader "to see *that* bit" of the Sloans' lives that lies outside the frame of their immediate attention, like the halves of their two faces, which are in the dark. Shields once used a similar image of cutting in half to describe the phenomenon of gender limitation, which she believed beset many writers of fiction: "The world we are being offered as readers is only half-realized, a world divided down its middle."[16] Here we might extend the application of that image to embrace both sexes, where time itself becomes the marker of division, with men and women split between their lives in the present and their invisible, already predestined, futures, however ordinary or "unimaginable" these may turn out to be. In such a reading that final sentence might be read as a gesture of recuperation, binding the *Vierge Ouvrante* and the Sloans in a shared narrative of the human condition: "There should be some foreshadowing, those little brush strokes of possibility, so that when the dénouement does arrive, it will both surprise and satisfy some level of expectation" ("Pacing," *Startle* 78).

Through her narrative craft Shields performs an imaginative act of redemption, buying back two extraordinary moments in the lives of human beings separated by centuries, and where the figurative time bomb hidden inside the medieval statue opens up "space for strangeness to enter" between the present and the shadowy future. Likewise, boundaries between the present and the past are elided as surely as the dividing lines between realism, fantasy, and myth, for "Narrative that questions experience, repositions experience, expands or contracts experience, rearranges experience, dramatizes experience, and which brings, without apology: colour, interpretation, and political selection, has been with us since the earliest stirrings of the human tongue," as Shields declares in "Open Every Question" (*Startle* 120; "Narrative Hunger" 24).

NOTES

1. Carol Shields, "Pacing, Passion and Tension," in *Startle and Illuminate: Carol Shields on Writing*, eds. Anne Giardini and Nicholas Giardini (Toronto: Random House Canada, 2016), p.77.

2. Lewis Carroll, Alice's *Adventures in Wonderland, Through the Looking Glass, and The Hunting of the Snark* (London: Bodley Head, 1974), p.131.

3. Carol Shields, "Segue," in *Carol Shields: The Collected Stories* (Toronto: Random House Canada, 2003), p.17.

4. Howard, Blanche and Allison Howard, eds. *A Memoir of Friendship* (Toronto: Penguin Canada, 2007), p.180.

5. Carol Shields, "Be Bold All the Way Through," *Startle* 144.

6. Carol Shields, "In Ontario: Reviewing *Friend of My Youth*," *London Review of Books*, 7 February 1991: 23.

7. Simone Vauthier, "Closure in Carol Shields's *Various Miracles*," *Reverberations: Explorations in the Canadian Short Story* (Toronto: Anansi, 1993), p.117.

8. All Carol Shields's short stories are republished in *Carol Shields: The Collected Stories*. Page references in my essay are taken from this edition.

9. Marina Warner, *Alone of All Her Sex: The Myth and the Cult of the Virgin Mary* (London: Weidenfeld and Nicholson, 1976), p.14.

10. Carol Shields, *The Republic of Love* (London: Flamingo, 1993), p.287.

11. Margaret Atwood, "Carol Shields Who Died Last Week," in *Curious Pursuits: Occasional Writings 1907–2005* (London: Virago, 2005), 341–44.

12. Carol Shields, "Arriving Late: Starting Over, "in *How Stories Mean*, eds. John Metcalf and J.R.(Tim) Struthers (Erin, Ontario: Porcupine's Quill, 1993), p. 246.

13. Phillipa Berry, "Postmodernism and Post-Religion," in *The Cambridge Companion to Postmodernism*, ed. Steven Connor (Cambridge: Cambridge University Press, 2000), p.170.

14. With their emphasis on the crucial role of woman in the cycle of redemption, these Vierges Ouvrantes were also regarded as idolatrous. For the same reason, they are of intense interest to contemporary feminist

theologians and art historians. See the authoritative study by Elina Gertsman, *Worlds Within: Opening the Medieval Shrine Madonna* (Penn State University Press, 2015) which considers the significance of these popular and controversial sculptures.

15. See "51 idées de Vierge Ouvrante" https://www.pinterest.co.uk/phillilpefavre)/vierge-ouvrante for multiple visual images. Accessed 15 August 2021.

16. Carol Shields, "The Same Ticking Clock," *How Stories Mean*, 90.

WORKS CITED

Atwood, Margaret. "Carol Shields Who Died Last Week, Wrote Books That Were Full of Delights." *Curious Pursuits: Occasional Writings 1970–2005*. London: Virago, 2005, 341–44.

Berry, Phillipa. "Postmodernism and Post-Religion," *Cambridge Companion to Postmodernism*. ed. Steven Connor. Cambridge: Cambridge UP, 2000, 168–81.

Carroll, Lewis. [1865, 1872, 1876] *Alice's Adventures in Wonderland, Through the Looking Glass, and the Hunting of the Snark*. [1865, 1972, 1876]. London: Bodley Head, 1974.

Gertsman, Elina. *Worlds Within: Opening the Medieval Shrine Madonna*. Penn State University Press, 2015.

Giardini, Anne and Nicholas Giardini, eds. *Startle and Illuminate: Carol Shields on Writing*. Toronto: Random House Canada, 2016.

Shields, Carol. *The Collected Stories*. Toronto: Random House Canada, 2003a.

———. "Hinterland." In *The Collected Stories*, 277–96. Toronto: Random House Canada, 2003b.

———. "Home." In *The Collected Stories*, 178–86. Toronto: Random House Canada, 2003c.

Vauthier, Simone. "Closure in Carol Shields's *Various Miracles*." *Reverberations: Explorations in the Canadian Short Story*. Toronto: Anansi, 1993, 114–131.

Warner, Marina. *Alone of All Her Sex: The Myth and the Cult of the Virgin Mary*. Oxford: Oxford University Press, 2013.

"Be a Little Crazy: Astonish Me": Carol Shields's Improvisational Flair in *Dressing Up for the Carnival*

Nora Foster Stovel

Carol Shields, most famous for her ten novels, published fifty-six stories in three collections—*Various Miracles* (1985), *The Orange Fish* (1989), and *Dressing Up for the Carnival* (2000)—all republished after her death in *The Collected Stories* (2004), along with "Segue," based on her unfinished novel.[1] Each collection employs a literary or artistic focus: *Various Miracles* focuses on literary genres, *The Orange Fish* focuses on literature and the other arts, and *Dressing Up For the Carnival* focuses on theatrical performativity, as its title suggests. This title inevitably evokes Mikhail Bakhtin's theory of carnival that he argues in his study of Rabelais, as Coral Ann Howells affirms in her essay on *Dressing Up for the Carnival*, "Space for Strangeness: Carol Shields's Short Stories," which she calls "Shields's postmodern version of the carnivalesque" (154).

Unlike Shields's first two collections, *Dressing Up for the Carnival* employs a framework, beginning with the title story, "Dressing Up for the

N. F. Stovel (✉)
University of Alberta, Edmonton, AB, Canada

© The Author(s), under exclusive license to Springer Nature
Switzerland AG 2023
N. F. Stovel (ed.), *Relating Carol Shields's Essays and Fiction*,
https://doi.org/10.1007/978-3-031-11480-9_5

Carnival," and concluding with the final story, "Dressing Down," suggesting preparation for life and then for death. It hinges on "Absence," the central story on which the others pivot, as many stories focus on absence, loss, or renunciation. Alex Ramon claims the stories are all interconnected by "the loss of 'ordinary items,' by the trope of absence and by an exploration of the strategies devised by protagonists to bear the lacks and deficiencies which characterize their lives" (Ramon 2008, 151).

Shields creates "an artifact out of absence,"[2] however, as she explores the *self* in relation to the *other*. For example, Mandy Eliot, in the title story, carrying her brother's football helmet, suddenly "*is* her brother" (7), while "X," enjoying "the embrace of happiness" during his wife's absence at bingo, "waltzes about in his wife's lace-trimmed night-gown" (8), suggesting that dressing up in the costume of the other enables the self to flourish.

"Dressing Up for the Carnival" parallels the title stories of both *Various Miracles* and *The Orange Fish* by introducing a series of characters "whose good fortune it is to materialize in the panoply of Shields's colorful street parade" (131), in the words of Barbara Love. This panoply allows Shields to list cameos and vignettes, and, through them, the topic of the collection, the life and death of the self in relation to the other. In "An Endangered Species," her review of *Dressing Up for the Carnival,* Joyce Carol Oates claims, "The quick-silver opening story, a sort of musical overture, glides rapidly about an unspecified Canadian city [...] with Woolfian bravura" (4–5)—or, she could say, with the whimsical curiosity of Dylan Thomas in *Under Milk Wood.*

Eleven individuals in this title story are characterized by an object that becomes a talisman, like Shields's eponymous orange fish, that transforms their sense of self: a yellow skirt, a mango, a pram, a bouquet of daffodils, a chignon, a copy of Samuel Beckett's *Waiting for Godot,* and a tag that proclaims, "I SKIED HAPPY MOUNTAIN" (7), leading onlookers to wonder, "Who does she think she *is*?" (8).[3] Shields freeze-frames individuals in disguise at that moment when they see themselves: Roger, holding his mango, "freezes and sees himself freshly" (2–3). This talisman inspires a new self-image, challenging the "shrivelled fate" he envisioned (3). Oates notes, "Shields both celebrates and gently mocks the human need to mythologize the self" (5).[4]

Tamara, the first character named, is "no longer just Tamara, clerk-receptionist for the Youth Employment Bureau, but a woman in a yellow skirt. A passionate woman dressed in yellow. A Passionate, Vibrant Woman

About To Begin Her Day. Her Life" (2). The theatricality of the story is manifest: Tamara is dressing up for the carnival of life, donning her costume, for life is viewed as performance art.[5] "We cannot live without our illusions," Shields claims, because these illusions allow "[v]istas of possibility [to] unfold" (8)—vistas that Shields pursues to their logical, or sometimes illogical, conclusions.[6] "Dressing Up for the Carnival" functions as an ideal introduction to the collection in another way, as it includes references to motifs in other stories, including "Weather," "Windows," "Mirrors," and a beating heart related to the ending of "Stop!"

Dressing Up for the Carnival includes several stories—"Weather," "Windows," "Mirrors," "Reportage," "Absence," and "Stop!"—that read like absurdist creative-writing improvisations. For example, what if there were a tax on windows, what if meteorologists went on strike and there were no weather, or what if a Roman arena were discovered in Manitoba? Shields imagines an alternate reality "beneath a trapdoor labelled '"What if—"'.[7] As Shields reflects in her essay "Boxcars, Coat Hangers and Other Devices," "Diurnal surfaces could be observed by a fiction writer with a kind of deliberate squint that distorts but also sharpens beyond ordinary vision, bringing forward what might be called the subjunctive mode of one's self or others, a world of dreams, possibilities, and parallel realities" (*Startle* 29). In *Dressing Up for the Carnival,* Shields explores that subjunctive mode, imagining parallel realities.[8]

This *what-if* dimension, suggesting theatrical "improvs," reflects Shields's interest in drama, in which improvisation plays an important role, as she was intimately involved in theatre during her two decades in Winnipeg, both as a frequent theatre-goer and as a published and produced playwright.[9] These '"What if"' stories suggest absurdity, such as the Roman arena unearthed in the midst of the Canadian prairies, that recalls the Theatre of the Absurd plays by Samuel Beckett, Harold Pinter, and Edward Albee that Carol and Don Shields enjoyed at the Black Hole Theatre Company and Winnipeg's Prairie Theatre Exchange during the last two decades of the twentieth century when they resided in Winnipeg.[10]

Moreover, the improvisational quality of these stories also reflects Shields's role as an instructor of creative-writing courses, which she taught for several years at the Universities of Ottawa, Manitoba, and Winnipeg. While dramatic improvisations would be an appropriate focus for Shields, I will focus on her use of improvisational exercises in her creative-writing courses, as explicated by her essay "Be a Little Crazy; Astonish Me" in

Startle and Illuminate: Carol Shields on Writing,[11] for her essays illuminate her fiction, as I argue in my introduction to this collection.

I suggest that Shields's improvisational techniques in her stories are inspired by her experience of teaching creative writing, as recorded in "Be a Little Crazy; Astonish Me" (*Startle* 37–48), and as illustrated by her several "What-if" stories in *Dressing Up for the Carnival*

In "Be a Little Crazy; Astonish Me" Shields notes that authors—such as Eugene O'Neill, Tennessee Williams, Arthur Miller, and Flannery O'Connor—took creative-writing courses (37), while John Barth, John Ciardi, and Ralph Ellison taught them (39). Although, when the Library of Congress hosted a gathering of 500 creative-writing instructors in Washington, D.C. in 1973, the consensus was that no one knew how to teach writing and that only one percent of people who took creative-writing courses became writers, nevertheless, writing courses flourished, along with writers' retreats and writer-in-residence programs. The 1970s, Shields notes, was the age of the non-hierarchical experimental *workshop*— a concept Kingsley Amis claimed was responsible for the downfall of modern civilization—as creative-writing classes became "our salons, our 'left banks,' our wine bars, the laboratories of our literature" (40), in Shields's words.

Shields concludes her essay on creative writing, "Be a Little Crazy: Astonish Me," thus: "The human transactions that take place in writing class are enormously useful in the long run, perhaps more useful than the aesthetic transactions" (45). Her view that "social transactions" are more valuable than "aesthetic transactions" (40) is demonstrated in her story "Chemistry," in her 1989 *The Orange Fish* collection (11–33), where she transforms an actual creative writing course that she taught at the University of Ottawa into a fictional class on playing the recorder.[12]

Shields was clearly skilled in leading writing workshops, although, when she described one in her first published novel, *Small Ceremonies* (1976), she had never taught or even taken[13] one. Nevertheless, she later judges that, through guesswork, she got it right (40). Her protagonist, Judith Gill, describes the "warming-up exercises" her creative-writing seminar instructor assigns: "we were to describe such things as the experience of ecstasy or the effect of ennui, a dialogue between lovers one week and enemies the next" (68). While Judith calls such exercises "childish games," Furlong Eberhardt refers to his students' writing as "garbage" (70)—a view that Shields clearly condemns and ironizes. Judith reports of her fellow students' creations, "They were relentless, compulsive, unsparing, as though they had waited all their lives for these moments of catharsis, these Wednesday afternoon epiphanies" (68–9). When Furlong assigns the students to compose a novel, she discovers an "inability to manufacture situations" and envies her fellow students for "the ease with which they drifted off into fantasies, for although they strained my credulity, their inventiveness seemed endless" (69), recalling Shields's comment about dreams.

Shields explains that, on the contrary, in her own creative-writing seminars, "I try to establish an atmosphere of creativity, not correction" (41), by employing "kindness and trust" (40). She found it takes weeks to establish an atmosphere of trust in a class, for "it is only then that creative and critical skills begin to grow" (41). She judged that early writing programs "ran on the gas of criticism rather than creativity" (38): she recounts taking over a creative-writing course wherein her predecessor prohibited use of the first person as "masturbatory and therefore indecent" (42). It took her a full year to restore students' confidence in use of the first-person voice. One student confessed that reading his writing to a class was like taking off his clothes in public (40)—a concept that relates to the nudity of the final story, "Dressing Down." "Ideally, students are drawn out, cajoled, persuaded, questioned, nudged, niggled and encouraged to make a new and personal set of criteria," she believes, "rather than fed a critical line on one way to approach creating fiction" (38). "A creative writing teacher can to a certain extent give permission" (44), she allows, however.

The success of Shields's approach is confirmed by her student Wayson Choy, who became a successful writer and who extols her teaching in his essay "My Seen-Sang, Carol Shields: A Memoir of a Master Teacher," wherein he celebrates "Carol Shields's characteristic 'goodness'" (299). She taught him more than "technique and craft" (299); she encouraged him to explore his own "personal history": "Write what you know about" (300). Above all, she urged him to "'Be creative'" (302). Her creative-writing student Martin Levin observes her dual self, recalling that she "hid an astringent sharpness beneath an exterior of sweet agreeableness" (305).

Shields rejects the idea that "writing is God-given" (37). Just as she remarked that Jane Austen understood that writing was creating scenes, so she believes that one can teach "certain skills involved in writing: setting up a scene and furnishing it, situating a narrative in time and space, controlling the flow of information, creating a mood, deciding who is telling the story and why" (39). She distinguishes between *art* and *craft*: while *art* cannot be taught, students can be given "a few basic tools that permit them to self-evolve" (37), as she believes instructors can teach "aspect[s] of writing," including "tension, tone, voice" (43).

In "Be a Little Crazy; Astonish Me" she explains her approach to teaching creative writing through using improvisations, such as assigning students to describe a scene "without using any adjectives" (44). She recalls, "I might for instance pass around a photograph of a human hand, and ask them to write for six minutes, using the voice of the owner of the hand" (43). Shields's notes for her creative-writing courses in the National Library reveal that she frequently improvised assignments for her students. Anne and Nicholas Giardini, her daughter and grandson, editors of *Startle and Illuminate: Carol Shields on Writing*, list some assignments recalled by Shields's former writing students, including:

> Write 250 words about one person giving a gift that is refused.
>   Write something in which the world is a blank slate, without history. (47) [14]

Martin Levin recalls that Shields asked students to "'Write an entire story in a single sentence" or "a paragraph on 'Why did the surgeon sell the pink ballet slipper?'" (305–6). In "'Controlled Chaos' and Carol Shields's 'A View from the Edge of the Edge,'" Marta Dvořák recalls that Shields arrived to teach a creative-writing workshop at the Université de Rennes armed with "a small white plastic coffee spoon, which she held up to trigger considerations on creation and its origins—namely the relations between craft and art, derivation and invention, formal constraint and artistic freedom." Dvořák continues, "She invited students to jot down a word the object had brought to mind, then to make a sentence which included that word, a sentence which in turn needed to be included in a paragraph on whatever they chose." She concludes, "The results read out were of a startling freshness and diversity" (95). She adds that in "A View from the Edge of the Edge" Shields "stresses how art is melded with craft, which can be learned [… and which] includes managing chance and chaos."[15]

Shields's descriptions of her teaching, plus her students' evaluations, housed in her archives, reveal what a gifted teacher she was, encouraging students to "Be bold *all the way through*" (*Startle* 146). She repeated exercises, urging students to "'Take it further this time.'" She recalls, "It's as though they need someone to say: Be a little crazy. Astonish me" (43). The title of her essay recalls Russian ballet impresario Sergei Diaghilev's famous response: when asked by artist Jean Cocteau what kind of design he wanted, he replied simply, "*Etonne-moi.*"

Just as the narrator of "Absence" elects "to create a story that possesses a granddaughter, a Boston fern, a golden apple, and a small blue cradle" (103),[16] so Shields perhaps set her students, or herself, the improvisational task of writing a story about a scarf, *soup du jour*, or dying for love. Perhaps she assigned students to write a story featuring keys, a steering wheel muff, or the next best kiss. Maybe she asked them to write a story imagining a moratorium on weather, a tax on windows, the discovery of a Roman arena in southern Manitoba, or a typewriter in which the letter "i" is defunct. The editors of *Startle and Illuminate: Carol Shields on Writing*, suggest some improvisational writing assignments following "Be a Little Crazy: Astonish Me," such as a story including "a needle, a ticket stub and a glass of milk" (47)—another example of what Dvořák, in "'Controlled Chaos' and Carol Shields's 'A View from the Edge of the Edge'" in this text, terms an "amplifying device of chaotic enumeration." She notes "Shields's hallmark inventories aspiring to exhaustivity, particularly her *chaotic* enumeration, a disorderly and open-ended accumulation."

Focusing on the essentially playful quality of Shields's short fiction, as Neil Besner argues in "The Short of It: Carol Shields's Stories,"[17] included in this text and as illuminated by "Be a Little Crazy: Astonish Me," her essay on creative-writing courses, let us explore what she discovers beneath the trapdoor labelled "What if" in her improvisational stories "Reportage," "Weather," "Windows," "Mirrors," "Absence," and "Stop!"

"Reportage," perhaps her most absurdist story, explores the repercussions of the discovery of a Roman arena in Manitoba—an absurd eventuality both geographically and temporally. When drills seeking oil under "Billy's Basin" strike "remnants of antiquity" (122) in the form of "three supine Ionic columns" (124), a circular tiered amphitheater is revealed. The discovery of such a "major historical monument of classical proportions" (123) transforms a peaceful agrarian community into a busy tourist attraction, stimulating the local economy. The Sandy Banks beer hall is renamed "the Forum" (125), while the owner of the old Orchard place, where the arena was unearthed, guides tours instead of growing grain and sells postcards in place of wheat, inciting envy south of the border and inspiring American scientists to scour Minnesota with lasergraphs.

Shields frequently employs Austen's technique of canvassing various individuals' responses, as in *Pride and Prejudice*, wherein each member of the Bennet family reveals her intelligence or lack of same in her response to Mr. Bennet's reading aloud of Mr. Collins's letter of introduction. In "Reportage" half a dozen reactions to the discovery are recorded, one of them presented in dramatic dialogue form (124–5) that recalls Shields's own interest in playwriting. Dr. Elizabeth Jane Harkness at the Interpretive Centre considers that the markings resemble the "cup-and-ring carvings of prehistory" and is offended by the "'Eurocentric'" dismissal of the markings as mere "'doodles'" (125).

Citizens envision extending the "takeaway trade" to open-air concerts or operas, as in Verona's Roman amphitheater, or even "Disney-on-ice" (126). The thesis of Shields's story, apart from its satirical thrust and humorous absurdism, is a metaphysical consideration of relations of time and place—"the metaphysics of time, Kiros and Chronos, and the disjunctive nature of space/matter" (123), a subject that Mavis Orchard, who has "an unflinching attachment to the quotidian" (123), as opposed to the ancient and historical, studied in college philosophy courses. Only Ruby Webbers, the Latin teacher, is appalled by the damage done to this agrarian community and asks rhetorically, "do beautiful monuments ever think of the lives they smash?" (127). Ruby commands this "monolithic enterprise" (126) to "Vanish," dismissing it as "a ridiculous old phantom" (127), thus raising the possibility that it is all mere illusion, a *"trompe l'oeil"* (118).

Three stories—"Weather," "Windows," and "Mirrors"—all portray middle-aged married couples dealing with deprivations or even voluntary renunciations that necessitate inventiveness to enable them to adjust to their deficiencies or sacrifices.

In "Weather," the National Association of Meteorologists goes on strike, resulting, absurdly, in a cessation of weather. Deadlocked, arbitration breaks down, extending the strike and plunging the population into depression, as the deprivation of weather inspires an "existential limbo" (Ramon 2008, 154). Speculation abounds: are they striking for better wages, pension plans, or working conditions? Equally absurdly, the government considers calling in the troops, but the weatherless situation remains unalleviated, as Shields plays with magic realism.[18]

Weather deprivation also instigates an existential malaise in the nameless narrator and even more in her unnamed husband, "an outdoor man by nature" (29), who works in a plant nursery. It impacts both their sense of self and their relationship, as they are "dislocated in time and space" (30), placing a moratorium on their "rare tender moments" (28). Even their garden suffers, as their "Mexican Ecstasy" tomatoes hang unripening on the vine, symbolizing the loss of their erotic ardor. *Ennui* triumphs: "This lack of mattering smarted like a deerfly's sting" (31).

The narrator recalls a rustic barometer composed of a wooden house from which a girl-doll and boy-doll dressed in Alpine costumes emerge to predict sunny or cloudy weather respectively (31–2), like the one Margaret Atwood describes in *Surfacing* (1972),[19] leading her to question such gendered signification. Finally, the strike is settled, as public appreciation and gratitude, the lack of which triggered the strike, is written into the meteorologists' contract. The resurgence of weather, signaled by a midnight breeze and "the ballet-slipper sound of raindrops on the garage roof" (34), triggers a rapprochement between husband and wife, leading them to sleep in each other's arms. It reinvigorates the couple and their commitment to the quotidian, so that they "have curiosity enough to rise and begin another day." It rekindles their intimacy, demonstrating that "the two of [them] have learned the trick of inhabiting parallel weather systems," of creating their own imagined weather (34–5). Shields's employment of absurdism, yoking weather and strike arbitration, like Monty Python's oxymoronic "Ministry of Silly Walks" or its "Graduate Seminar for Village Idiots," emphasizes the relationship between the subjective self and external reality.

"Windows" postulates a "Window Tax" (109) that citizens may evade through eliminating their windows by bricking or boarding them up, creating an "*Obscura maxima*" (113). Bizarre as such an edict may appear now, a tax on windows was actually levied in eighteenth-century Britain, as mentioned by Jane Austen in *Mansfield Park*, and footnoted in the Penguin edition, for which Shields composed the preface.[20] Thus, multiple windows ostentatiously proclaimed the owners' wealth. Such a sacrifice is difficult for anyone, but is specially challenging for "M. J. and I" (115), the nameless narrator and her husband, always referred to by his initials, who are both artists and require natural light to create "that accident we call art" (111). "'Be bold,'" the narrator exhorts herself, recalling Shields's advice to creative-writing classes, "Be bold *all the way through*" (146).

When their application to the government for "professional dispensation" (110) is rejected, they brick up their appropriately named "picture window" (109), referred to as their "panoramic vista" (110). Deletion of their "wondrous apertures to the world" causes their "retreat to medieval darkness," to the primitive underground world [... of] caves or burrows" (114). Rejecting "nature's studio" (113) in the great outdoors and "the perpetual distortion of artificial light" (114–5), they suffer from deprivation, similar to the previous couple's weather deprivation. This affects their self-consciousness, instigating "a curious amnesia of the self" and impacting their erotic relationship (114), causing a moratorium on the "long love affair" (115) of their marriage, as does the cessation of weather in the previous story. Thus, Shields demonstrates the influence of one's quotidian context on one's psyche and the relationship between self and other, as well as the interconnections between art and life.[21]

But, as Shields quotes Leonardo da Vinci's maxim in her final story, "Segue," "Art breathes from containment and suffocates from freedom" (*Collected Stories* 11). Thus, the narrator of "Windows" is inspired by necessity to invent, or create, a literal *picture window* that appears to let in light: "Not real light, of course, but the idea of light" (120). Shields invokes Plato's numinous theory of forms, suggesting that *idea* is preferable to actuality or that art is preferable to reality. She attempts to "make light dance" (119) on the surface of the glass, while she creates a "trompe l'oeil" (118) in painting the oak moldings of the frame. Twice she employs the word "squint," perhaps deliberately recalling her suggestion, alluded to previously, that "Diurnal surfaces could be observed by a fiction writer with a kind of deliberate squint that distorts but also sharpens beyond ordinary vision."

Like the Alpine pair, "Windows" reflects on the equipoise of husband and wife, day and night, light and dark, symbolizing the relationship between reality and art. Husband and wife now wake and sleep in opposition in "an unspoken equipoise" (115), as she works by day and he by night in a quotidian variation on the barometer couple of "Weather," thus also interfering with their "*vie intime*" (150). The mauve (119) tint that appears overnight on the wife's window reveals the contribution of M. J.— whose predilection for lavender (115) has been noted earlier—to the project and represents their artistic cooperation. Art triumphs over limitation, affirming the truth of da Vinci's maxim, while improving on reality, thus "bringing forward what might be called the subjunctive mode of one's self or others, a world of dreams, possibilities, and parallel realities" (29). In one of their "rare moments of tenderness" (119), the pair simultaneously apply the final brush strokes that complete the illusion of light—"infinitely more alluring than light itself [...] better than a window, the window that would rest in the folds of the mind as all that was ideal and desirable in the opening, beckoning sensuous world" (120). "The moment was beautiful" (120), the narrator declares. The wife's description of her creation of this metaphorical window on the world, complete with life-like frame and mullions, highlights painting as performance, just as Shields's self-reflexive metafiction forefronts writing as performance, as Dvořák has argued.[22]

"Mirrors" is another "What-if" story: what if one foreswore mirrors? A nameless couple, seeking a form of asceticism, or renunciation, elects "a voluntary forswearing of mirrors" (76), treating themselves to "an annual season of non-reflectiveness" (67) at their summer cottage that frees them from self-consciousness. While "Weather" suggests the influence of one's context on one's psyche, and "Windows" extends that topic to encompass the resulting subject's perception of external reality, "Mirrors" depicts the subject's self-reflection. The wife considers mirrors *magical*, because they resemble windows, the silver backing alone creating that "miracle of reflection" (75), as Shields plays once again with the double meaning of the word *reflection*.

Although mirrors are "good-luck charms," or compasses that help locate oneself in the world, as Shields suggests, and although they are usually associated with women—especially mermaids, whom she celebrates in *The Republic of Love*, who rise out of the sea "with a comb and mirror in hand" (*RL* 73–4)—the wife, who has always struggled with her weight and mourned her physical failures, enjoys a mirrorless summer wherein she is not obliged to witness the full "panorama" (68) of her figure. "Her concerns, her nightmares, her regrets, her suspicions" (75) may all be wiped clean by this "single act of forfeiture" (67), this "voluntary foreswearing of mirrors" (76). The husband, from whose viewpoint the story is presented, and who is relieved by their "mirrorless" (67) situation, following a love affair, is spared the pain of seeing his guilt reflected in the glass (74).

The couple meticulously clear their cottage of mirrors, including the one embraced by the pair of arms over the bureau (69), and even the little round mirror in the wife's purse compact—although the circle of glue that secured it remains as a reminder. Shields repeats the circle metaphor in the name "Big Circle Lake" (66, 75), where their cottage is located, in their "circle of friends" (68), and in the Roman arena discovered in Manitoba in "Reportage" and described as a "gorgeous multi-tiered, almost perfect circle" (126).

This "deprivation" (65), Shields writes, "signals dissent" (67), a "sacrifice" that frees their "better selves" (65). Eventually, however, the husband of "Mirrors" "developed a distaste [...] for acts of abnegation, finding something theatrical and childish about cultivated denial" (76).

"Living without mirrors is cumbersome and inconvenient" (76), he concludes, rejecting renunciation.

What happens if you don't have mirrors? You become each other's mirror, Shields suggests, for the pair find "the miracle of reflection" in each other's faces, as they mirror each other, because a "twinned current flowed between them" (75). Although this couple, married for 35 years, still perceive each other as *strangers* (72, 76),[23] mirroring allows them to rediscover unity, as the husband, viewing their reflection in a restaurant mirror, declares, "'Hello, us'" (72). When he awakens to find his wife reading in bed, "Their eyes held, caught on the thread of a shared joke: the two of them at this moment had become each other, at home behind the screen of each other's face" (77). No longer strangers, they become one flesh.

The mirror symbolizes life: just as it can endure forever, so the wife can obliterate "[h]er concerns, her nightmares, her regrets, her suspicions" (75). Since she is her husband's mirror, perhaps she already knows of his affair, even without his confession. "We are creatures of the moment, these tales say, yet our victories, though only momentary, can be golden," judges John Bemrose in "Enriching a Fictional Universe" (1). Many Shields short stories, including "Eros," celebrate the renewed intimacy of a somewhat estranged middle-aged couple (205).[24] The epiphanic conclusion of "Mirrors" exemplifies "the epiphanies or transcendent moments" that Elke D'Hoker argues, in "Moments of Being: Carol Shields's Short Fiction," punctuate Shields's stories (152).

"Weather" and "Mirrors" both feature abstinence, but "Stop!" marks the epitome of renunciation. What if a queen renounced everything—from flowers to food, from music to time, from clothing to courtiers, and even the king? "Stop!" acts as a fulcrum for *Dressing Up for the Carnival*, as it reflects several of the "What if" stories in the collection: the queen's harp is smashed and buried deep in the palace garden (62); palace windows are bricked up; weather is "disallowed" and meteorologists dismissed (63), as the queen becomes intolerant of all aspects of her environment. Clocks and calendars are destroyed, and all symbols of time are forbidden. Even Spring Rites are cancelled. Eventually, the queen becomes allergic to the sheer sequentiality of time and language, as they demand "a progression that invites that toxic essence, that mystery" (63). Ultimately, she lives blindfolded, unthinking, her ears stopped, but she cannot stop the "literal dance," the "deadly arithmetic" (63) of her heart, as Shields carries renunciation to its logical conclusion in this quirky tale—recalling Marian McAlpine's renunciations in Margaret Atwood's first published novel, *The*

Edible Woman (1961). Finally, the queen disappears from her kingdom altogether: "absent" (61), she anticipates Shields's best "What-if" story, "Absence."

Shields's profound statement about "the metaphysics of time, Kiros and Chronos, and the disjunctive nature of space/matter" in "Reportage" (123) may recall the diurnal structure of "dressing *up*" for life and "dressing *down*" for death. This existential framework hinges on the central, pivotal story "Absence," as mentioned.[25] The real subject of *Dressing Up for the Carnival* is selfhood and its relation to the other—the spouse, the lover—*and* to external reality: "Subject, object, and the nature of reality," as James Ramsay explains his father's work to Lily Briscoe in Woolf's *To the Lighthouse*, or "object and subject sternly fused," as Shields writes in "Absence" (107), where she "pursues 'the real mystery' of the self, of the other, of the creative process itself," as Marta Dvořák claims in "Carol Shields and the poetics of the quotidian." Just as a character in "The Next Best Kiss" delivers a paper titled "End of the Self" about "the instability of the self, the self as the sum of incalculable misunderstandings, and the selfishness of even claiming a self" (186), so Shields notes "the insularity of the soul" (198) as "the self was placed on trial" (197) and characterizes narrative at the end of "Absence" as "the arabesque of the unfolded self" (107).

"Absence" is the most profound of the "what-if" stories in this collection because it goes to the heart not only of language but also of selfhood *and* the relationship between them. The problem involves a different kind of key from those in the preceding story of that name: one letter that is never named in the story—"a slender, one-legged vowel, erect but humble, whose dot of amazement had never before mattered"—is defunct on her "too-clever-by-half sparky-larky computer" (105). The consequences are linguistic *and* metaphysical, inspiring a rhapsody on language and reflections on selfhood.

Like "The Circus Animals' Desertion" by William Butler Yeats, Shields's fictional woman writer creates a work of art from the inability to write, because she must "make an artifact out of absence" (103)—*improvising*, in a word. The loss of the crucial vowel, which is never employed in the story, causes the gerund (as in the word *being*) to drop through "language's trapdoor," forcing the writer to select words from "her well-loved garden" of vocabulary, even making her resort to her thesaurus, like murdered poet Mary Swann in Shields's 1987 novel *Swann*. "Absence gestures at meaning" (169), Shields claims in "Invention" (*DC* 165–75), and thus opens up possibilities, because nature abhors a vacuum.

The broken key, "the very letter that attaches to the hungry self" (103) that Shields calls "the lonely self, the misunderstood self" in "Be a Little Crazy: Astonish Me" (41), demands "a parallel surrender, a correspondence of economy subtracted from the very alphabet of the self" (106).[26] As well as posing a challenge to selfhood, this absence also creates a sense of freedom that inspires the writer to wonder why she remained "enclosed by the tough, lonely pronoun of her body when the whole world beckoned?" (106). As Aritha van Herk comments in "Extrapolations from *Miracles*," "Taking on the entire subjectivity of the word 'I,' the story is written without one word containing the letter 'I,' and yet resonates with the 'lonely pronoun' of all bodies." Nevertheless, as van Herk claims, the story emerges from the narrator's "cast-off self," from "the dark eye of her eye, the stubborn self" (106).

"Several thousand years ago a woman sat down at a table and began to write" constitutes the refrain of this archetypal story. In the final sentence—"'A woman sat down and wrote,' *she wrote*" (107, emphasis added)—the last two words transform the story from realism to metafictionality, a hallmark of Shields's first short story collection *Various Miracles* (1985).[27] Thus, "our woman" writer, despite the *absence* of the I/eye of the narrator, has the last word (103).

As Marta Dvořák observes in "'Controlled Chaos' and Carol Shields's 'A View from the Edge of the Edge,'" "the specularity of 'Absence' in which our woman writer stages a woman writer protagonist writing about a woman writer writing [...] shifts the focus from story to story*telling*." Thus, "It metatextually calls attention not only to the fabricated nature of the textual product, but also to its process...." Shields adds, "The metatextual discourse of 'Absence' openly substitutes itself for narrative and turns the process, mechanics, or even business of writing into content," a process she suggests is "arguably designed to foreground writing as performance" (107). In a parallel scene in *Unless*, Reta Winters reflects, "I would become a woman writing about a woman writing about women writing, and that would lead straight to an echo chamber of infinite regress in company with the little Dutch girl, the girl on the bathroom cleanser, the vision multiplied, but in receding perspective" (*Unless* 269). "Writing is performance," Shields declares in her essay "Myths That Keep You from Writing" (*Startle* 16).[28] "Absence" provides an ideal example of this performative phenomenon because "*absence* gestures at meaning," as Shields affirms in her story "Invention" (169, emphasis added).

"Absence," which opens with the woman writer setting herself the challenge of composing "a story that possessed a granddaughter, a Boston fern, a golden apple, and a small blue cradle" (103) and facing the additional challenge of composing it on a typewriter on which the letter *i* is defunct, may be Shields's most improvisational story. Before she composed the quirky, absurdist "What-if" stories that compose *Dressing Up for the Carnival*, perhaps Shields assigned herself the challenge that she posed to her students: "Be a Little Crazy: Astonish Me."

NOTES

1. See Nora Foster Stovel's "'Fragments on My Apple': Carol Shields's Unfinished Novel" for a discussion of Shields's draft of her final novel, titled "A Moment's Moment."
2. *Dressing Up for the Carnival*, page 103. Print. Unless otherwise specified, all parenthetical references to Shields's short stories will be to this collection.
3. Shields's repetition of the rhetorical question "Who does she think she is?" (8) may constitute a deliberate tribute to Alice Munro, whom Shields referred to as "the divine Alice," and whose short story collection *Who Do You Think You Are?* was published in 1978.

    Ramon argues that the characters' "performance-based survival strategies" include "props" that are "at once the totems that make their performances possible and the crutches that offer psychological support" (Ramon 2008, 153).
4. In her essay "An Aesthetics of the Ordinary in *Dressing Up for the Carnival*" Marta Dvořák writes, "Defying the linear plot of conventional short story structure, the title story of the collection is constructed upon the rhetorical devices of seriation and hypotyposis" (136).
5. Shields begins certain novels—*Happenstance, Swann*, and *The Republic of Love*—with her protagonists—Brenda Bowman, Sarah Maloney, and Fay MacLeod—dressing for the day.

    As Marta Dvořák claims in "An Aesthetics of the Ordinary in *Dressing Up for the Carnival*," Shields "suggests that the self is a performance, that being is a representation, a construction [... as] all the characters envisage life as a spectacle, and represent themselves to themselves as well as to others on the stage of the world" (Dvořák 2003, 139).

6. Ramon claims, "Performance permits the creation of a parallel story which momentarily liberates the protagonists from the master-narratives of their everyday existences" (Ramon 2008, 153).

7. *Startle and Illuminate: Carol Shields on Writing*, page 32. Unless otherwise specified, all parenthetical references to Shields's essays will be to the Giardini collection.

   In "The quotidian is where it's at," a review of *Dressing Up for the Carnival*, Laura Moss affirms, "several of the stories are extrapolations on 'what if' stories" (194–96).

8. In her essay "Space for Strangeness: Carol Shields's Short Stories" in this collection Coral Ann Howells explains how Shields's stories in both *Various Miracles* and *The Orange Fish* allow us to enter "a world of dreams and possibilities and parallel realities."

9. See Nora Foster Stovel's "*Thirteen Hands*: A Power Play by Carol Shields" for a discussion of her plays. The married couple in "Mirrors" enjoy "*serious* drama" in off-Broadway theatres—"plays that coolly examine the psychological positioning of men and women in our century. This torn, perplexing century. Men and women who resemble themselves" (66).

10. Shields's "What-if" stories demonstrate what Dvořák terms, in "'Controlled Chaos' and Carol Shields's 'A View from the Edge of the Edge" in this volume, "the modernist and postmodern break with realism and its rule of plausibility."

11. This essay was first delivered as a 1990 talk titled "Creative Writing Courses" in Trier, Germany. Unless otherwise specified, all parenthetical references to Shields's essays will be to this essay.

12. In my May 2003 interview with Shields, she told me that, in her first class at the University of Ottawa, a night course in creative writing, she had a class of "mature" women and "puerile" men, so different that she thought the room would overbalance. She said she was rather "school-marmish" at first. She told Eleanor Wachtel, "I taught at the university [Ottawa] for the first time that year – creative writing – and I really loved it. I had one of those evening classes where you get people of all ages who have an extraordinary sense of solidarity and love for each other" (Wachtel, 1989, 32). Her story "Chemistry" was inspired by this class, although she altered the course subject matter from a creative-writing class to a class in playing the recorder. She remained friends with some of the women who kept in touch with her and also kept on writing. Later, she taught creative writing one year at the University of British Columbia.

13. Although Shields claims in "Be a Little Crazy; Astonish Me" that she had never taken a creative-writing course, she mentions in her essay "Writers Are Readers First" that she took a creative-writing course in high school (*SI* 11).

14. Creative-writing assignments were cited courtesy of D. Belanger and M. Zlotnik, from English 4–350 at the University of Manitoba, 1994–1995.
15. Marta Dvořák's essay is included in this collection. Unless otherwise specified, all references to Dvořák's essays will be to this text.
16. This opening improvisational list in "Absence" is, according to Dvořák, an "amplifying device of chaotic enumeration." Shields comments in "The Short Story (and Women Writers)," "I was for some reason drawn to randomness and disorder" (*Startle* 99).
17. Neil Besner argues in his essay "The Short of It: Carol Shields's Stories" (45–55) included in this collection that Shields's stories demonstrate experimentation, playfulness, and performativity.
18. Shields introduces the subject of weather in her opening story, "Dressing Up for the Carnival": Tamara, dressing for her day, "never checks the weather before she dresses," as she considers that "her clothes *are* the weather" (2).
19. Atwood's unnamed narrator thought as a child that the couple "controlled the weather instead of merely responding to it" (*Surfacing* 20). Shields pursues that notion, suggesting that meteorologists create the weather, rather than merely commenting on it.
20. Carol Shields's introduction to the 2001 Modern Library edition of *Mansfield Park* by Jane Austen, pages ix-xii. Shields wrote to Blanche Howard on 5 November 1997, "I reread *Mansfield Park* this summer to see if I could figure out why Jane loved Fanny when no one else could. I found a few clues, not many, and have done a short essay for the salon.com on it" (*MF* 375). She wrote to Howard on 1 December 1997, "Am just finishing a rather odd little story about the Window Tax, which I am sure you know about. But I set it in contemporary times" (*MF* 379). In "The Visual Arts," an unpublished talk delivered to the Royal Canadian Academy of Arts in Winnipeg in 1997, the fortieth anniversary of the founding of the Canada Council, as she observes, Shields talked about the new tax on windows in late eighteenth-century England that led to the bricking up of windows and the "window artists" who painted windows on walls, making stone resemble glass through which light shone—"Not real light, of course, but the idea of light, which is infinitely more powerful than light itself"—echoing her story "Windows" verbatim.
21. In his essay "The Short of It: Carol Shields's Stories" in this collection, Neil Besner claims of "Weather," "Shields is intent on making small plausible worlds with one element gone missing, or gone awry, or recurring variously, miraculously—calling into question our more common understanding of sequence, of causality, of narrative chains, of plot" (49)—invoking the subjunctive, one could say.

22. Shields's narrator highlights the word "mullions," as Shields does with so many words, and she includes a self-reflexive note on the use of her phrase "*most especially*" (117). Interestingly, the narrator suggests that it might be better if she were married to a "civil engineer" (111), as Shields herself was.

23. In her essay "Where Curiosity Leads," Shields states, "even partners in long, happy marriages remained, ultimately, strangers, one to the other" (*Startle* 83).

24. In her essay "Space for Strangeness: Carol Shields's Short Stories" in this collection, Coral Ann Howells observes that the middle-aged couple in the story "Hinterland" from *The Orange Fish* (1989) achieve a state of "marital intimacy."

25. Shields situates "Absence" as the twelfth in a collection of twenty-two stories, thus placing it at the centre of the collection.

26. As Dvořák claims in "An Aesthetics of the Ordinary in *Dressing Up for the Carnival*," Shields pursues "'the real mystery of the self,' of the other, of the creative process itself."

27. In "The Short Story (and Women Writers)" (*Startle* 97–108), Shields defends her innovative, experimental approach to the story genre in her first collection, *Various Miracles* (1985) (98–9).

28. In her essay "'Controlled Chaos' and Carol Shields's 'A View from the Edge of the Edge'" in this collection, Dvořák notes, "The metatextual discourse of 'Absence' openly substitutes itself for narrative and turns the process, mechanics, or even business of writing into content," a technique she suggests is "arguably designed to foreground writing as performance." In her earlier essay "Disappearance and 'the vision multiplied,'" Dvořák explored Shields's writerly craft from the angle of workmanship and play, highlighting her recurrent recourse to self-imposed formal constraints, such as handicapping herself by composing "Absence" as a lipogram, voluntarily depriving herself of the use of the letter 'i,' thus foregrounding writing as performance.

    In his essay "The Short of It: Carol Shields's Stories" in this collection, Besner considers Shields's "seriously playful stories," particularly "Absence" from *Dressing Up for the Carnival*, in which, he writes, "tellingly, both the letter and the pronoun 'I' have been excluded, producing," he claims, "a selfless, if wholly self-conscious meditation on a woman writing without or beyond or outside of a self." He continues, "She is in a Room of her Own Making and Writing; but the voice, the writer, is without an I" (49). He finds here "meaningful play and experiment at the level of language" that he finds replicated in Shields's novels *The Stone Diaries* and *Unless*. He adds, "this is play and experiment *shown* as such, performing as such; or, in other words, these instances signify, they mean, as enactment, demonstration, performance" (50).

WORKS CITED

Amis, Kingsley. *Jake's Thing*. London: Hutchinson, 1978. Print.

Atwood, Margaret. *Surfacing*. Toronto: McClelland and Stewart. 1972. Print.

Bemrose, John. "Enriching a fictional universe." Rev. of *Dressing up for the Carnival*. *Maclean's* vol 113, issue 12 (3 Mar 2000): n. p.

Besner, Neil. "The Short of It: Carol Shields's Stories." In *Relating Carol Shields's Essays and Fiction: Crossing Borders*. Ed. Nora Foster Stovel. London: Palgrave Macmillan, 2022. 45–55. Print.

Choy, Wayson. "My Seen-Sang, Carol Shields: A Memoir of a Master Teacher." *The Worlds of Carol Shields*. Ed David Staines. Reappraisals: Canadian Writers. Ottawa: U of Ottawa P., 2014. 305–311. Print.

D'Hoker, Elke. "Moments of Being: Carol Shields's Short Fiction." *Studies in Canadian Literature/Etudes en Littérature Canadienne* 33.1 (2008): 151–168. Print.

Dvořák, Marta. "An Aesthetics of the Ordinary in *Dressing Up for the Carnival*." *Carol Shields: The Arts of a Writing Life*. Ed. Neil K. Besner. Winnipeg: Prairie Fire P, 1995. 133–144.

———. "Carol Shields and the poetics of the quotidian." *Journal of the Short Story in English*, 38 (Spring 2002). 2–10. Print.

———. "'Controlled Chaos' and Carol Shields's 'A View from the Edge of the Edge.'" In *Relating Carol Shields's Essays and Fiction: Crossing Borders*. Ed. Nora Foster Stovel. London: Palgrave Macmillan, 2022. 95–111. Print.

Giardini, Anne, and Nicholas Giardini. *Startle and Illuminate: Carol Shields on Writing*. Toronto: Random House Canada, 2016. Print.

Blanche Howard, and Allison Howard. *A Memoir of Friendship: The Letters between Carol Shields and Blanche Howard*. Toronto: Viking Canada, 2007. Print.

Howells, Coral Ann. "Space for Strangeness: Carol Shields's Short Stories." Print.

Levin, Martin. "Carol Shields." *The Worlds of Carol Shields*. Ed David Staines. Reappraisals: Canadian Writers. Ottawa: U of Ottawa P., 2014. 305–311. Print.

Love, Barbara. Rev. of *Dressing up for the Carnival*. *Library Journal* Vol. 125, No 1, March 2000, p 131. Print.

Moss, Laura. "The Quotidian Is Where It's At." *Canadian Literature*, Issue 172 (Spring 2002). 194–196. Print.

Oates, Joyce Carol. Rev. of *Dressing up for the Carnival*. *New York Times Review of Books*, vol 47, no 11, 29 Jun 2000, pp 38–41. Print.

Ramon, Alex. *Liminal Spaces: The Double Art of Carol Shields*. Newcastle: Cambridge Scholars, 2009. Print.

Shields, Carol. "Absence." *Dressing Up for the Carnival. Carol Shields: The Collected Stories*. Toronto: Random House Canada, 2004a. 103–7. Print.

———. "Be a Little Crazy: Astonish Me." *Startle and Illuminate: Carol Shields on Writing*. 31–45. Print.

———. "Be Bold All the Way Through." *Startle and Illuminate: Carol Shields on Writing*. 141–8. Print.

———. "Boxcars, Coat Hangers and Other Devices." *Startle and Illuminate: Carol Shields on Writing*. 23–30. Print.

———. "Chemistry." *The Orange Fish*. Toronto: Random House Canada,1989, 11–33. Print.

———. "Creative Writing Courses," a lecture given in Trier, Germany, April 1990. Print.

———. "Dressing Down." *Dressing Up for the Carnival. Carol Shields: The Collected Stories*. Toronto: Random House Canada, 2004b. 221–37. Print.

———. "Dressing Up for the Carnival." *Dressing Up for the Carnival. Carol Shields: The Collected Stories*. Toronto: Random House Canada, 2004c. 397–403. Print.

———. "Dressing Up for the Carnival." *Dressing Up for the Carnival*. Toronto: Random House Canada, 2000a. 1–8. Print.

———. "Dying for Love." *Dressing Up for the Carnival*. Toronto: Random House Canada, 2000b. 41–52. Print.

———. "Eros." *Dressing Up for the Carnival. Carol Shields: The Collected Stories*. Toronto: Random House Canada, 2004d. 205–20. Print.

———. "Introduction." *Mansfield Park*. Jane Austen. The Modern Library Classics. 2001 Modern Library pbk. ed. New York: Modern Library, 2001. Print.

———. "Invention." *Dressing Up for the Carnival*. Toronto: Random House Canada, 2000c. 165–75. Print.

———. "Mirrors." *Dressing Up for the Carnival*. Toronto: Random House Canada, 2000d. 65–78. Print.

———. "Myths that Keep Us from Writing." *Startle and Illuminate: Carol Shields on Writing*. 15–21. Print.

———. "The Next Best Kiss." *Dressing Up for the Carnival. Carol Shields: The Collected Stories*. Toronto: Random House Canada, 2004e. 185–204. Print.

———. Preface to *Mansfield Park*. Print.

———. "Reportage." *Dressing Up for the Carnival*. Toronto: Random House Canada, 2000e. 121–8. Print.

———. "Segue." *The Collected Stories*. Toronto: Random House Canada, 2004f. 1–20. Print.

———. "The Short Story (and Women Writers)." *Startle and Illuminate: Carol Shields on Writing*. Toronto: Random House Canada, 2016. 97–108. Print.

———. *Small Ceremonies* (1976). Toronto; New York: McGraw-Hill Ryerson, 1976. Print.

———. "Stop!" *Dressing Up for the Carnival*. Toronto: Random House Canada, 2000f. 61–4. Print.

———. *Unless*. London; New York: Fourth Estate, 2002. Print.

————. "Weather." *Dressing Up for the Carnival*. Toronto: Random House Canada, 2000g. 27–36. Print.

————. "Windows." *Dressing Up for the Carnival*. Toronto: Random House Canada, 2000h. 109–120. Print.

Stovel, Nora Foster. "'Fragments on My Apple': Carol Shields's Unfinished Novel." *Canadian Literature* 217 (Summer 2013): 186–96. Print.

————. "*Thirteen Hands*: A Power Play by Carol Shields." *The Worlds of Carol Shields*. Edited by David Staines. Ottawa: U of Ottawa P, 2014. 363–75. Print.

Van Herk, Aritha. "Extrapolations from Miracles." *Room of One's Own* 13.1–2 (1989): 99–108. Print.

"Controlled Chaos" and Carol Shields's "A View from the Edge of the Edge"

Marta Dvořák

In May 1996, Carol Shields was among the ten Canadian writers invited to the prestigious French literary festival promoting foreign books in translation, *Les Belles Etrangères*. She took part in a televised round-table discussion in Paris with Timothy Findley, Jane Urquhart, and John Ralston Saul which I had been asked to chair, and she kindly accepted my invitation to give a reading (along with David Adams Richards) at the Université de Rennes[1] where I was then teaching. While Richards then attended a university panel on translation, Shields tutored a creative-writing workshop. She arrived at the workshop carrying a small white plastic coffee spoon which she held up to trigger considerations on creation and its origins—namely the relations between craft and art, derivation and invention, formal constraint and artistic freedom. She invited students to jot down a word the object had brought to mind, then to make a sentence which included that word, a sentence which in turn needed to be included in a paragraph on whatever they chose. The results read out were of a startling freshness and diversity. The practical advice she gave the aspiring authors included a

M. Dvořák (✉)
Canadian and World Literatures at the Sorbonne, Paris, France

personal tip on how "to prime the pump": not to write themselves dry, but always to leave part of an unfolding idea for the next day.

> The air of ideas is the only air worth breathing.
> —(Edith Wharton, *The Age of Innocence*)

Carol Shields and the Extra-ordinary, an essay collection I co-edited with Manina Jones, opens with a previously unpublished piece by Shields, "A View from the Edge of the Edge,"[2] whose considerations I shall weave into this discussion. The book concludes with Aritha van Herk's ficto-critical tribute to Shields's craft, deconstructing vintage features of her writing practice and using them like building blocks. Van Herk stresses "Carol Shields's ineffable ability to make stories mean more than they might" (van Herk 257), and she grieves that "Carol Shields, with the same outrageous courtesy and quiet, has died" (268). I, too, wish to pay tribute to this exceptional writer who was also exceptionally modest, wise, and good—quick to recognize neediness there where we might deplore excessive ego. Adhering to Virginia Woolf's modernist call to arms in the essay "Modern Fiction," "Let us not take it for granted that life exists more in what is commonly thought big than in what is commonly thought small" (Woolf, *Collected Essays* 107), Carol found beauty and wonder in small things.[3] The play *Thirteen Hands* that later brought us together one November day in Paris[4] is a perfect illustration. It collapses the whole round earth and time itself into a square bridge table around which north and south confront east and west in a fluid dynamic pointing back to origins and ahead to infinity. The concept of rupture as an unending continuum of transmission underlies the staggered replacements of the bridge club's original founders and in turn of their substitutes. The same but not quite, analogous to the way Robert Kroetsch's stone hammer (i.e., story) undergoes a dizzying spiral of changes of hand standing for the (de)creation process, as old as the last Ice Age, "the retreating, the recreating ice" (Kroetsch 265). Shields's characters, designated John Bunyan fashion only by their function, carry the weight of allegory but bear themselves as lightly as your next-door neighbor. North *was* my neighbor in fact, sitting next to me like a perfectly ordinary spectator until she suddenly began to talk with the actors already on stage, thereby disclosing the dramatic in the apparently dull, and blurring the boundaries between natural speech and prepared script.

Carol accepted the arbitrary scheme of things in life just as admirably as she harnessed chance on the page. Over our last lunch together on what she knew would be her last trip to the France she loved,[5] she learned that Manina and I had had to reschedule (to March 2003) the Sorbonne conference on her work that she had hoped to attend,[6] and told me with stunning simplicity, "Oh, I won't be around by then." She went on working, though, and, in the spring of 2002, I learned from Margaret Atwood, who was in Paris to promote the French translation of *Blind Assassin*, that Shields's new novel was much awaited and already held to be superb. That fall I heard from Mavis Gallant that Carol was "having a good period." Being awarded the Charles Taylor Prize and being shortlisted for the Booker and the Giller may have had something to do with it. But one could also impute her good period to the late friendship that had blossomed with the Mavis Gallant Carol referred to in private as "the divine Mavis" and which came to provide astonishing comfort to both. Shields first used the term with me in November 2001, before her play's opening night. Neither of us felt comfortable about my giving Gallant's telephone number without her prior permission, so I offered to ask Mavis to call Carol. Shields explained the "divine Mavis" once again in the following personal e-mail in which she thanked me for having asked the Gallant she had never met to telephone her:

> Dear Marta,
>   What a good soul you are! And yes, I was astonished to hear from Mavis Gallant and to find her so beautifully sympathetic. I don't have her mailing address or her email—or even if she has one, nor her phone number.
>   When my daughters and I talk about Canadian writers we always talk about the divine Alice, and then, immediately, the divine Mavis (that's the extent of our divinity division, just two members).
>   I am doing small tasks these days; today it is a short preface to a book of plays. A curious comfort to tick off these tasks.
>   much love, c̄

Gallant later confided that they at present called each other regularly for long conversations about writing and life, sharing perceptions in a way Mavis had not experienced since her close friend Anne Hébert had died—other writers' conversations in her experience tending to revolve around agents and contracts. Similar in vision and aesthetic agenda, both Gallant and Shields liked to subtly show the spectacle of the human comedy from a high altitude with little corrective intent[8] but rather a benevolent amusement involving both appraisal and sympathy. Both liked to equate characters with the items to be found in their kitchen drawers, and both, along with Margaret Laurence, Alice Munro, and Bronwen Wallace, tended to transform objects into signs housing an ontological stance.[9] In the last months of her life, Carol's e-mails revealed an ongoing interest in Manina's and my scholarly project, as well as an amazing (and increasingly sunny) productivity of her own:

> *Dear Marta,*
>
> *I cannot tell you what an honour the colloquia international is for me. I have read through the program, marvelling at all the ideas and points of view. I don't have to tell you how much I would love to be there, mar-rs en Paris [sic], joining in the discussion (though there would be a good deal I would be unable to follow). I wonder if you would give all my good wishes to all who are there—I know several of them but not all.*
>
> *Flowers are budding out here in Victoria; winter seems to have vanished. With the help of my daughter Sara we have made* Unless *into a play, which will be produced in England next year and in Canada in three theatres. The play turned out funnier than the much sadder book.*
>
> *I will look forward to seeing the papers, and I want to wish you the best of luck. Putting together a colloquium takes enormous energy; it doesn't just happen!*
>
> *much love, carol* [10]

Like the Gallant who declared that she had "lived in writing like a spoonful of water in a river" (Gallant, "Preface" to *Collected Stories* 3), Shields was half in life and half in books. In "A View from the Edge of the Edge," she confesses to never having been able to "separate [her] reading and [her] writing life" ("A View" 19), and she traces her writings to the books she ingested and digested as a child. Which books were involved in shaping her tastes was a question of pure chance, which made the bonding even stronger. As the author remarks in "A View": the books that "*happen* to lie within easy reach, the family books, the in-house books" are precisely those which "have a way of entering our bodies more simply and completely" (20, stress added). She thus sees happenstance as the catalysis if not the organizing principle behind the beginning writer, who, in the well-known words of Gallant, "has to choose, tear to pieces, spit out, chew up and assimilate as naturally as a young animal" (Gallant, "What Is Style?" 37). While the young Shields's textual companions were chosen beforehand, were there "by default" (20), they also represented randomness in other ways. They were as an "eclectic sampling" as Anne Shirley's readings in *Anne of Green Gables*—all typical of "the *randomness* of early reading lists" (21). The texts themselves carried a strong streak of "*coincidence*" which to the young Shields seemed to be along with sentimentality "one of the strands of American existence" (21, stresses added). The mouthpieces of the mature writer subsequently identify coincidence as "carelessness or luck or distraction or necessity" (*Dressing Up* 178), and integrate it into a cosmological assessment: "The mythic heavings of the universe" (Shields, *Mary Swann* 21). In "A View," Shields explains that her writing life did indeed begin soon after her reading life. Her childhood writings took the form of stories, "often with a supernatural theme and a trick ending," little poems "about spring," and later, once she had "mastered the mechanics of meter, *sonnets* about spring" (19, original stress). The key words here light up first of all what was "derivative in the extreme" (19) about her early work: the stock imagery and structures of any budding writer replicating "in-house" formulas that happen to be there. The programmed surprise ending systematically (and predictably) deployed by writers like Maupassant and O. Henry was already denounced by Woolf in "Phases of Fiction" for the artificial way it closes with a "pinch of gunpowder" which explodes "when we tread on its tail" (Woolf, *Coll. Essays* II 61). While Alice Munro called on the twist ending in a story like "Prue," printed in *The New Yorker* in 1981 (and reprinted in Leon Rooke and John Metcalf's anthology (19)*82 Best Canadian Stories*),[11] the mature Shields, like Gallant, would elaborate a more impressionistic, elliptical aesthetic of indeterminacy whose repeated leitmotifs leave a wake of meaning which gently fades rather than clinching the circumference and significance of the whole story. So, while Shields in "A View" stresses the role of imitation and derivation in an artist's development, she also calls attention to what her creative-writing tutorial in Rennes would be all about: how art is melded with craft, which can be learned (the mechanics of rhythm, say). And how the craft which can lead to inventive reconfiguration significantly includes managing chance and chaos.

The scientific and technological debates on chaos dynamics have seeped into public consciousness and (post)modern cultural discourse. Umberto Eco's essay, *The Aesthetics of Chaosmos*,[12] already famously engaged with James Joyce's oeuvre via the dialectic between two world views: medieval and Renaissance thought (and its preoccupation with order and moderation) and the modernist avant-garde (and its fascination with disorder and excess). As illustrates the essay "A View," Shields's outlook and (as a corollary) her fictional production are quite naturally informed by the theory of chaotics, which postulates a paradoxical system in which the only phenomenal determinacy lies in the certainty of unpredictability. The writer calls out for "the rich variables of a *randomly* evoked, organically spilling, unselfconscious, *disorderly*, unruly, uncharted and uncharitable pouring out of voice" (23) and draws attention to "that very seething, smoking, *chaotic*, multicultural *muddle* which is, in fact, our reality" (23, stresses added). "Muddle" is a homely word which encapsulates the complex jumble in our knowledge society's tentatively integrative conceptual frameworks of reference. "A View from the Edge of the Edge" shows how hard it is to locate the edge. Many have posited, like Shields, that a British reading public long perceived Canadian literature as coming "from the exotic margins of the planet, the far edge" ("A View" 18). Others have held that, like a poor cousin, CanLit is not exotic enough. In her introduction to the Clarendon Lectures she gave at Oxford University, Margaret Atwood suggested that the British find Canadian literature too boringly similar, "lacking the exoticism of Africa, the strange fauna of Australia, or the romance of India" (Atwood, *Strange Things* 2). Centre and edge in Shields's essay repeatedly melt like Dali's clocks. Winnipeg, where the writer was living at the time, is smack in the middle of the country (and continent) but is "certainly not the literary centre of Canada" ("A View" 19). Shields states she was born "in the centre of the United States," but then points out that "Midwesterners were, culturally, at the edge" (19). She helps readers tick off a check list. First, Shields's home town Chicago, one of the largest cities in the United States, but not even the capital of Illinois, wields little political power. Second, Shields comes from the middle class, also "at the edge"—"the middle being nowhere near the centre" (19). She grew up in a "leafy green *suburb*, of a relatively happy family" which doubly places her "at life's margin"—at least in "romantic literary terms" (19, stress added).

Contributing to the muddle is the discernible clash between centripetal and centrifugal tensions. One can detect the centrifugal view of modernity—the flux of geographical and social mobility leading outward from city to nation to world—which collides with a nostalgic centripetal belief system straining back to a certain rootedness or unity. Shields confesses that part of her "yearns for that degree of cultural saturation, a whole tradition compacted like a gemstone" which small nations like Hungary—completely other in language and history—possess. She envies such peoples' feeling that, even among strangers at a bus stop or in a café "every cultural moment is secured, *and* refracted and enlarged, by common references, quotations, allusions, nuances, a body, in fact, of shared belief" (22, original stress). Yet she confesses that another part of her would deplore any cultural unity whose homogeneity would make her feel "confined"

(22). She finds "the shape and force of a national literature" valid only if it is fluid and does not cement literature "belly-to-belly to the national destiny" in a Tarzanist way.[13] She argues, "People are bonded and nourished by a common literature, but only if it has flourished *naturally*, unproved by politicians and flag-wavers and the prescriptive notions of the Academy" (25, stress added). Shields either does not fear her own contradictions or else chooses to ignore the ultimate muddle of her own fraught position. She declares that "nations are fortunate if they possess texts …whose spirit is universally shared… and understood even by those who have never read it and never will" (25). In this, she is unpredictably Back to Go, to the cultural saturation of a small country like Hungary, not deemed oppressive this time simply because it has spilled out of its borders. Cultural hegemony here seems to be scrambled with an attraction to cross-cultural Ur-myth and a certain idealist Unity.

> Maybe none of this is about control.
> —(Margaret Atwood, *The Handmaid's Tale*)

The discussion which follows moves from the particular ("A View") to the general, and from the essay genre grounded in ideas to fiction with its rhetorical and aesthetic agenda. I focus in a hands-on fashion on certain features of chaotics which are undeniably operative in Shields's oeuvre and ponder why a writer who likes to investigate connections and correspondences should cultivate randomness, if not the better to flaunt her control. Like Atwood's rhetoric of denial figuring above as epigraph to this section, which underlines the interplay between uttering and the truth or virtual value of the utterance, these features might be taken as an abdication of, or challenge to, the notions of author/ity or authorial power which inhabit conventional linear narrative grounded in logic and causality. The traits include various strategies of recursion (applying a function to its own values to engineer an infinite sequence of values) and bifurcation (the random changes or deviations in trajectory cascading through a system). One can remark among the writer's incremental figures the vertical pile-ups of repetition and variation and even of "scenic epanalepsis" (Vauthier 126). Simone Vauthier has quite an eye when she analyses Shields's closure of "Mrs. Turner Cutting the Grass": "Oh *what a* sight is Mrs. Turner cutting her grass and *how*, like an ornament, she shines" (Shields, *Various Miracles* 25, my stresses). Vauthier notably distinguishes the exclamatory assertion, "Oh, what a sight" (which is a variation of the story's opening declarative sentence, "*is* a sight") from the very final *grammatical* exclamation, "how she shines," whose spiritual connotations, the critic argues, "resemanticize the word *sight*" (Vauthier 127, final stress original) so that readers are brought to embrace the sight of the ungraceful Mrs. Turner as "gracing our world" (Vauthier 127). The critic judiciously remarks that the recursive procedure (which spirals back but also deflects) produces the pleasure of recognition but also makes us toe the line, ultimately changing our readerly response to the character to "what was *expected*" (Vauthier 127, my stress).[14]

In the fraught relation between apparently fortuitous co-occurrences and authorial control, readers can equally note Shields's fondness for the humble parenthesis.[15] Operating within the dynamics of replication and augmentation, the parenthetical segment is ostensibly appended to saturate the meaning unfolding in linear fashion. But as Shields, like Atwood, is well aware, its intrusion actually disrupts and sidetracks us away from the discursive sequence centrifugally, sending us every which way like the mad editor Kinbote's reader in Nabokov's a/mazing *Pale Fire*, analogous to a rat in a maze, "free to go anywhere, as long as it stays within the maze" (Atwood, *Handmaid* 174). The rat may well be meant to learn that "the path to a maze's goal is always shortened by turning away from the goal" (Shields, *Larry's Party* 152). It can be valuable to hold up to the light a single sentence from *Larry's Party*. In the segment below, Larry's house mirrors the airlessness and confinement of his marital life.

> The walls, the kitchen floor, the tight circle of second-hand appliances, the tiny corner table with its chairs pushed neatly in—these objects refuse to acknowledge him, though he's the one—isn't he?—who brought the scene into being, and who is now trapped in the bubble of his own dread. (*LP* 94)

This hypotactic sentence moves in a spiral pattern from its structurally complex subject in constant augmentation which doubles back, condensed and reduplicated (the appositional "these objects"). The discursive curve arrives at the psychological predicate ("him," our focalizer) which morphs, echoic, into a new subject position that we readers are prepared to follow on another overlapping round. But a parenthesis (framed by dashes) stops us dead in our tracks, all the harder as it takes the shape of a rhetorical question. The question unsettles readerly faith in the truth which subjectivity allegedly offers, all the while on a higher plane it invites an existential questioning of subjectivity and agency. So does that experimental tour de force, "Love So Fleeting, Love So Fine," in which the focalizer falls in love with a sign ("Wendy is back!").[16] The protagonist infers that the Wendy in question enjoys huge popularity with customers.

> The store manager—a fatherly type—might even refer to it as "phenomenal." (Else, why this sign in his window? And why the Christmas bonus already set aside for her?) (*VM* 118)

The sequence's first parenthesis framed by dashes derails us onto a parallel track, into another "life." In the double utterance of the parenthesis which follows, the focalizer's viewpoint (appraising the manager as "fatherly") morphs into voice. The interpolated questions escalate from purely rhetorical to informational (the set aside Christmas bonus). Or rather *pseudo*-informational, since the information requirement regulating the use of the definite article (*the* Christmas bonus) has not been met: no such thing has been mentioned in the world of the framing story. A ventriloquized voice which takes on omniscience thus projects readers into a parallel reality that the true authorial presence controls from a high altitude. A parallel, horizontal reality somehow collides with a vertical suprareality which the story's ending enigmatically suggests can "widen for an instant the eye of the comprehended world" (*VM* 122).

And what are we to make of Shields's systematic recourse to self-reflexive embedding, from "Various Miracles" and its collision of framing and framed narratives to the specularity of "Absence" in which our woman writer stages a woman writer protagonist writing about a woman writer writing—a specularity reiterated and expanded in *Unless*:

> I would become a woman writing about a woman writing about women writing, and that would lead straight to an echo chamber of infinite regress in company with the little Dutch girl, the girl on the bathroom cleanser, the vision multiplied, but in receding perspective. (Shields, *Unless* 269)

The specular parallelisms call up the same unending series of possibilities in text and world which Atwood evokes as "the reflections in two mirrors set facing one another, stretching on, replica after replica, to the vanishing point " (Atwood, *Handmaid* 165).[17] Like Atwood's self-conscious fiction, which turns the narration into "the very substance" of the content (Hutcheon, *Narcissistic Narrative* 28), Shields's embedding shifts the focus from story to story*telling*. It metatextually calls attention not only to the fabricated nature of the textual product, but also to its process, involving the fluidity of random movement as well as the fixed structures of design. The author foregrounds both by having her novel *Unless* feed on her story "A Scarf," in the recursive manner of David Hockney's Polaroid composites. In Hockney's analogous snapshots of body segments arranged vertically (separated by both white frame and by space between the snaps), his figures' anatomical overlaps evoke connections but challenge a congruent fit, as do the space–time distortions (stemming from slightly different vantage points and time of day).

Even more obvious than the above devices are Shields's hallmark inventories aspiring to exhaustivity, particularly her *chaotic* enumeration, a disorderly and open-ended accumulation of terms not of the same nature. These lists control chaos, in the manner of the objects designed to deceive[18] which in *Larry's Party* stand for the body, the self, the world, and the novel itself. One can hold up the random contents of a cracked china cup: "a single hairpin, a handful of thumbtacks, a stub of a candle, half an eraser, a blackened French coin, a book of matches from the Informatic Centre, a rubber band or two, and a few paper clips" (*Dressing Up* 101). Still, a close reading senses a certain haunting. One can divine that the author draws up the list of broken, mismatched objects with inchoate relations of inclusion in mind, to suggest a certain fit or indeterminate ordering principle. Entropy comes to mind, as do desire and despair. The cup's contents are revealed to be "the unsorted detritus of economy and mystery" (*Dressing Up* 102) which stands for life. *Is that all there is* implicitly wonders the no-longer-young single woman reading *The Sands of Desire*, who in a fury of revolt throws the contents out the window. A disorderly series of word sentences concurrent with the objects rattling down concludes the sequence: "Ping. Tut. Tsk, Tick. Gone." (102) The opening onomatopoeic lexeme, a phonetic intensive, shifts to the phonic symbols of regret, reproach, transitoriness, and—through the final odd man out—the irremediable, tinged with mortality.

Like many fellow postmodernists, then, Shields adheres to an aesthetic practice that Umberto Eco identifies in *L'Oeuvre ouverte* as that of systematically resorting to disorder, chance, and indeterminacy to the extent of setting them up as values (Eco, *Oeuvre* 9–10). Postmodernists like Shields have borrowed the agenda from Romantics like Byron, who gave the impression that his verse was spontaneous and free-flowing, despite self-imposed straitjackets such as the *terza rima*. The Romantic break with Neoclassical composure and balance has been mirrored by the modernist and postmodern break with realism and its rule of plausibility. So, Shields dismisses conventional narrative links and shows in "Keys" that a story can "happen" through a mere structural lay-out passing a random object from hand to hand. A story can happen through bald undisguised spatial or temporal patterns which paradoxically signal the writer's fingerprint.[19] In "Invitations" (*Various Miracles*), the seriation is purely temporal. Each juxtaposed scene begins by the name of the day of the week and involves the anonymous protagonist's finding in her mailbox yet another invitation, to events of escalating importance. These trigger corresponding variations in the planned accoutrement which also contribute to setting up a readerly predictable, reconstruction-inviting pattern. The seriation elsewhere can be purely spatial. In "Home," Shields places in contiguity within the enclosed space of a London-bound plane an assemblage of protagonists, whose individual portraits she introduces in a combinatory but mechanical fashion that triggers readerly anticipation. The theme and variations rooting in one fixed space characters of different ages, sexes, and occupations calls up Chaucer's Prologue to *The Canterbury Tales*, bringing together people from all walks of life: upper and lower class, male and female, town and country, educated and ignorant, lecherous and virtuous. In her portrait of a period, Shields never fleshes out the narrative relationships, which are as conspicuously absent as "the million invisible filaments of connection, trivial or profound, which bind the people one to the other and to the small green planet they call home" (*VM* 156). Yet with one stroke of the pen, the author playfully sketches in visible connections. The cosmological assessment is incongruously tacked on to an ironic observation: each of the 109 passengers stepping off the New York flight, "without exception—is wearing blue jeans" (156). A close look at a well-known sequence from the story showcases another paradox:

> By some extraordinary coincidence (or cosmic dispensation or whatever), each person on the London-bound flight that night was, for a moment, filled with the steam of perfect happiness. Whether it was the oxygen-enriched air of the fusiform cabin, *or* the duckling with orange sauce, *or* the soufflé-soft buttocks of the stewardess sashaying to and fro with her coffee pot, *or* the unchartable currents of air bouncing against the sides of the vessel, *or* some random thought dredged out of the darkness of the aircraft and fueled by the proximity of strangers—whatever it was, each of the 100 passengers—one after another, from rows one to twenty-five, like little lights going on—experienced an intense, simultaneous sensation of joy. (*VM* 152–3, stresses added)

The narrative strategy of implausible simultaneity grounds the co-occurrence in a seriation underlined by polysyndeton (unnecessarily redu-plicating the coordinator "or"). One can see that Shields flaunts randomness as system not through common speech meant to be heard, but through a structurally complex, elevated, hypotactic register which is *contrived* to stress relations of subordination and coordination and which requires slow silent reading (and even rereading).

The extravagant number and eclectic nature of the causal connections which the writer exhibits as merely endless possibilities is in amused opposition with the advice of the fictional publisher in the first story of the collection, "Various Miracles."[20] The writer-protagonist Camilla has been told that she has relied too heavily on the artifice of coincidence (playfully equated with miracle). She has consequently rewritten her manuscript so that "Wherever fate, chance or happenstance had ruled, there was now logic, causality and science" (*VM* 16). Not so the narrator of "Invention," who in an appropriately digressive fashion, challenges the notion of perfectibility along with that of scientific or technological progress by proclaiming that "invention is random and accidental" (*Dressing Up* 178). This authorial mouthpiece resorts to playful seria-tion, periphrastic parallelisms, and juxtapositions that engineer unusual equivalences between gunpowder and the hoola hoop, say, or chairs and Darwinism. A double instance of chaotic enumeration in subject and predicate once more ends with an odd man out—that incongruous ele-ment not of the same nature which derails any semblance of an ordering principle: "Other people—through carelessness or luck or distraction or necessity—invented keys, chairs, wheels, thermometers, and the theory of evolution" (*DU* 178).

Further complicated by the technically unmediated free indirect dis-course of multiview marked by a profusion of modalizers, interjections, shifters, embryonic sentences, and markers of emphasis (such as exclama-tions, rhetorical questions, and italics) and behind which the gently mock-ing stance of the implied author is perceptible, Shields's works seem to be designed according to the "controlled chaos and contrived panic" (*Larry's Party* 313) inherent in the art of the maze: that apparently random pattern which leads to a goal, prize, or destination—"what the puzzling, branch-ing path is all about" (*LP* 149). Just what in Shields's case may that goal or prize be? Look at one last inventory to search for an enlightening metonymic function. The opening list in "Absence" announces that the writer protagonist wants to "create a story that possessed a granddaughter, a Boston fern, a golden apple, and a small blue cradle" (*DU* 108). The amplifying device of chaotic enumeration suspends and postpones, suggesting that there is always something left to be said or added. Its disorderly contiguity of seemingly arbitrary terms different in nature implicitly seeks to produce correspondences or relations of inclusion on multiple planes (concrete/abstract; particular/general). The power to make the desired connections, to trace a pattern out of the apparently disconnected and incoherent, would seem to be both the challenge and the prize. But whose power is at stake in this postmodern world which has declared the death of the author and the empowerment of the reader? The answer nestles in the story's following line: "*Some hand must move* the pen along or press the keys *and steer, somehow*, the granddaughter towards the Boston fern or *place* the golden apple at the foot of the blue cradle" (111, stresses added). In passing, one can note the analogies with the hands moving the pen in Rennes who were told to create a story that possessed a plastic coffee spoon, to be placed into a sentence and then steered/ stirred into a narrative.

The metatextual discourse of "Absence" openly substitutes itself for narrative and turns the process, mechanics, or even business of writing into content. Shields grounds the metatext in the alethic modality governed by the operators of necessity (*must*) and (im)possibility (*somehow*). She thus plays out the core issue of power and control on the highest plane, that of authorship and authority, involving the concepts of freedom and constraint in the writing and reading processes and in that literary space created between the producer and the receiver.[21] My chapter in *Carol Shields and the Extra-Ordinary*, "Disappearance and 'the vision multiplied,'" already explored the writer's craft from the angle of workmanship and play, lighting up Shields's recurrent recourse to self-imposed formal constraints. I focused on how the author handicapped herself by composing "Absence" as a lipogram, voluntarily depriving herself of the use of one letter—a handicap all the more challenging as it involves the common vowel "i". Such constraints, freely chosen, are arguably designed to foreground writing as performance, even combat. Shields's declaration that some (iron? velvet?) hand must move and steer and place this next to that, somehow, calls attention to the dexterity, even virtuosity, with which a writer can wield the building material available to her, and puts on display the control of an authorial presence which guides projected readers toward a desired interpretation, or even *goads* less alert readers toward an intended meaning. In the manner of Early Modern, Mannerist artists from Ariosto and Tasso to John Donne, fond of parabasis, false perspectives, and *trompe l'oeil*, the statement claims for the writer the romantic power of a demiurge, reflecting in receding perspective an arguable original grand Design, or perhaps controlled chaos.

NOTES

1. Shields and Richards also generously agreed to read and talk with the general public at the Rennes School of Fine Arts.
2. The piece was originally an address Shields delivered at Harvard University on 10 February 1997.
3. I use "Carol" as a term of address when the personal material I integrate into the discourse offers insights regarding the woman in her life and cultural habitat. I meant to use "Shields" for everything involving *what* happens on her pages and *how*. But questions of inclination, taste, talent, perception, influences, and experience—all vital to the vocation and craft of writing—make it hard to compartmentalise the person, Carol, from the writer, Shields, so the switches in terms of address are rather fluid. They inhabit the to-ing and fro-ing of my text/note dialogue, which contributes to the plurality of arrangement allowing readers to revisit previous understandings.
4. I had lunch with Carol (already very ill) and her husband Don when she came to Paris for the first performance in France of her play, *Thirteen Hands/Treize Mains* (translated, adapted, and directed by Rachel Salik), at Théâtre 13. The opening night we attended was on 20 November 2001, but the play ran till 30 December.
5. Carol seemed full of vitality, and initiated a sunshine-drenched walk from her Ile-Saint-Louis hotel to the Abbey (CanLit) Bookshop in the Latin Quarter. But in the evening, at the end of the performance, as people milled around her, she was too exhausted to stand.
6. The colloquium provided the matrix of *Carol Shields and the Extra-Ordinary*, and among the writer's final professional acts was the 31 May 2003 letter giving us official permission to include her Harvard address.
7. Shields, 3 December 2001 e-mail to Dvořák.
8. Despite the author's early love for didactic books, stemming from "a didactic Methodist Sunday School," a "didactically charged classroom," and "well-meaning didactic parents," which brought her to conclude that "this was the natural way of the world, half of humanity bent on improving the other half" ("A View" 20), Shields's irony is not the brand that seeks to reform.

9. "There is no stone, shrub, chair, or door that does not offer arrows of implicit meanings or promises of epiphany," declares a narrator providing objective correlatives in the domains of both nature and culture (Shields, *Dressing Up* 163). Regarding Munro, for instance, see Dvořák, "The Other Side of Dailiness: Alice Munro's Melding of Realism and Romance."

10. Shields, 8 February 2003 e-mail to Dvořák.

11. Rooke and Metcalf point out in their Preface that "Prue" is a story "owing everything to its ending, which casts back a very different light upon the complexion of the whole" (Rooke and Metcalf 8).

12. The essay *The Aesthetics of Chaosmos* was first published as the last chapter in Eco's *Opera Aperto* (1962), then dropped from later editions, and published on its own in 1966.

13. I borrow the term "Tarzanist" from Barbara Godard, who pointed out that writers like Morley Callaghan and Mavis Gallant were "caught in the crossfire of the Tarzanist/cosmopolitan debate in Canadian culture," marginalised because "physical setting, not a particular mode of perception, has determined Canadianness for the critical establishment" (Godard 75–76).

14. Neil Besner also addresses the issues of perception and performance in Shields's story.

15. The Vauthier *Reverberations* chapter I cite was originally published as "On Carol Shields's 'Mrs. Turner Cutting the Grass'" in *Commonwealth* 11:2 (Spring 1989): 63–74.

16. By deconstructing and glossing a simple sign in the window of a shoe store, the story's protagonist (re)constructs the entire existence of a self rendered so thick with life that he falls in love with it/her.

17. Actually, both Shields and Atwood are among the postmodern writers that Woolf in her first self-published short story predicted would increasingly realise the importance of such reflections and set out to explore their depths, "leaving the description of reality more and more out of their stories, taking a knowledge of it for granted" (Woolf, *The Mark on the Wall* 6)

18. The primary object in *Larry's Party* is of course the maze, but the author lumps it together with a list of material and immaterial riddles standing for fate, that ultimate, unpredictable, divine "sleight of hand, the clown's wink, the comic [and cosmic] shrug" (*Larry's Party* 152).

19. Woolf was among the first modernists to celebrate a slice of space-time in her story " The Mark on the Wall " (1917), evoking " the old lady about to pour out tea and the young man about to hit the tennis ball in the back garden of the suburban villa as one rushes past in the train " (Woolf, *The Mark on the Wall* 3).

20. In his chapter Besner identifies "serious play" as one of the vital features of Shields's writing. Calling attention to her fun with form, he playfully (sorry) calls the author "Shields Ludens."
21. Warren Cariou, too, engages with the concept of contrivance—with respect to the maze and *Larry's Party* in particular, and to endings and art in general.

WORKS CITED

Atwood, Margaret. *The Handmaid's Tale*. Toronto: McClelland and Stewart, 1985.
———. *Strange Things: The Malevolent North in Canadian Literature*. Oxford: Clarendon Press, 1995.
Dvořák, Marta. "Disappearance and 'the Vision Multiplied': Writing as Performance." *Carol Shields and the Extra-Ordinary*. Ed. Marta Dvořák and Manina Jones. Montreal & Kingston: McGill-Queen's UP, 2007. 223–237.
———. "The Other Side of Dailiness: Alice Munro's Melding of Realism and Romance in *Dance of the Happy Shades*." *Etudes anglaises* 67.3, July-Sept. 2014. 302–17.
Dvořák, Marta and Manina Jones, ed. *Carol Shields and the Extra-Ordinary*. Montreal & Kingston: McGill-Queen's UP, 2007.
Eco, Umberto. *L'Oeuvre ouverte*. Paris: Seuil, 1965.
———. *The Aesthetics of Chaosmos. The Middle Ages of James Joyce*. Trans. Ellen Esrock. Cambridge, Mass.: Harvard UP, 1989.
Gallant, Mavis. "Preface." 1996. *The Collected Stories*. New York: Alfred A. Knopf, Everyman's Library, 2016. 3–16.
———. "What Is Style?" *Canadian Forum*, September 1982. 6, 37. Rpt. in Gallant, *Paris Notebooks*. Toronto: Macmillan of Canada, 1988. 176–179.
Godard, Barbara. "Modalities of the Edge, Towards a Semiotics of Irony: The Case of Mavis Gallant." *Essays on Canadian Writing* 42 (special Gallant issue), winter 1990. 72–101.
Hutcheon, Linda. *Narcissistic Narrative: The Metafictional Paradox*. New York: Methuen, 1988.
Kroetsch, Robert. "Stone Hammer Poem," in *Field Notes*, 1981. Rpt. in *The New Oxford Book of Canadian Verse*, ed. M. Atwood. Toronto: Oxford UP, 1983. 264–269.
Rooke, Leon and John Metcalf. *82 Best Canadian Stories*. Ottawa: Oberon, 1982.
Shields, Carol. *Dressing Up for the Carnival*. London: Fourth Estate, 2000.
———. e-mail to Marta Dvořák, 3 December 2001.
———. e-mail to Marta Dvořák, 8 February 2003.

————. *Larry's Party.* London: Fourth Estate, 1997.

————. *Mary Swann.* Hammersmith, London: Flamingo/ HarperCollins Publishers, 1993.

————. *Thirteen Hands and Other Plays.* Vintage Canada, 2002.

————. *Unless.* Toronto: Random House Canada, 2002.

————. *Various Miracles.* Toronto: Stoddart, General, 1989.

————. "A View from the Edge of the Edge." *Carol Shields and the Extra-Ordinary.* Ed. Marta Dvořák and Manina Jones. 17–29.

Van Herk, Aritha. "Mischiefs, Misfits, and Miracles." *Carol Shields and the Extra-Ordinary.* Ed. Marta Dvořák and Manina Jones. 256–270.

Vauthier, Simone. *Reverberations: Explorations in the Canadian Short Story.* Concord, Ont: Anansi Press, 1993.

Woolf, Virginia. *Collected Essays* Vol. II. Ed. Leonard Woolf. London: Chatto & Windus, 1972.

————. *The Mark on the Wall and Other Short Fiction* Ed. David Bradshaw. Oxford: Oxford UP, 2001.

PART II

Essays on Carol Shields's Novels

"The Alchemy of Re-Imagined Reality": Biographical Gothicism in Carol Shields's *Swann: A Mystery*

Cynthia Sugars

[T]he birth of the reader must be at the cost of the death of the Author.
—Roland Barthes, "The Death of the Author" (148)

We are as writers responsible—or are we?—for our offered up passions and for our buried themes, even those buried out of sight of our own eyes…
—Carol Shields, "What You Use and What You Protect" (51)

Like many writers, Carol Shields struggled with the guilt of literary author-ship, the complicated guilt that Alice Munro expressed so well in her story "Family Furnishings." To write is to plunder the lives of others, admits Shields in "To Write Is to Raid," but for Shields it is this soupçon of reality that lends the imaginative structure its power, what she calls "the experience-plus-imagination recipe that makes fiction possible" (31). It is

C. Sugars (✉)
University of Ottawa, Ottawa, ON, Canada

© The Author(s), under exclusive license to Springer Nature Switzerland AG 2023
N. F. Stovel (ed.), *Relating Carol Shields's Essays and Fiction*,
https://doi.org/10.1007/978-3-031-11480-9_7

not surprising, then, that Shields herself confessed her fascination with "that subjunctive branch of people (*mea culpa*) who were curious about the details of *other* ordinary people—so curious, in fact, that they became biographers or novelists" ("Where Curiosity Leads" 85). Paradoxically, this self-reflexive interest in biographers and writers informed her fascination with the "*unknowability*" of others (83).

It is this fixation on the unknowability, the sheer "otherness" of others (83), that constitutes the core of *Swann: A Mystery*. Here the academics and biographers gather to discuss the life and oeuvre of another "othered" and fictionally disguised figure—that of Mary Swann herself. But the smoke-screen "self," inevitably, eludes their grasp. As Sarah Gamble puts it, "*Swann* makes an important point, which is that to tie a story down to a single author is to isolate it and deprive it of that connection to other narratives that would give it meaning" (58).

Sometime in the early 1970s, Carol Shields, then a Master's student at the University of Ottawa, sat in the audience at one of the university's Canadian Literature symposia (see McMullen), the very same symposium series that hosted a conference dedicated to the work of Carol Shields in 2012. Registered as a Master's student in the university's English Department from 1969 to 1975, Shields was struck by the intensity of the emotional investments of academics and authors who took part in the annual colloquia, an experience that would inform her work thereafter. Later, Shields would criticize the participants in a conference dedicated to Susanna Moodie for agonizing over lifeless minutiae at the expense of the imaginative "rearranging and pushing towards something new" that constituted the true power of Moodie's text ("The Short Story" 98).

Indeed, the University of Ottawa symposia and others later found themselves raided to produce their fictional alter ego, the famous "Swann Symposium" that concludes Shields's 1987 novel *Swann*. The Swann Symposium is surely a parodic nod to some of the Ottawa symposia that contributed to Shields's emergent literary bio-critical aesthetic. In "To Write Is to Raid," Shields quotes Kennedy Fraser's words that "[h]onest, personal writing…is a great service rendered the living by the dead" (qtd. in Shields 35). This theme is explored in Wendy Roy's and Smaro Kamboureli's contributions to this collection, in which the authors discuss the self-reflexive nature of Shields's fiction whereby the business of writing-about-writing is embedded within a narrative storyline and structure. As Nora Foster Stovel notes in her introduction to this volume, not only did Shields use her essays to "quest for new forms to trace the 'arc' of a human life," but much of Shields's work "is a polemic that can be read in conjunction with her essays as a nurturance of the craft and politics of writing both for writers of fiction and for academics who read and study Shields's fiction."

It is hard not to think of the various convolutions of significance of these words as they apply to Mary Swann—a dead (murdered) author whose personal writing inspires an immense fan base, but which is itself filtered through a number of biographical disguises. "[W]rite first...*disguise* later" ("To Write" 33), says Shields. The multiple levels of biographical disguise in *Swann* are tantalizing, as Shields grapples with questions of literary influence and biographical fictionalization, particularly as she conjures the ghosts of Canadian literary predecessors through her presentation of the uncanny bio-critical afterlife of Mary Swann.

In the novel, Shields is interested in the allure, even the *necessity*, of literary ancestors, not only as sites of individual projection but also as forms of communal emplacement and connection. Although she satirizes the ways literary critics engage in this quest, this concern self-reflexively evokes her own compulsion for literary precursors in her bio-critical studies of Susanna Moodie and Jane Austen, a theme that Shields also explored in *Small Ceremonies*, in which Moodie, like Swann, functions as an enticing textual cipher. Nevertheless, literature, even if it is "nothing more than the art of creative rearrangement" (Gamble 44), indebtedness, and slippery signification, creates an imagined community and shared currency—between authors, between authors and readers, among readers. As one character in the novel perceives it, literature "binds one human being to the next and shortens the distance we must travel to discover that our most private perceptions are universally felt" (179), a thought that is echoed in Shields's allusion to the "murmured chorus" that sustains us in the texts we read ("To Write" 34). As Shields magisterially put it in "Narrative Hunger and the Overflowing Cupboard," it "might be a project for the narratives of the next millennium...[to ask] how we've come to record what separates us rather than what brings us together" (33).

And so, literature compels us to commune with ghosts. Stephen Greenblatt memorably described this as "a desire to speak with the dead" (1)—a sentiment echoed in Shields's sense that writing "is a great service rendered the living by the dead" ("To Write" 35). As Margaret Atwood puts it in *Negotiating with the Dead*, "dead bodies can talk if you know how to listen to them, and they *want* to talk" (163). We *want* to speak with ghosts, and it is through literature that this communing becomes possible, since writing, in "chart[ing] a process of thought," survives as the "voice" of the dead (Atwood 158). Which is not to say that writing offers a transparent window onto past ancestors. As Shields puts it in describing the "alchemy of re-imagined reality" ("To Write" 32), we have before us "the author's *willed impression* of the world...a smoke screen, a concealing cape, an occluded mirror, a kaleidoscope, a magic lantern,...the subjunctive self" ("What You Use" 64).

Shields's parody of the colloquium in *Swann*, I would argue, is not in the interests of wholly debunking such gatherings, nor in the name of a cynical rejection of literary scholarship. Rather, it emerges from an aware-ness of the importance that literary authors continue to have for personal and communal needs. Shields questions the projections and blindnesses that inform these needs, to be sure, particularly in the reconstruction of female precursors, but she does not place herself outside of this dynamic, as is evident in her essay "To Write Is to Raid" (34–35). Indeed, the nar-rative of *Swann* is itself presided over by the ghosts of two significant female Canadian literary predecessors: the legendary Saskatchewan lyricist Sarah Binks (from the 1940s) and British Columbia poet Pat Lowther (from the 1970s). Shields's meta-perspective on her novel's own parodic stance finds its clearest expression in these two Canadian literary intertexts that go into the construction of Mary Swann, particularly since what binds together the various critics in the novel is their search for literary precursors.

Swann, in one sense, is Shields's tribute to her fellow (though not con-temporaneous) University of Manitoba professor Paul Hiebert, who retired from the university in 1953; indeed, *Swann* was published in the same year that Hiebert died. Hiebert was the author of the 1947 satirical novel, *Sarah Binks*, a novel that poses as a biography of a Saskatchewan poet named Sarah Binks. In its portrayal of the academics, biographers, and groupies who grapple over the reputation of the poet Mary Swann, Shields's novel offers a satirical reworking, exactly 40 years later, of *Sarah Binks*, about the fictional and dubiously talented "Songstress of Saskatchewan" (vii). In both texts, the biography and literary legacy of the absent poet are fabricated through scraps of poetry, sentimental pro-nouncements, and scattered biographical details, evoking the often-willed distortion of academic sleuthing and celebrity boosterism. More insis-tently, it is the humble and rural origins of Binks, like Swann, that make the "miracle" of her supposed talent all the more exceptional. Binks's fic-tional biographer "takes exception" to the theory that Binks was "an iso-lated genius" who "sprang spontaneously" from the soil (x). Instead, he insists that she has been integrally shaped by the fabric and historical legacy of her Saskatchewan environment; "her roots go deep," he maintains (x). As he puts it, Binks was "the product of her friends, of her books, and of the little incidents which shaped her life" (viii). This is echoed in Mary Swann's meagre and mysterious origins: a farm wife who has left no identifiable legacy; an overworked and tired woman who lived in squalor, had few refined tastes, no literary influences, and had not been farther than Belleville in her entire life. How *could* an individual of so restricted experience write the heartfelt and probing verses that she did? Well might the critics ask this question. At the Swann Symposium, critics debate whether or not Mary Swann did produce the works that are attributed to her (ironic, of course, given that we discover that she, in fact, did not write most of them). In the life of Sarah Binks, a similar question arises through a controversy about the authorship of her poetry: Professor Marrowfat speculates that "Sarah could not have written these poems...because she lacked the profound philosophical background which characterizes the poems" (78). This is further complicated when we later learn that the foremost "Binksian," Miss Rosalind Drool, who is credited with the discovery of Sarah Binks (much like Sarah Maloney in *Swann*), "permitted her sweeping admiration" of Binks's work "to carry her beyond the reading of it into the actual addition of several verses of her own," a fact that "has made it difficult, according to Professor Marrowfat, 'to decide which is Binks and which is Drool'" (150).

That Sarah Binks is a fictional invention, the subject of a mock literary biography, offers a further reflection on Shields's novel in which the theme of biographical invention is overtly explored. Not only is Swann, in a sense, a fabrication of the scholars who promote her work, but her invent-edness becomes highlighted the more the novel proceeds, since the "evidence" of Swann's existence is slowly disappearing (the photograph of her; the pen she used to write with; her notebook; the last remaining copies of her book *Swann's Songs*; the original manuscripts; and the reminiscences themselves). Both texts reveal Swann and Binks to be ciphers, textual constructs, both as fictional creations of their authors, but also in the sense that the "author" position is itself a construction fabricated by a community of readers. In both texts, a seminal literary manuscript is destroyed by the keepers of the poet's reputation: Cruzzi's wife Hildë in *Swann* uses the manuscript to dispose of fish scraps, while in *Sarah Binks* an original manuscript is "used for kindling by the curator" of "Binksiana" (51).[1] Shields makes the connection even more explicit in Frederic Cruzzi's letter to Sarah Maloney in the novel: "A manuscript is, after all, only a crude representation...and might just as usefully be employed as kindling for a fire or in the wrapping of fishbones" (192). In both texts, the critical blindnesses of literary academics are mocked. The parallel extends to the verses themselves, of course. Sarah Binks, according to her biographer, is the poet of the unabashedly "trivial" (xiv), as is Mary Swann; they both attempt to link the trivial with the profound (as does Carol Shields throughout her work). At the same time, however, the parodic effect of both novels is expressly that the poetry does not merit the kind of literary-critical attention that it receives—at least, this is true of Sarah Binks...in Mary Swann's case it is a little more ambiguous.

What establishes the parodic effect in *Sarah Binks* is the gap between the sentiment and the quality of the verse. In short, Binks's poetry is no good. Gerald Noonan explores the parodic workings in *Sarah Binks* in his 1978 article in *Studies in Canadian Literature*. According to Noonan, there is a split effect in the reading experience of *Sarah Binks*, for on the one hand her writing has the mark of "trivia" upon it, but, on the other hand, the reader experiences a sense of nostalgia for a time when it may have been possible to have believed in the profundity of such a confined world. Sarah's life is significant expressly because it is of a time that is no more. Noonan describes this effect as one of both "incongruity and nostalgia," which is in turn dependent upon the reader's "unconscious awareness of the discrepancy between Hiebert's and Sarah's understanding" (3). As Noonan writes, "We both recognize the incongruous reality and feel a nostalgia for a lost possibility" (4). This element of nostalgia, I would argue, is absent in Shields's text. But there is something else at work here, for it is through the figure of Pat Lowther that Shields enables us to effect this cross-over. By superimposing Lowther's tale atop Binks's, the story becomes a feminist commentary about the invisibility (from literature, if not elsewhere) of women's lives. The sweet songstress of Saskatchewan, in other words, points to the sinister specter of misogyny.

Shields's Mary Swann evokes numerous parallels with the real-life Canadian poet Pat Lowther, who, like Swann, was violently murdered by her husband in 1975.[2] Indeed, the title of Shields's 1992 novel, *The Stone Diaries*, echoes Lowther's posthumous poetry collection *A Stone Diary* (1977), the text which, like *Swann's Songs*, Lowther had submitted to a publisher shortly before her disappearance and which, in turn, clinched her literary reputation. Shields, in fact, had met Pat Lowther during her student days at the University of Ottawa when Lowther was a visiting reader on the campus in 1974 (Wiesenthal 301); the two established a passing friendship, both publishing poetry collections in 1974 that were reviewed together in the *Canadian Forum*. The parallels between Lowther and Swann in the novel are substantial. Both women were bludgeoned to death with a hammer by their husbands; both submitted a major poetry manuscript to a publisher shortly before their deaths which was published posthumously; both are authors of posthumous poetry collections whose composition and "authenticity" are uncertain (in Swann's case, because the poems were inadvertently destroyed by Hildë Cruzzi; in Lowther's case, because her husband had plundered her manuscripts to amass "evidence" from her poems that she was having an extra-marital affair, and subsequently Lowther's personal papers were rifled through by others as they became material for a criminal investigation); both achieved notoriety, in part through the fact of their untimely end; both had their name linked to a public institution: in Lowther's case, to the "Pat Lowther Memorial Award" given by the League of Canadian Poets, in Swann's case, to the "Mary Swann Memorial Room" in the local Nadeau museum.

More interestingly in terms of the storyline of *Swann*, an obvious parallel exists in the posthumous deification—indeed gothicization—of the two poets. The celebration of Mary Swann as a martyr/victim (and, indeed, as a kind of ghost who haunts her readers) echoes the propagation of the "poet as victim" myth which circulated in the wake of Lowther's death. In her biography of Lowther, Christine Wiesenthal outlines the posthumous construction of Lowther as "the proverbial sacrificial lamb" (83). The myth (and subsequent controversy that followed) began with a 1975 tribute to Lowther that was aired on Peter Gzowksi's CBC radio program shortly after her death. As Wiesenthal describes it, the "'special report' opened with a recorded reading by Pat Lowther of a short poem entitled 'Nightmare'" (75). The poem is a quirky piece of black humour, very much in the vein of Margaret Atwood, and at the end of the reading Lowther chuckled in response to the humorous concluding line: "I try to cry out:/ *I'm harmless!*/ but the words can't/ get through my fangs" (76). Wiesenthal explores the ways Lowther's "mordantly clever little 'Nightmare'"—and Lowther's work overall—was "re-recorded as 'a true nightmare' for the living, [a slippage that] requires no explanation or apology" (76). The Gzowski tribute inspired a subsequent feature article in the 1976 *Canadian Magazine* written by Paul Grescoe. Entitled "Eulogy of a Poet" and subtitled "Poet as Victim," Grescoe's article traced what he termed "the soul-scarring experience of Lowther's life," which he felt formed the impetus of her uncannily evocative verse. The tributes initiated a series of controversies and debates about who could legitimately claim insight into the poet's life (poet Andy Wainwright, who took issue with the maudlin tone that had entered into discussions of Lowther's life at the expense of her work, was castigated as "an East Coast stranger") and the extent to which one could read the life (and death) into the poems. Critics' insistence on reading Lowther's death into her work is echoed in the ways Shields's biographer-critics seek fleeting glimpses of the "real" traumatized Mary Swann in her writing, simplistically reducing her work to a biographical reflection of her suffering (the very literary approach that is so steadfastly mocked in the reductive poems written by Sarah Binks!). It is not surprising, therefore, that Sarah Maloney in the novel compares Mary Swann's legacy to that of Sylvia Plath (82), a comparison that was made about Lowther as well.[3] In the case of Swann, the profundity that is attributed to the poems is applied in hindsight; the death, in other words, renders the poetry significant, but primarily because of the death.

It would seem that Shields in a sense updated Sarah Binks as a literary foremother through the overlay of Pat Lowther. But by superimposing a gothic prototype atop a satirical one, and a "real" dead author atop a "fake" dead author, the satirical effect of the portrayal of Mary Swann is altered. But why? This is where I want to argue that Shields's novel takes us beyond satire through its very play on the poststructuralist motif of the "death of the author." Shields told Eleanor Wachtel in an interview that when she wrote *Swann* she was "reading a lot of postmodern criticism" (118). The desire to pin down the *real* Mary Swann in the novel becomes parodied as a delusion, since Swann (and indeed her works) exist only as simulacra. But is Shields parodying the earnestness with which critics inflate the reputation and intentionality of their literary icons or is she making fun of the murdering of the author function itself, which, echoing Roland Barthes, leaves behind a text that is—literally—no more than "a tissue of quotations" (146)?

In the novel, the death of the author is literalized and Mary Swann would seem to evaporate in its wake, an outcome that echoes the standard criticism raised by many feminist and postcolonial theorists to the effect that the author was declared dead just as many authors from marginalized constituencies were finding a voice. As Shields said of the novel in her interview with Wachtel, "How can you ever know anything about a person who's been so effectively erased from the world?" (41). Interestingly, Morton Jimroy, Swann's biographer, feels he is committing literary-critical homicide in the very act of constructing a false public face for Mary Swann. He accuses himself "of burying Swann's grainy likeness, keeping her out of sight and shutting her up, a miniature act of murder" (110). There is something particularly troubling about this since, as Jimroy observes, Swann lived a life that was beneath the radar, "a life lived...in the avoidance of biography" (110). To represent Swann accurately is to bury her even further, thereby compounding the social and historical erasure of wives and working-class women that has dominated generations of Western patriarchal society. For Shields, the quotidian world of women's lives is one of the many things that is not available in the narrative cupboard. Swann is thus the paradigmatic "dead" female author—dead, and erased, as a result of misogynistic male violence. She is also the paradigmatic poststructuralist author—dead in the sense that the work (and, indeed, the written biography) exists outside of the author function—a function that overwrites the historical silencing and oppression of women within which Mary Swann is deeply embedded. Given this context, if all that is left of Swann is a series of trace fragments (and a series of false traces), what are we to make of the real-life "authors"—Sarah Binks and Pat Lowther—who hover, metadiscursively, in the background of Mary Swann? In other words, Shields's invocation of two pivotal iconic Canadian literary intertexts in her portrayal of Mary Swann needs to be considered before we can sum up her approach in this book, which has been widely described as a literary-critical and anti-national satire.

Shields's satirical gothic adds an important twist to the novel. As *Swann* playfully calls attention to the failed quest for the suffusing presence of literary precursors, it is itself presided over (haunted?) by the presence of very prominent literary precursors. In so doing, Shields's novel plays out the very "ghost-of-a-ghost" (38) function that Jonathan Kertzer identifies as being at the heart of Canadian literary culture: the sense that poetic ancestors are neither *sui generis* nor posthumous but rather a kind of unresolvable "empty set" which persists in haunting the Canadian literary establishment. This is what Kertzer identifies as the absent *genius loci* in Canadian culture, the emblem that should unite spirit and place (40). Kertzer argues that Canadian authors and scholars will remain haunted "as long as they conceive of literature as the voice of a *genius loci*" (47), that the urgency to link spirit with place is precisely the romantic move that Canadian history disallows. In Kertzer's sense, it is not the Barthesian death of the author that is at issue, but rather the cultural-historical legacy of Canada, in which national cultural discourse was built upon a foundation of ambivalence, displacement, and instability. A claim to indigenous authorship, in the sense of a localized emergence from place (which is what critics seek in Mary Swann), is absent. "The ghost cannot be captured," Kertzer writes, "since it is a spectre of thought, banished by the same reflex that seeks it" (38). Mary Swann is just such a ghost: a ghost who refuses to haunt. And *that*, expressly, is the problem. Her readers, all of them, desire evidence of an authenticating haunting—a local woman who has achieved apotheosis—and in so doing, they are partially responsible for bludgeoning the author beyond recognition. Swann, in this role, becomes the gothic victim or ghost who is hounded and pursued by scholars who want her to take up residence in them. Sarah Maloney expresses this desire quite literally: "I'm tempted to grope under the band of my skirt, grab hold of my flesh and see...whether it's Mary Swann who has taken up residence there" (58).

For the critics within the novel, it is the origins of genius that pose the greatest conundrum. Yet Shields's novel inhabits a curious position with respect to this process, since it engages with the question of cultural inheritance and legacy in seemingly contradictory ways. On the one hand, the critics in the novel are obsessed with the question of literary precursors. Sarah Maloney, for example, is perturbed by Swann's apparent lack of literary influences: "There's a gap that needs explaining....How did Mary Swann, untaught country woman, know how to make that kind of murky metaphorical connection. Who taught her what was possible?" (55). Sarah grapples with this conundrum: not so much a Bloomian anxiety of influence as an anxiety of non-influence. "Back to the same old problem," she says to herself. "Mary Swann hadn't read any modern poetry. She didn't *have* any influences" (55). Morton Jimroy, Swann's biographer, is similarly obsessed with identifying Swann's poetic precursors. When he asks her daughter what poetry she remembers her mother reading, the daughter is unequivocal: "'[None] that I can remember. Unless you count Mother Goose as poetry'" (93). At the conference itself, critic Syd Buswell appalls the crowd by dispelling the question of literary influence head on: there is no modernist poetry contained in the Nadeau public library, he pronounces with satisfaction (259–60). The "mystery" of Mary Swann is thus not the one that is ostensibly posed by the novel—i.e., the burglar who is removing the last traces of Swann's existence from the historical record—but rather how a genius managed to arise in such lowly Canadian origins (or, to invoke Kertzer's language, how a *genius loci* might be imagined to have arisen there). As Sarah Maloney puzzles, "therein...hangs the central mystery:...Where in those bleak Ontario acres...did she find the sparks that converted emblematic substance into rolling poetry?" (31). The critics in the novel are flummoxed by this idea and troubled by it. In their view, just as there is no "death" of the author in the sense that Barthes meant it, so is there no "origin" of the author without a genealogical tradition to precede it. In a moment of striking self-perception, Sarah notes that "The fact that art could be created in such a void was, for some reason, deeply disturbing" (44), which, I think, takes us to the heart of Shields's novel. The disturbing element might be the possibility of literature arising in a vacuum, for what does that say about cultural inheritance and continuity? Does that render all of us as alone as Mary Swann, exiled to a metaphorical boneyard of cultural isolationism? Buswell, who suspects Swann of being a fraud, is only voicing what all the other critics already know: that they are pursuing a specter of their own desires. Critics want to implant Swann as a *genius loci*, a spirit who both emerges from the land and speaks its authentic "voice" in poetry, yet they are anxious about the notion of a *sui generis* (or self-generated) author because it undermines any sense of literary, cultural, and communal continuity. In both instances, they are propelled by a yearning for cultural inheritance, a desire for literary genealogy alongside a subconscious awareness that genealogy may need to be invented.

The novel, then, performs the death of the author in tandem with its characters' fruitless resuscitation of the signifying author (since they obsessively engage in outmoded biographical and intentionalist forms of literary analysis). As Barthes states, the writer "is born simultaneously with the text, [and] is in no way equipped with a being preceding or exceeding the writing" (145). And yet, overlaid atop the absent Mary Swann hover the specters of Binks and Lowther, both of whom, in different ways, have been integrally identified with their biographies. On a metatextual level, then, Shields performs the very quest for literary precursors that her text appears to be satirizing. If she fills in for the absence of ghosts by making the very absence itself a figure of influence, she also takes her satire one step further by gothicizing the haunting poet Mary Swann. As a literary intertext, *Sarah Binks* on its own might bolster the satirical portrait of the dubiously talented Mary Swann. If it were left here, Shields's satire would seem to be unrelenting in its commentary on Canadian colonial culture (in the spirit of Stephen Leacock's Mariposa). But when Binks is merged with Pat Lowther, a touch of *gravitas* is leant to the portrayal of Swann, and the satire becomes gothicized in becoming haunted by its own subject: the *return* of the dead author. This process charts the enabling construction of a willed haunting that transforms the "ghost of a ghost" (that is, Swann and Binks, who are both fictions) into the "ghost of a (once living) poet."

Shields appears to be saying something about the need for literary haunting as a source of spiritual-cultural sustenance—"all that murmured chorus" of dead women writers, as she describes it in "To Write Is to Raid" (34). Does the quest for precursors falsify the endeavor or is the need authentic as a need? The novel circles around this unresolved tension. Swann, in effect, is a communal—and, indeed, a textual—creation. Her mythology has been generated by the literary establishment; her poems are partially written by her publisher; her biography is invented by the local Nadeau librarian; and, in the end, the symposium participants have to rewrite, from memory, everything she is thought to have written. If on the one hand this can be read as a puncturing of the insistence on national labels and literary traditions, it also testifies to the important function that art serves for communal identity. In the end, are we to think that Swann's legacy has been subject to distortion, as Hammill asserts (130), or are we to think that it is the haunting effect, finally, which constitutes the power and pleasure of all literary—and literary-critical—artifice? As Morton Jimroy says of the miracle of the literary effect: "When he thought of the revolution of planets, the emergence of species, the balance of mathematics, he could not see that any of these was more amazing than the impertinent human wish to reach into the sea of common language and extract from it the rich dark beautiful words that could be arranged in such a way that the unsayable might be said. Poetry was the prism that refracted all of life" (86). By channeling Pat Lowther through Sarah Binks, Shields is able to parody the compromised celebration of literary ancestors while conjuring the human need to connect with a lived past through literature. The tragedy of *Swann*, then, is the source of its parody: the more the author is dead, the more one wishes to commune with her. In part a send-up of the literary establishment's inexorable and fatuous reinvention of its authors, the novel also provides a self-conscious meditation on the urgent compulsion for literary ancestors in the construction of cultural tradition and collective identity.

Given *Swann*'s apparent deconstruction of national and authorial identity markers, it is ironic that the novel sets itself firmly within an identifiable Canadian literary trajectory, not only lending a touch of poignancy to its portrayal of Mary Swann, but also suggesting that localized, even national, culture is not entirely superfluous in an apparently postmodern, postnational era. Moreover, by transposing the Saskatchewan and B.C. origins of Binks and Lowther into rural Ontario, Shields places her mystery firmly within Canada's celebrated Southern Ontario Gothic tradition, which in many instances (as in the case of Alice Munro) figures the gothic as a function of the quotidian and the local. Shields's novel thus charts and enacts both the making and unmaking of a national poet—a commemorative fusion of Binks and Lowther—through her fictional creation of a haunting literary legend whose authority and origins are evocative, yet spectral. *Swann* thus adopts a metatextual reflection on its satirical narrative through its real-life poetic gothic intertext, exploring the ways a community embraces literary ghosts in the urge to secure a form of collective memory that may—or may not—be a will of the wisp, but which is no less necessary for all that. This is the "narrative hunger" that Shields writes so eloquently about, and it is what sparks the act of communal creation that concludes the novel. As Kathy Barbour puts it, the poetry that Swann's followers compose at the novel's end can be seen as "re-embodying the eclipsed presence of Mary Swann, the author" (279), herself a figural embodiment of other literary predecessors. This "alchemy of re-imagined reality" ("To Write" 32), to quote Shields again, structures the novel, while also pointing to the gaps that inhere in any act of literary or memorial representation.

Shields is teasingly materialist in her account of the writer's method: "those who have chosen a writing life have already surrendered a portion of their DNA. There are all those clues in their work, all those revealing gaps…, *all those teeth*" ("What You Use" 59). This sounds like Sarah Maloney's mother's embedded twin, "a compacted little bundle of bone and hair, which…became absorbed into her body" (56). The work becomes the host, which houses things that connect to the author but of which he/she may be unaware. As Shields puts it, the written work embeds things that are "buried out of sight of [the author's] own eyes" ("What You Use" 51). And yet, Mary Swann leaves no such embedded messaging, no DNA trace (neither literal nor metaphoric) by which one might assign her geographical or cultural emplacement. This is the circuit of desire that constitutes the voraciousness of the symposium members. Shields satisfies this hunger by sleight of hand, through her own metatextual literary cupboard: embedding the ancestral ghosts of two Canadian literary predecessors that oversee her act of creation. In the end, this leaves us, the academics who study Shields's work, no closer to identifying Swann's substance. It is not in our/their toolkit—or should I say, our kitchen drawer. Swann's essence, notwithstanding her shared genealogy with Binks and Lowther, inheres in the "lost things" of the novel's closing poem (which is itself a pastiche of "lost" phrases), things that have "withdrawn/into themselves" to become part of a broader narrative of feminine, communal, and cultural loss, the swan song of which the literary cupboard has long been deplorably out of stock.

NOTES

1. This "manuscript," the author tells us, was a board from one of the buildings of the Binks's farm upon which was written a poem (51).
2. The connection between the two has been noted by a few critics, including Catherine Addison in her review of *Swann* in *Canadian Literature* when the novel was first published. Addison notes Swann's "resemblance to Pat Lowther" in that each is a "female poet murdered by her husband," but asserts that the resemblance ends there (159). I am proposing that the parallel is more extensive, and indeed more suggestive, than this.
3. In their reviews of *A Stone Diary*, both Gary Geddes and Christopher Levenson sought to distance themselves from any comparison of Lowther's legacy with Sylvia Plath. Levenson warned against the propagation of "a Canadian Plath cult" (352).

WORKS CITED

Addison, Catherine. "Lost Things." Rev. of *Swann: A Mystery*, by Carol Shields. *Canadian Literature* 121 (Summer 1989): 158–60.

Atwood, Margaret. *Negotiating with the Dead: A Writer on Writing*. Cambridge: Cambridge UP, 2002.

Barbour, Kathy. "The Swann Who Laid the Golden Egg: A Cautionary Tale of Deconstructionist Cannibalism in *Swann*." *Carol Shields, Narrative Hunger, and the Possibilities of Fiction*. Ed. Edward Eden and Dee Goertz. Toronto: U of Toronto P, 2003. 255–82.

Barthes, Roland. "The Death of the Author." *Image—Music –Text*. Trans. Stephen Heath. New York: Hill and Wang, 1977. 142–48.

Gamble, Sarah. "Filling the Creative Void: Narrative Dilemmas in *Small Ceremonies*, the *Happenstance* Novels, and *Swann*." *Carol Shields, Narrative Hunger, and the Possibilities of Fiction*. Ed. Edward Eden and Dee Goertz. Toronto: U of Toronto P, 2003. 39–60.

Geddes, Gary. Review of *A Stone Diary*. *Globe and Mail* 9 Apr. 1977: E27.

Giardini, Anne, and Nicholas Giardini, eds. *Startle and Illuminate: Carol Shields on Writing*. Toronto: Random House Canada, 2016.

Gzowski, Peter. "Pat Lowther Tribute." *Gzowski on FM*. CBC Radio. 2 Nov. 1975.

Greenblatt, Stephen. *Shakespearean Negotiations: The Circulation of Social Energy in Renaissance England*. Berkeley: U of California P, 1988.

Grescoe, Paul. "Eulogy for a Poet." *Canadian Magazine* 5 June 1976: 13, 16–19.

Hammill, Faye. "Influential Circles: Carol Shields and the Canadian Literature Canon." *Literary Culture and Female Authorship in Canada, 1760–2000*. Amsterdam: Rodopi, 2003. 115–33.

Hiebert, Paul. *Sarah Binks*. London: Oxford UP, 1947.

Kertzer, Jonathan. *Worrying the Nation: Imagining a National Literature in English Canada*. Toronto: U of Toronto P, 1998.

Levenson, Christopher. Review of *A Stone Diary*. *Queen's Quarterly* 85 (1978): 352–54.

Lowther, Pat. *The Collected Works of Pat Lowther*. Ed. Christine Wiesenthal. Edmonton: NeWest, 2010.

McMullen, Lorraine. "Carol Shields and the University of Ottawa: Some Reminiscences." *Prairie Fire* 16.1 (Spring 1995): 132–37.

Noonan, Gerald. "Incongruity and Nostalgia in *Sarah Binks*." *Studies in Canadian Literature* 3.2 (1978). Online version: http://journals.hil.unb.ca/index.php/scl/article/view/7898/8955. Accessed 23 January 2013.

Shields, Carol. "Narrative Hunger and the Overflowing Cupboard." *Narrative Hunger, and the Possibilities of Fiction*. Ed. Edward Eden and Dee Goertz. Toronto: U of Toronto P, 19–36.

———. "The Short Story (and Women Writers)." Giardini 97–107.

———. *Small Ceremonies: A Novel*. Toronto: McGraw-Hill, Ryerson, 1976.

———. *Swann: A Mystery*. New York: Viking, 1987.

———. "To Write Is to Raid." Giardini 31–36.

———. "What You Use and What You Protect." Giardini 49–66.

———. "Where Curiosity Leads." Giardini 83–92.

Wachtel, Eleanor. *Random Illuminations: Conversations with Carol Shields*. Fredericton: Goose Lane, 2007.

Wiesenthal, Christine. *The Half-Lives of Pat Lowther*. Toronto: U of Toronto P, 2005.

Transforming Love: Critical and Religious Discourses in Carol Shields's *The Republic of Love*

Brenda Beckman-Long

In Anne and Nicholas Giardini's edition *Startle and Illuminate*, a collection of reflections on writing from the Shields archive, an entire chapter is devoted to "The Love Story" (*Giardini* 93–6). Here Carol Shields detects a current skepticism about romance narratives, especially in the historical wake of the sexual revolution and recent popular culture. In Hollywood and Harlequin romances, love is, she says, "no more than a cocktail of chemicals and sentimental echoes"; and yet, she questions the contemporary view that "love no longer powers and transforms ourselves and our society" (*Giardini* 94). She recalls writers from the past, such as Jane Austen and the Venerable Bede, who find love to be redemptive and a "story worth risking" (96). Shields is inspired by Bede's medieval vision of a bird flying from darkness into a bright public space, a banquet hall. She describes *The Republic of Love* (1992) as "my own attempt to write A Love Novel," and a story of not one individual but two people flying side by

B. Beckman-Long (✉)
Briercrest College, University of Saskatchewan, Caronport, SK, Canada

© The Author(s), under exclusive license to Springer Nature
Switzerland AG 2023
N. F. Stovel (ed.), *Relating Carol Shields's Essays and Fiction*,
https://doi.org/10.1007/978-3-031-11480-9_8

side (*Giardini* 94). Her novel interrogates and renews the language of love that has been "trivialized in our society" (Shields, qtd. in De Roo 55). As she states in an earlier essay, "Arriving Late," Shields seeks to reclaim the novel form itself as a public space for performing "an inquiry into language" (251). By writing about a woman who is writing about love, Shields uses a complex *mise en abyme*, or story within a story, to blend romance and metafiction, creating in her novel an embedded cultural critique. Just as she uses the essay, a traditionally masculine form, to express a personal artistic vision that is peculiarly feminine (Verduyn 22, Stovel 2–3), she uses the novel too for this purpose. In this narrative space, her aim is to reinscribe today the historical and enduring themes of love, interconnection, and, above all, the love of others.

Feminist critics rightly find in *The Republic of Love* a parody designed to reclaim the romance genre that is so frequently dismissed as being minor, mainly because it is women's writing. Faye Hammill and Taïna Tuhkunen find in Shields's novel a self-reflexive commentary and work of metafiction (Hammill 62, Tuhkunen 158). Tuhkunen demonstrates some ambivalence, however, saying Shields flirts with the popular romance, to which a "feminist scholar might prefer plugging her ears" (111). But Clara Thomas argues correctly that Shields uses the female body as the grounds for interrogating a feminine identity and self-representation (Thomas 156). Perry Nodelman misjudges the novel, conversely, as "not really all that different from the kind Harlequin publishes" (112). Yet, as I argue elsewhere, Shields uses the romance to develop two subjects, masculine and feminine, to question the generic assumption of a singular and autonomous subject, and a disembodied "self" (Beckman-Long 66).[1] The love stories of Fay McLeod and Tom Avery are interwoven and involve a romance, its deconstruction, and its renewal in order to renegotiate the public space—and common ground—that is the novel form.

In both Fay and Tom, Shields depicts characters whose vision is consequently enlarged. Like her characters, Shields is self-consciously aware that the language or "syntax of love" is "co-opted" by greeting cards and rock lyrics, such as the Beatles' tune "I wanna hold your haaaand" (*RL* 244). She also knows that "gender shifts in the last half-century have bred distrust," as she states in "The Love Story" (*Giardini* 95). Resisting both the superficiality of popular culture and the cynicism of critics, Shields's narrator actively engages evolving feminisms to renew the language of love.[2] But that is not all she does. She participates in both critical and religious turns in recent literary history. More than a decade after the novel's publication (and the death of Jacques Derrida), literary critic Stanley Fish declared in a news column that religion would succeed "high theory" as the "center of intellectual energy in the academy" (C4). Fish notes increased tensions between civil and religious realms, particularly as "religion is transgressing the boundary between private and public" spaces (C1). Such crossovers did escalate, following the attacks on the World Trade Center by Al-Quaeda leader Osama Bin Laden on September 11, 2001. Still, Fish remarks that religion has always been present in the literary field, especially in medieval and Renaissance studies. For much the same reason, Shields cites Bede in "The Love Story."

Shields knows such crossovers persist too in feminist theory, its mantra being the personal is political. "All my books," she claimed, "examine those moments" of epiphany and renewed vision (Shields, qtd. in De Roo 45). As a writer-critic she re-examines worlds of "dreams, possibilities, and parallel realities" ("Arriving Late" 247). She explores gaps, ruptures, and silences to show an absence of words in contemporary English for mystical and "transcendental experiences" (*Giardini* 126). As she stated early in her career, "Language has always seemed to me to be a kind of proof of our spiritual nature" (Shields, qtd. in De Roo 45). She later qualified this view by explaining, "I am not religious, though I was brought up in the Methodist Church" (Shields qtd. in Wachtel 33). Whether in her speech, stories, or essays, she recalls her Methodist upbringing to illustrate an ongoing need, even in contemporary secular society, for communities of readers; she calls them "compassionate and ethical citizens," underlining the value of reading itself as a transformative experience that offers an experience of otherness (*Giardini* 3, 5–7).[3] As Coral Ann Howells observes elsewhere in Shields's short fiction, religious discourse and Christian iconography, such as statues of the Virgin Mary, are a kind of "cultural haunting" that can be traced in Shields's "post-Christian" stories (64). She seeks to expand the vision of her characters and readers alike. Thus, carvings of the Virgin and related image of the mermaid loom large in *The Republic of Love.*

Before Fish made his critical statement, Shields made an important observation of her own in an interview with broadcaster Eleanor Wachtel. She insisted, "Some postmodernists think there is no point beyond the language game but I think there can be" (44). She flatly denied the death of the novel. Regarding *The Republic of Love*, she told another critic, Marjorie Anderson, "The mermaid is one of the most interesting parts of our [cultural] iconography" (149). Fay, the main character and museum curator, studies the cultural "persistence of spiritual beliefs" (*RL* 220). A feminine icon, the mermaid evokes both the cult of the Virgin and Western individualism, because she is "always alone," and independent, as if to represent an autonomous "self" (Shields, qtd. in Anderson 149). Shields interrogates and re-examines these contradictions and ideological beliefs in her novel. As a writer, her express purpose is "to embrace contradiction and tentativeness," while conducting an inquiry into language and its gaps ("Arriving Late" 249–50). Shields demonstrates in her work, and in Fay's work too, that women writers are often ahead of literary critics, by the means of a fictional, feminist narrative performance of a cultural critique.

The Republic of Love is a prime example of a complex metafictional narrative which, in Shields's hands, becomes a creative and political gesture that escapes simple categories. Being a writer and critic, she uses embedded critical and religious discourses to renew the language of love. The novel opens and closes, for example, with references to the liturgical calendar. Its time frame spans the period from Good Friday to Christmas, signaling a thematic movement from death to life. The plot moves, similarly, from the death of a relationship in Fay and Peter Knightley's breakup, to the birth of a marriage in Fay and Tom's wedding. Again in "The Love Story," Shields admits that the handling of time shifted as she wrote her fictional romance:

> The original structure for *The Republic of Love* failed. My plan was to write a love story (a tricky business in these cynical times) by using a short notation from each day of a year, giving my book 365 related segments. This proved impossible, for I soon saw my novel swelling toward what looked like a thousand pages. I abandoned the plan and chose daily segments stretching from Easter to Christmas, a more manageable framework. (*Giardini* 26)

The novel's form changes in her writing process to emphasize its complex purpose.

In the novel's opening, Fay notes that it is Good Friday. She stresses that it is the "ultimate day of contradictions" with its "pagan roots" (5). She refers to a social practice in some rural communities in England, whereby people roll beer through the streets in lieu of animal sacrifices. Cultural anthropologist René Girard would describe this kind of ritual as an "act of collective substitution" intended to "protect the entire community from its own violence" (77). This *scapegoat effect*, to borrow his term, performs the social function of maintaining order and unity by redirecting violence (Girard 80–82). At the same time, such a ritual act veils the violent and exclusionary nature of scapegoating (92). He calls this effect a form of *méconnaissance*, a misrecognition or effect that myths also create, as Shields is evidently aware. Like Girard and other cultural critics, such as Margaret Visser (258–59), Shields draws attention to the scapegoat effect in myths and stories that circulate even now. By doing so, she recalls the sacrificial and religious origins of contemporary cultural discourses and practices. Like Stanley Fish, she is not a promoter of such practices, but a critic and observer of ongoing tensions between sociopolitical and religious practices.

In *The Republic of Love,* "visions of the Holy Virgin" (289) are presented as "corruption[s] of Christian symbol" (205). Shields has stated in interviews that the "mythology of virginity" and related ceremonial acts, though secularized, persist in today's culture (Shields, qtd. in Wachtel 37, 43). The fictional Fay draws similar conclusions in her writing practices. The curator and folklorist initially explores the "ritualized exchange" of vows in the traditional marriage ceremony (221). The "sacred pledge" makes public the "private pledge" of a mutual commitment (298), which is embodied in the mirroring words "I love you, I love you" (221). Later, Fay explores the global and pervasive mermaid myth, finding it to be "at once private and collective" (351). In Fay's research about medieval French architectural details, Inuit soapstone carvings, and public images and exhibitions at the Louvre and Vatican museums, she traces the objectification of women through a figure of the feminine that has not "a whit of intelligence about her," only a fleshy "writhing" body. As she remarks of many mermaids, "They're starved and vapid and stupid as fish [...] maddened by love" (222). She recalls the same phenomenon in Hollywood films including the movie *Splash* starring Tom Hanks (14). Once again, she remarks in a public lecture at Winnipeg's folklore center, "We know how visions of the Holy Virgin are multiplied and reinforced by the blessed communities" (189–90), whether they appear in the Vatican or the Louvre, the Arctic, or the Loire delta. In her explorations of mermaid sightings in France, she learns that young women, though often dismissed and silenced, find paradoxical meaning in mermaid myths and an uncanny self-recognition in the marginalized status of such stories and icons. Fay sees in folklore studies, generally, the "collapsing edge of elaborate religious observance," and she regards her field as a way of connecting language, theory, and action (219). She recognizes the interrelation of narrative and social practices, especially the subordination and disempowerment of women in Western cultures. While Fay's writing uses psychoanalytic and Jungian theories to frame her cultural critique, her shifting views indicate evolving feminisms and not, in Shields's words, "a closed system of belief" (Shields, qtd. in Anderson 149). Fay's views on historical and cultural stereotypes of gender are shaped by a combination of theoretical research and personal experience; yet, her own beliefs and cultural assumptions elude her, especially her beliefs in objectivity, rationality, and autonomy. Nevertheless, as she continues her research, she is compelled to pursue not only ideas but also love and community, thus assuming in her own life a "self" that is not entirely autonomous; unlike a Western and masculine "self," hers is portrayed by Shields as a relational and embodied "self" of the type identified by second- and third-wave feminists in the 1980s and 1990s.

In her personal experience, especially in the developing romance with broadcaster Tom Avery, Fay's desire for "rapturous union" eventually finds fulfillment in the marriage ceremony she once studied in a supposedly objective and detached manner. Unlike her parents, she chooses to participate in a civil ceremony rather than a church wedding. The ceremony's printed text is noticeably "creased" from general and repeated use; nevertheless, it is meaningful, due to the "particularity" of Fay's sexual desire for Tom (364). The creased text is also a *mise en abyme* for a narrative fold, or "pocket" in the novel's plot ("Arriving Late" 249), with a double reversal of the decision to marry. Here, the narrative fold is a feminist double strategy that is both political and self-reflexive. As critical theorist Paul Smith argues, "The effect of feminism's double-play is [...] to have cast doubt on the adequacy of the poststructuralist shibboleth [dogma] of the decentred 'subject'" (151). Fay comes to represent a feminist subject that is not decentred, but performative and embodied. While the marriage ceremony attempts to codify love and fix it in language, its words are renewed in Fay's personal speech act and public banns. The text of the marriage ceremony codifies love, *"the most elusive of human bonds"* (*RL* 359, original italics); yet, the words are enacted and renewed in a spoken personal pledge and social contract, to which Fay affixes a signature in her own hand. In effect, the printed text becomes meaningful again in the present by engaging the body.

Shields's novel shows, then, that the body cannot be reduced to language or theory. Fay's decision to marry is actually motivated by a bodily crisis in her desire for a child. Perhaps the desire for motherhood is a part of the text to which a feminist would, like Taïna Tuhkunen, prefer to turn a deaf ear. After Fay has left Tom because of a lingering fear of commitment and loss of freedom, she later returns, because she can neither sleep nor bear the "cup" of pain that is his physical absence (336, 348). She then remembers an "archaic phrase," alluding to the Anglican marriage ceremony and Form of Solemnization of Matrimony, which reads "*with my body I thee worship*," a word suggesting "honour" (336, original italics). An embodied memory motivates her return. The phrase belongs to a tripartite vow: "With this ring I thee wed, with my body I thee worship, and with all my worldly goods I thee endow."[4] As Shields was likely aware, the vow appears in many editions of *The Book of Common Prayer*, albeit with spelling variations, extending to the 1552 first edition and its origins in Catholic ritual. By evoking such a long historical view, the narrator's third-person perspective in Shields's text exceeds Fay's limited perspective. Shields's text thus troubles and complicates Fay's feminist point of view, unsettling even the reader's assumptions. Fay again confronts the assumptions derived from her academic studies, namely "the insularity of the Western tradition," as well as "the weight of the patriarchy" (220). In their silent thoughts, Fay and Tom have equally faced a gnawing loneliness. In "The Love Story," Shields stresses that her novel is "as much about loneliness as it is about love" (*Giardini* 94). Fay is described as a "woman not even on speaking terms with her own loneliness" (154), just as Tom is a "loner" (167). Moreover, Tom is thrice divorced, and Fay is recovering from three breakups. With Fay, Tom feels miraculously "liberated" from the "capsized faith of the single life" (254) and his continual search for "intimacy" and commitment (299). For both Fay and Tom, the needs and desires of the body exceed gender ideologies and cultural assumptions about an autonomous "self." Shields treats an autonomous selfhood as a kind of cultural fiction, and she treats self-representation or autobiographical discourse as a space from which the body is conspicuously absent.

Fay's grief ends only when she prostrates her body at Tom's door. To understand this strange, almost worshipful gesture and the novel's final pages, it is important to consider Shields's theoretical reasons for emphasizing the body. In "The Love Story," Shields recalls a moment of epiphany, similar to that of Fay. An uncle's spontaneous kiss on her aunt's neck represents an "ardour" that Shields never forgot (*Giardini* 93). No potboiler or critical theory could erase the memory of that love, and its transforming power, in an ordinary woman's life. In her novel, Shields again explores the body and personal narratives as sites of communication, and, as other women's life writing shows, "rich grounds for thinking through the relationships between identity and representation" (Gilmore 84). The body resists representation to the extent that, once Fay has exhausted her theories and self-knowledge, she lays herself down on Tom's doorstep. The body must finally be acknowledged, in the words of feminist theorist Susanna Egan, as "a significant component of identity" (5). Shields's novel parodies the popular romance and, simultaneously, presents a feminist critique of the politics of self-representation, in relation to gender and Western individualism.

Fay's startling gesture of self-sacrifice is inspired by a self-sacrificing elder who also reversed a decision not to marry (365). Onion Boyle is a "nonbeliever" (110), a modern rationalist who thinks the body is nothing more than "a bundle of protoplasm" (153). A second-wave feminist, she shunned marriage to pursue a career as a pathologist. But when her long-time lover suffers a stroke, she thinks she has made an error and marries him at his bedside. Grieving her subsequent loss of a husband, she counsels Fay to correct her error in rejecting Tom. Despite Onion's crisis, she confers on Fay the "blessing" that she silently craved from her godmother (272, 364). By contrast, Fay's father, Richard McLeod, who was once a "true believer" in love (255), has given up marriage in a false sacrifice to his masculine autonomy upon retirement. But now an "act of God," a traumatic experience, in which he has narrowly escaped being killed by a fallen airplane wheel, reminds him of his "mortality" and need for the other (364). As if "out of the blue" (357), he calls Peggy McLeod and returns home to resume his marriage, renewing his sacred pledge. He, too, becomes an elder who models for Fay the need for a loving sacrifice of individual freedom, for the sake of the emotional and physical rapture that comes from a vital union.

In Shields's novel, all the primary characters, including Fay, Tom, Onion, and Richard, experience the body's "hunger for the food of love" (366). Fay acts on her experience to renew her engagement with Tom. His commitment to Fay has already found expression in the words of the hymn "Abide with Me" (243). Her commitment comes now in words derived from historical and sacred texts, such as *The Book of Common Prayer*: "I pledge you my troth" (359). These words signify a promise of loyalty or truth. Again, the archaic phrase can be traced to several sources since the sixteenth century.[5] In Shields's text, the female body is then reinscribed in language and action, and the language of love is renewed in personal and public discourses that are both critical and religious in nature.

In a narrative collage of religious and civil discourses, the novel troubles binary divisions, such as the sacred and profane, masculine and feminine, language and the body.[6] Still, Fay thinks, "Love renewed is not precisely love redeemed" (364). Instead, it is transformed. Even the central and pivotal chapter of the novel is entitled "The Sacred and the Profane." In this chapter, which covers Fay's earlier research in Paris, she encounters a local friar for whom she feels an unspoken affection, and she meets a fellow scholar whose greeting, "Ah, my dear," inspires the silent thought "*ravish me*" (149). These words allude to seventeenth-century metaphysical poets George Herbert and John Donne in "Love (III)" (l. 9) and "Batter My Heart" (l. 14). The sonnet by Donne, Dean of Saint Paul's Cathedral in London, turns on the paradox that only in the bonds of love can one truly be free. At the same time, Fay recognizes that "love is not necessarily patient .... nor kind" (224). Here, she contradicts the words of Saint Paul: "love is patient and kind" (1 Cor. 13:4). Her lived experience teaches her that love is often "selfish" (15). After her father left her mother, she thought of him as "selfish" and his love as a "metaphysical ruin" (319). Yet, Fay resembles her father. They think they have freely desired romance, but they have both imitated literary models, such as Emma Woodhouse or Don Quixote. Richard constructed models of windmills to fill his time, and Fay rejected Knightly, for his rather pedantic "finger" (14), at the novel's outset. Both father and daughter demonstrate what Girard would call "the imitative nature of desire" (42). In contrast to selfishness, it is still possible to demonstrate "positive" desire in the "willingness to give oneself to others" (Girard 70). Eventually, Fay's action of prostrating herself at Tom's door gestures toward a positive sacrifice in the sense of a "renunciation of metaphysical desire" for personal and individual autonomy (Girard 48–49). Shields thereby creates a double twist that Girard would associate with parody in historical texts by Miguel de Cervantes Saavedra and Fyodor Dostoyevsky. Like Cervantes, Shields undermines the romantic myth of original desire by exposing it as a symptom of Western individualism and middle-class romanticism.

With this historical view in mind, we may turn again to Shields's advice to writers in "The Love Story." In her essay and novel alike, she re-examines the work of Austen, just as she also does in her literary biography, *Jane Austen: A Life* (2001). In a historical moment when the Enlightenment's models of individualism and autonomous selfhood emerge in Western culture, Austen's novels embody a new ideal of equality in marriage, and Austen reaches an expanding middle-class audience. In her own time, Shields acknowledges a fifty percent incidence of marital breakdown and growing numbers of common-law, same-sex, and blended-family relationships. These social changes mean that heterosexual unions that can stand the test of time find less frequent representation than they once did in fiction. Regarding both the limits and possibilities of a romance narrative, Shields further reflects: "Two people meet, fall in love, and integrate their histories. Crises arrive, but the marriage holds firm. Really? Who would expect readers to believe this fairy tale?" (*Giardini* 128). At the same time, she questions a critical assumption that there is no audience for such narrative representations. She reassesses the necessity of exploring narrative gaps today, asserting that "the union of two souls, the merging of contraries...can be as complex, as potentially dynamic and as open to catharsis as the most shattering divorce" or breakup (129). This is clearly the case in *The Republic of Love*, in which a cultural critique is embedded, recalling the kind of social commentary often observed in Austen and designed to "convert the fluff of romance into something more nourishing" for readers (*Austen* 30). As Shields herself points out, "It might be a project for the narratives to come, asking why the rub of disunity strikes larger sparks than the rewards of accommodation." In other words, she questions why we now "privilege what separates us above that which brings us together" (*Giardini* 29). Shields denies neither the social relevance nor ethical imperative to love. Rather, she seeks to engage with the subject of love in an immediate socio-historical context.[6]

In *The Republic of Love*, Shields's language of love exceeds and enriches a romantic discourse to include critical, religious, and civil discourses, connecting them, finally, with the overarching theme of loving one's neighbors. As Fay recognizes, "Love is, after all, a republic" (224). This epiphany is reinforced in the novel's title. Shields's text underscores Fay and Tom's interconnection with one another and also with their family, friends, and neighbors. The curator and critic, Fay, values her social "network" (77) as much as the broadcaster, Tom, values his "circles of listeners" (323). The public space of talk radio—like the novel's public space—inspires the knowledge that "love's got an infrastructure, too. Love your neighbor" (362). These words allude to the gospel according to Matthew: "You shall love your neighbour as yourself" (Matt. 22:39). Fay and Tom arrive at a social vision and cultural practice of "citizenship in each other's lives" (247)—and citizenship in the lives of others. Furthermore, the novel ends, not with a wedding (as Austen's novels do), but a book launch, its cover image being a beckoning mermaid. This image on Fay's *Mermaids of the Inner Mind* is at once a *mise en abyme*, and a figure for the reader, in an individual and collective call to attend to "a deep longing" and the "hunger for the food of love" (366). The communion provided by the "food of love" is emphasized in these words from the last line of Shields's own book; moreover, the female novelist's intended emphasis is apparent in an archival manuscript, where she sets off in a separate paragraph her final words.[7] As her daughter Anne Giardini comments in her Foreword to this edition, the mermaids in *The Republic of Love* could as easily have become, for Shields, the subject of an essay rather than a novel (Giardini vii). In both the novel and her essay, "The Love Story," Shields's advice to writers is clear. She advises the contemporary writer to be a writer-critic. That means answering an ethical and social call for love in action. She calls upon writers—and readers—to become loving, empathic, and responsible citizens.

NOTES

1. For more discussion of the body and self-reflexivity, and the complexity here of Shields's feminist critique and engagement as a writer-critic with a long tradition of women's fiction, autobiography and life writing, see Brenda Beckman-Long (85).
2. For critical discussions of the embodied subject, see Judith Butler or Lorna Irvine. Shields describes the romances of popular writer Danielle Steel as "a light diversion from the serious problems that trouble us," but she says, "I am interested in writing away the invisibility of women's lives, looking at writing as an act of redemption" (*Giardini* 106, 123).
3. A writer who likes to escape and exceed categories, Shields declares, "The best way to introduce yourself to the basis of storytelling is through fairy tales and the Old Testament. Storytelling reminds you to use freedom in story—to jump into it" (*Giardini* 147).
4. I refer to *The Two Books of Common Prayer*, 2nd ed., edited by Edward Cardwell, Oxford U P, 1838, p. 353, which is available online at Google Books (books.google.ca).
5. See *The Two Books of Common Prayer*, p. 353; variations of this phrase can be found for instance in the 1789 U. S. *Book of Common Prayer* and the 1552 *Book of Common Prayer*.
6. I therefore disagree with Lorna Irvine's view that the novel is "attentive to the body's earthiness, and singularly uninterested in its more spiritual…man-

ifestations" (141). Shields eschews the binary division of body and soul, preferring to show instead their interconnection.

7. This quotation from an archival manuscript comes from the *Carol Shields Fonds* in the Literary Manuscripts Collection of Library and Archives Canada in Ottawa. See *Carol Shields Fonds*. 1954–1998. Literary Manuscripts Collection. Ottawa: Library and Archives Canada. 1994, 1997. LMS-0212 1994-13 38, f. 6, p.615.

WORKS CITED

Anderson, Marjorie. "Interview with Carol Shields." *Prairie Fire*, vol. 16, no. 1, 1995, pp. 139–50.

Beckman-Long, Brenda. *Carol Shields and the Writer-Critic*. U of Toronto P, 2016.

Butler, Judith. *Gender Trouble: Feminism and the Subversion of Identity*, Routledge, 1999.

Carol Shields Fonds. 1954–1998. Literary Manuscripts Collection. Ottawa: Library and Archives Canada. 1994, 1997.

De Roo, Harvey. "A Little Like Flying: An Interview with Carol Shields." *West Coast Review*, vol. 23, no. 3, 1988, pp 38–56.

Donne, John. "Batter My Heart." *The Literature of Renaissance England*, ed. John Hollander and Frank Kermode, Oxford U P, 1973, p. 552.

Egan, Susanna. *Mirror Talk: Genres of Crisis in Contemporary Autobiography*. Chapel Hill: U of North Carolina P, 1999.

Fish, Stanley. "One University, Under God?" *Chronicle of Higher Education*, vol. 51, no. 18, 2005, pp. C1, C4.

Giardini, Anne. Foreword. *Relating Carol Shields's Essays and Fiction: Crossing Borders*. Ed. Nora Foster Stovel. Palgrave Macmillan, 2022.

Giardini, Anne and Nicholas Giardini. *Startle and Illuminate*. Toronto: Random House, 2016.

Gilmore, Leigh. *Autobiographics: A Feminist Theory of Women's Self-Representation*. Ithaca: Cornell UP, 1994.

Girard, René. *The Girard Reader*, ed. James G. Williams, Crossroad, 1996.

Hammill, Faye. "*The Republic of Love* and Popular Romance." *Carol Shields, Narrative Hunger, and the Possibilities of Fiction*, ed. Edward Eden and Dee Goertz, U of Toronto P, 2003, pp. 61–83.

Herbert, George. "Love (III)." *The Literature of Renaissance England*, ed. John Hollander and Frank Kermode, Oxford U P, 1973, p. 678.

Howells, Coral Ann. "Space for Strangeness: Carol Shields's Short Stories." *Relating Carol Shields's Essays and Fiction: Crossing Borders*. Ed. Nora Foster Stovel. Palgrave Macmillan, 2022.

Irvine, Lorna. "A Knowable Country: Embodied Omniscience in Carol Shields's *The Republic of Love* and *Larry's Party*." *Carol Shields and the Extra-Ordinary*, ed. Marta Dvořák and Manina Jones, McGill-Queen's U P, 2007, pp. 139–56.

Nodelman, Perry. "Living in the Republic of Love: Carol Shields's Winnipeg." *Carol Shields: The Arts of a Writing Life*, ed. Neil K. Besner, Prairie Fire Press, 2003, pp. 105–24.

Shields, Carol. "Arriving Late: Starting Over." *How Stories Mean*, ed. John Metcalf and J. R. Struthers, Porcupine's Quill, 1993, pp. 244–51.

Shields, Carol. *Jane Austen: A Life*. Viking, 2001.

Shields, Carol. *The Republic of Love*. 1992. Vintage, 1994.

Smith, Paul. *Discerning the Subject*. U of Minnesota P, 1988.

Stovel, Nora. Introduction. "'Crossing Borders,' Breaking Rules: Carol Shields's 'Strategy for Survival.'" *Relating Carol Shields's Essays and Fiction: Crossing Borders*. Ed. Nora Foster Stovel. London: Palgrave Macmillan, 2022.

The Book of Common Prayer. General Synod of the Anglican Church of Canada, 1962.

The Holy Bible. Revised Standard Version, Collins, 1952.

Thomas, Clara. "Carol Shields's *The Republic of Love* and *The Stone Diaries*." *"Union in Partition": Essays in Honour of Jeanne Delbaere*, ed. Gilbert Debusscher and Marc Maufort, Liège Language and Literature, 1997, pp. 153–60.

Tuhkunen, Taïna. "Carol Shields's *The Republic of Love*, or How to Ravish a Genre." *Carol Shields and the Extra-Ordinary*, ed. Marta Dvořák and Manina Jones, McGill-Queen's U P, 2007, pp. 97–114.

Verduyn, Christl. "(Es)Saying It Her Way: Carol Shields as Essayist." *Relating Carol Shields's Essays and Fiction: Crossing Borders*. Ed. Nora Foster Stovel. Palgrave Macmillan, 2022.

Visser, Margaret. *The Geometry of Love: Space, Time Mystery and Meaning in an Ordinary Church*. Toronto: Harper Flamingo Canada, 2000.

Wachtel, Eleanor. "Interview with Carol Shields." *Room of One's Own: A Feminist Journal of Literature and Criticism*, vol. 13, no. 1–2, 1989, pp. 5–45.

Shields's Theory of Fiction Writing and the Limitations of Remembrance in *The Stone Diaries*

Christian Riegel

This chapter focuses on the inextricable interconnection of Carol Shields's fiction and essays that Nora Foster Stovel signals in the introduction to this volume as inherent qualities of Shields's writing. My interest is in how we can read Shields's essays as a means of gaining insight into her fiction-writing approaches, arguing that reading her essays generates a theory of fiction writing useful to define the generic and literary historical underpinnings of her fiction. Christl Verduyn comments, in the prologue to this volume, on how Shields employs the essay genre as a "highly flexible mode of writing" in a "unique and expansionary manner" (22), echoing Anne Giardini's articulation of Shields's essays as "highly imaginative" in her preface. To be attuned to the possibilities of the essay form that Shields embraces is thus to recognize what Aritha van Herk, in her epilogue, identifies as "consequence" (239). In van Herk's opinion, Shields steps away from event, from the primacy of plot: the notion of consequence invites us

C. Riegel (✉)
Campion College, University of Regina, Regina, SK, Canada

145

N. F. Stovel (ed.), *Relating Carol Shields's Essays and Fiction*,
https://doi.org/10.1007/978-3-031-11480-9_9

to read the essays laterally, an activity out of which a theory of fiction writing emerges.

In several of her essays collected in *Startle and Illuminate: Carol Shields on Writing*, Shields writes about the concerns of narrative, genre, and subject that course through her literary oeuvre, focusing on the challenges to and departures from literary convention that she undertakes in her fiction. As she writes in "Writers Are Readers First," "I understood that the books I should write were the very books I wanted to read, the books I wasn't able to find in the library" (12). Shields gives significant consideration to how she fashions new kinds of books, reflecting a tension between the conventional in fiction writing and the desire to break from tradition. To write fiction for Shields is to push against the boundaries of what fiction can be, while also to recognize the long sweep of literary history. Her essays express a theory of fiction writing that overtly signals this duality, encompassing questions such as the nature of fiction, the role of women in the twentieth century, and form and genre. As she remarks in her essay "Open Every Question, Every Possibility," her novels are constructed out of social, cultural, and historical concerns that reach back millennia, a simultaneous looking back and forward: "We need perhaps to turn back to that twilight of the gods where our stories were born. And ahead to narrative's full potential" ("Open"[1] 129).

In her 1993 novel, *The Stone Diaries*, Shields embraces this movement between tradition and the books she finds lacking in literary culture, creating a novel that in its complexity leaves its readers on intrinsically unstable ground, requiring contemplation of the nature of the text, and underscoring the theory of fiction writing articulated in her essays. In *The Stone Diaries*, Shields "employs common postmodern aesthetic strategies—the fragmented narrator, hybrid genre, and metafictional narrative," while joining them "with a thematic insistence on the transformative female imagination, foraying into new parts of the aesthetic field" (Johnson 203) to achieve the potential she identifies in "Open Every Question, Every Possibility." This chapter examines how Shields articulates the complex possibilities of fiction in her exploration of loss and how the dead are memorialized in *The Stone Diaries*. Shields challenges conventions, transfiguring conventional elegiac writing to define the nature of how death in the mid-to-late twentieth century is considered, defining textual memorializing as a fraught endeavor.

While various aspects of how she creates texts has received critical attention in relation to *The Stone Diaries*, the way Shields addresses notions of loss, and in particular the role of the textual articulation of grief to memorialize the dead, has not been explored. The novel opens with the protagonist's mother's death, is subsequently concerned with the way the protagonist and other family members respond to this breach in their lives, deals with the arc of a woman's life, and is framed with characters engaging in memorial activities, signaling the importance of the way Shields engages her theory of fiction writing in relation to grief and memorializing. Shields cites Robert Alter's idea of "deep structures" (cited by Shields 125) in "Open Every Question, Every Possibility" to articulate what she sees as a long-standing history of narrative that invokes common shapes of expression: "Contemporary stories may be very different from the old tale of the bison hunt, but the long history of the teller and the tale does offer up a remarkably persistent pattern" (125). Though Shields refers specifically to the story of the hunt, her example serves as metaphor for the kinds of universal stories that have abounded in culture for millennia, including those relating to loss. When she refers to the "remarkably persistent pattern" of the old tale of the bison hunt, she also refers to other long-standing patterns of story that persist across the millennia, such as engaging loss. Shields thus inserts her own interests in women's experience and the nature of story into a long tradition of such writing. She makes innovative contributions to the way writers in the twentieth century have grappled with the changing nature of death and dying by shifting the discussion into fictional forms as responses to loss, a subject in which poetry has previously dominated.

The theory of fiction writing Shields develops in her essays challenges and departs from conventional fictional practices and serves as a fruitful lens through which to read her approach to engaging memorializing in *The Stone Diaries*. Shields writes of what she terms "narrative hunger," which she defines as an expansive desire for readers to find the plenitude of experience fulfilled through language that is deliberately organized as narrative. In "Open Every Question, Every Possibility," she provides the example of a homeless man she encounters in Paris. He exists in a world of signs that profoundly seeks narrative to organize them: "I remember once, in Paris, walking past a street person, sitting on his patch of pavement with a sign around his neck that said '*J'ai faim*.' When I saw him again an hour later he was eating an enormous ham sandwich, and it occurred to me that the sign around his neck should have been corrected to read '*J'ai eu faim*.'" Shields describes him as being "momentarily satisfied," but she is aware of how his immediate hunger is rooted in a broader and deeper sense of being in the world that is understood only through signs. She deems the man "conscious of...an enlarged or existential hunger—for a coded message, a threaded notation, an orderly account or story that would serve as a witness to his place in the world" (116). This concept of "narrative hunger" is elemental to Shields's elucidation of her theory of fiction writing, for narrative hunger is the desire for story relating to the world and is an expression of loss for that which cannot be contained in narrative. Story is inherently limiting, in that it cannot account for the wealth of experience. As she writes, "*Un*luckily, a good part of the world falls through the narrative sieve, washing through the fingers of the recorder's hands, and is lost" (116). Shields sets out to define further this sense of loss in relation to the plenitude of experience: "It is this simultaneous abundance and loss that I want to talk about—how, while the narrative cupboard is full to bursting, the reader is left fed, but still hungry" (116). To read is to engage in the tension between wanting to access the fullness of experience while simultaneously recognizing the inability of narrative to fulfill that desire—to recognize that signs are illusory in their ability to contain experience.

Language nevertheless still has purpose in its politically infused nature, Shields asserts: "I hope that you'll agree with me...that language is not disinterested, that it flows from a bank of cultural references, both private and shared. It flows with purpose, with, shall we say, an agenda" ("Open" 120). So, what, then, might be one aspect of that agenda? For Shields, an agenda involves refashioning and rethinking the norms of narratives that have arisen over thousands of years. "We've grown self-conscious about our fictions," she writes, to the point that "we've made rules about how our stories must be shaped. Rules about time and space, about conflict, rising action and the nature of story conclusions" (124). One purpose to writing is to challenge the ways in which "our narratives...have had their hair cut and permed" so that the "sleek literary line" (124) narratives conform to is shifted. Much of her oeuvre presents precisely such an agenda, which is to refashion and repurpose what the long sweep of literary culture presents us with, as she does when she engages with memorializing in *The Stone Diaries*.

To memorialize in the literary elegiac tradition is inherently to engage with language, and Shields is centrally interested in language for such purposes even as an uncertain tool. Shields writes in "Open Every Question, Every Possibility" that language attempts to capture "Experience, reality that is," but she also underscores its inadequacy, for language "plods behind" (119): "We can start, maybe, with the admission that both real events and their accompanying narratives are conveyed to us by words, and that words, words alone, will always fail in their attempt to express what we mean by reality. We cannot think without words—or so many believe—and thus the only defence against words is more words. But we need to remember that the labyrinth of language stands *beside* reality itself, a somewhat awkward, almost always distorted facsimile or matrix" (119). Seen as a labyrinth, language indicates its complexity in relation to experience, or reality, but also as signal for the way we respond through story or narrative in our attempts to capture that experience: "I hope I can begin with this shared notion: that both 'reality' and literature are joined in the need for language and that they labour under the crippling limitations that language imposes" (120). Shields perceives genre as crippling, for genre is an organizing structure for language wherein generic elements partake of the labyrinth of language. Her treatment of the elegiac is thus subject to the vagaries of this labyrinth and its qualities of incertitude, and her theory of fiction writing challenges the crippling function of genre.

In *The Stone Diaries*, Shields blurs generic boundaries, and this blurring is key to how her practice of writing generates a theory of fiction writing. Readers have noted various ways in which Shields engages her theory of fiction writing in *The Stone Diaries* to shift the way language and genre operate. Brenda Beckman Long describes the novel as a "narrative puzzle...[that] challenges readers' interpretive skills" (86), and this sense of a puzzle is central to the way Shields's theory operates, for fiction writing is more about posing challenges than about providing concrete answers. Wendy Roy contemplates the role of autobiography in *The Stone Diaries*, by noting that "Shields's novel undermines autobiography's traditional privileging of linear and cohesive narratives" (114), and acknowledges that the novel "crosses boundaries between autobiography and fiction" (117): thus, it must be seen as "metafiction that makes a critical comment on the genre of life writing" (118). Nora Foster Stovel, likewise, identifies the way Shields challenges conventional senses of genre to shift understanding of autobiography: "Shields's feminist mission in subverting traditional male, linear (auto)biography is to valorize the lives of ordinary women" (526). The life of Daisy Goodwill takes on parodic elements to, as Stovel remarks, "pivot" the typical understanding of autobiography "as usually written by famous people" (526). The idea of a "mission" is comparable to Shields's use of the word "agenda" in her essay "Open Every Question, Every Possibility," and the notion of a "pivot" reflects the desire

by Shields to offer "digressive feminine structures, as opposed to traditional male linear forms" (521). Stovel recognizes the relation of Daisy's
narrative to a memorial purpose when she writes that "Daisy's narrative is
also fossilized" (518). As Wasmeier remarks, "The complex relationship
between life, death and text is at the center of Carol Shields's fictional
(auto)biography…which reflects on the limits and possibilities of life writing, of life becoming text, of flowers turning into stone, and of self-
narrative as the writer's funeral monument to herself, preserving in stone,
as it were, and beyond death, the story of her life in her own voice" (qtd
in Stovel 518–19), showing that her larger concern with fiction writing as
a transformative vehicle is key to the way she engages the relation of death
to writing.

In doing so, Shields complexly engages with the shifting nature of elegiac writing in North America and by women in the twentieth century.
Melissa F. Zeiger, following Celeste Schenck and Juliana Schiesari, in
Beyond Consolation: Death, Sexuality, and the Changing Shapes of Elegy,
remarks on the changing nature of elegy in the twentieth century, noting
how elegy has historically prioritized male voices and male grief: "These
critics have directed attention to elegy as a site of male bonding, power
production, and authorial self-identification, and to the privileging of male
melancholia and concomitant appropriation of mourning by a melancholic
poet and cultural hero" (5). Male loss is privileged, while "women as characters and authors are systematically written out of the picture" (5).
"Women have," she argues, "been positively barred from the traditional
genre, and the elegies of women poets must be read as countertradition
with a revisionist agenda" (5–6). While Shields is not technically writing
elegy in *The Stone Diaries,* she does work out of the tradition by invoking
the trope of writing as an attempt to give presence to the dead; the "revisionist agenda," to quote Zeiger, that Shields employs is associated with
the agenda she writes of in "Open Every Question, Every Possibility," for
she is interested in resituating women's grief in fiction, rather than in the
male poetic space that is conventional in elegy. Her grieving women are
not melancholic nor are they heroic (though some of her men are dramati-
cally so).

While there is a tradition of writing elegiac fiction by women in Canada,
most notably by Margaret Laurence, Alice Munro, and Joy Kogawa, none
challenge the elegy's male-centric perspective as Shields does. Shields
aligns her approach with the practices of Robert Kroetsch in "Stone
Hammer Poem" (1973) and Eli Mandel in *Out of Place* (1977) and their

prairie-oriented elegies by exploring how text serves as memorial structure through its use of purposeful language. Shields is interested in the quotidian grief of her characters, rather than in the large emotional gestures prevalent in traditional elegy. She takes the revisionist sensibilities of Kroetsch and Mandel and inscribes what Zeiger would identify as a countertradition to write deliberately against the grand elegiac mode conventional for so many male writers in literary history in her interest in the day-to-day and "ordinary" grief of her characters. Useful to Shields is the way Kroetsch and Mandel refashion the poetic response to loss in their works. Kroetsch challenges the notion of how language itself can articulate grief with any solidity: Can it be anything more than a structure within which to explore one's melancholic relationship to the dead? Does the poem as construction then serve as memorial structure even when it cannot articulate a consoling work of mourning as is conventional in elegy?[2] Mandel departs more forcefully from the conventions of elegy by ascribing to the very structure of the text a memorial function in addition to its presentation of an active work of mourning: the complete work itself becomes a signaling structure. He models his work on Jewish Yizkor books, which arose after the Holocaust as a way for survivors to commemorate their lost communities. In the absence of the ability to return to their original communities, textual structures (the Yizkor Books themselves) serve as stand-ins, becoming memorial structures.[3] Thus, language, and text, become artefactual.

Where Kroetsch and Mandel write within the elegiac tradition by engaging in poetic expression, Shields asserts that fiction can and should serve the purpose by writing with the "agenda" to refashion what fiction can be. She writes in "Open Every Question, Every Possibility" that writers need to look "to narrative's full potential" (129), and her treatment of memorializing in *The Stone Diaries* addresses that assertion by showing how fiction can be a forceful medium to understand the nature of loss in the mid-to-late twentieth century. In "Boxcars, Coat Hangers and Other Devices," Shields writes about her aversion to conventional modes of constructing stories: "Suddenly, I wasn't interested in the problem-solution story I had grown up with. The form seemed crafted out of the old quest myth in which obstacles were overcome and victories realized. None of this seemed applicable in the lives of women, nor to most of the men I knew, whose stories had more to do with the texture of daily life and the spirit of community than with personal battles, goals, mountaintops, and prizes" (28). Dealing with loss, like other aspects of "the texture of [the] daily life" (28) of her female characters in *The Stone Diaries*, is muted: it is not a battle, but rather an experience to be accommodated and endured. Thus, when she tackles the question of how grief occurs in her era, she evokes it in terms of the twentieth century's fraught relationship to it: it is a part of ongoing daily life and not understood as a strong story arc with beginning, middle, and end. Jacques Derrida expresses the challenges to mourning in this era when he states bluntly: "mourning is interminable. Inconsolable. Irreconcilable....[T]hat is what whoever works at mourning knows" (143). For Shields, this sense of loss as a regular part of the every-day contributes to her understanding of her theory of fiction writing. She emphasizes her choice of material and how its nature serves to explicate a theoretical perspective on what fiction can be when she writes: "I felt emboldened enough to allow the fictions I was writing to fill up on the natural gas of the quotidian, and, without venturing into the inaccessible, to find new and possibly subversive structures" ("Boxcars" 28). To Shields, much of these subversive structures are departures from plot or, as she puts it, "to replace plot—which I more and more distrust" (29).

While Laurence, Munro, and Kogawa prominently write elegiac fiction, they do not challenge the nature of their expression as Shields does: Laurence wrote relatively straightforward works of mourning in many of her novels, where her protagonists in one way or another recognize the nature of their loss and labor through it to achieve consolation;[4] Alice Munro wrote what Karen E. Smythe observes as a work of mourning as "meaning-as-progress," where "the performance of the work of mourn-ing" is prioritized (14); and, while Kogawa's protagonists engage in inconsolable grief, they nevertheless work at mourning with the intention of unearthing deeply buried loss.[5] For all three, what Smythe identifies as an apprehension about effective mourning in Munro applies: they "simul-taneously employ, demonstrate, and question methods of mourning" (13). Shields, however, extends this sense of the uncertainty to challenge whether it can be effective *at all* in providing any sense of social, cultural, and familial guidance to her characters and whether or not "the problem-solution story" ("Boxcars" 28) has any application in a memorial text. The world her characters occupy in the twentieth century denies the possibility of recovery, recuperation, consolation, and certainty in the face of loss. In this regard, Shields anticipates the uncertain grief that Jonathan Safran Foer, for example, expresses in his 2005 novel, *Extremely Noisy & Incredibly Close*, where he challenges whether or not language can in any way address the nature of loss even while he constructs his novel as a memorial structure recognizing the complexity of losses relating to the 9/11 terror attacks. His novel serves as artefact, but it never offers more than a structure of language that enacts trauma, as none of his characters find consolation through the acts of grieving that they perform or find satisfaction in engaging with the work of mourning. The novel's memorial qualities serve primarily to signal to readers the complexity of existing in the contemporary period, a world devoid of the solidity that ritualized structures of mourning offered in previous eras. Shields should rightly be seen as being ahead of her time, figuring loss and memorializing as twenty-first century novelists do.

Shields's approach to death and dying nevertheless grows out of a mid-twentieth-century ethos that framed death and dying in a social world that did not provide adequate structures for its comprehension, even when she transcends this context. Geoffrey Gorer argued in 1955 in his seminal essay "The Pornography of Death" that death had become a taboo, as sex was in the Victorian age, forcing the consideration of death and dying away from the social realm. This vacuum in the public sphere caused the grieving subjects to struggle to find useful ways to deal with their loss. Ernst Becker in *The Denial of Death* (1973) coins the phrase of his book's title, and consequently public expressions of grief are deemed inappropriate, as they suggest a "loss of control...[and] often as a source of shame beyond even the guilt of survival" (Gilbert 264). Death, and how to grieve and remember the dead, are shifted into the private sphere, and thus the textual articulation of loss takes on many of the functions that were previously publicly sanctioned. Jahan Ramazani remarks that "the poetry of mourning for the dead assumes in the modern period an extraordinary diversity," as it responds to mass death and warfare, and to death being deemed a taboo subject (1), which applies well to *The Stone Diaries* and its anxious engagement with loss.

Shields contributes to the diversity of elegiac writing that Ramazani points to, working out ways in *The Stone Diaries* to signal her recognition of the fraught nature of dying and remembrance and finding means to express a memorial function to her novel. I have written elsewhere that "the fictional figuration of a work of mourning as a memorial structure relates well to a multitudinous understanding of how memorials function socially" ("Writing" 108), and a novel like *The Stone Diaries* provides a space within which an author can work out what is deemed private or inappropriate for the public sphere. Fiction becomes a *de facto* public space where the uncertainty of ritualized grief and memorializing can be addressed. The structure of *The Stone Diaries* creates a valid space for the articulation of grief and, by its existence as textual artifact, serves as a memorial object that readers engage with as they would a more conventionally understood memorial structure. James E. Young has influentially remarked that memorials should be considered as "memory-sites" (4) and that "a memorial may be a day, a conference, or a space, but it need not be a monument" (4). Following and extending Young, a work of fiction too can be a memorial or memory site, as Shields demonstrates in *The Stone Diaries*.

In keeping with the theory of fiction writing articulated in her essays, then, Shields takes up in *The Stone Diaries* the notion of a textual response to loss involving a memorial function that challenges the efficacy of language, fulfilling what Shields asserts as "an agenda" (120) in her essay "Open Every Question." In her agenda, Shields situates her novel as a memorial text, demonstrating how a novel can become a structure for remembrance, while also questioning how this construction can be an adequate response to death. When her characters grieve, they do so in ways that lead to ambiguous results, determining neither catharsis nor resolution to their loss. The physical matter of the novel as artefact asserts its memorial status, as incorporated between its two covers is a set of diaries that encompass one woman's life, from her birth to her death, and framing this narrative arc are familial considerations of remembrance as her granddaughter and son contemplate her life and death in this framing. As sign, the novel is similar to familiar memorials, which are physical structures that are "read" for their symbolism and significance. By constructing *The Stone Diaries* in this manner, Shields raises questions about remembrance and about the nature of the structures we employ to memorialize, and by doing so in language she re-visions the possibilities for memorial work in literature.

The first signal to Shields's structuring of the novel is the epigraph, an excerpt from a fictional poem, composed by Judith Downing, Daisy Goodwill's granddaughter. Downing notes that Daisy's "life/ could be called a monument" (np). If the life itself is monument, then the written life is a textual monument, and the "stone diaries" that readers encounter are that literary textual memorial. Placed immediately after the excerpt from the poem is a family tree spanning the life of two families—connected through Daisy's second marriage—beginning in the middle of the twentieth century and reaching to the 1990s. The presence of the family tree reinforces the memorial purpose of *The Stone Diaries*, for it underscores the reach of remembrance, beginning with Daisy's ancestors and extending to her progeny. The many descendants are one audience for the diaries, and extra-textual readers are another, and both are its community. Situated as it is, the family tree serves as a sort of preface to establish family links as key qualities of both community and family, and, through these connections, Daisy's story is threaded, signaling in variable ways to individual family members.

The conclusion of the novel also reinforces the structural nature of the memorial function of *The Stone Diaries*. Two interrelated passages signal this memorial essence, indicating the novel's status as artefact of remembrance. The first is the "Closing benediction," read by Daisy Goodwill's son Warren. He identifies a series of relationships to Daisy that move from the individual and personal to the broad and universal. Both are conventional qualities of memorial sites: references to individuals as well as larger epic considerations. "Daisy Goodwill Flett, wife, mother," states Warren, is also "citizen of our century" (361). His recognition of her relevance in memory as individual *and* as citizen of a particular epoch signals the role of the text to this point. Daisy's life can be read in relation to epic concerns as well as to personal ones. In its articulation of Daisy's life from birth to death, it provides textual space as memorial site, as James E. Young suggests. The second passage, which concludes the novel, appears as a brief exchange between anonymous mourners at the service:

> "The pansies, have you ever seen such ravishing pansies?"
> "She would have loved them."
> "Somehow, I expected to see a huge bank of daisies."
> "Daisies, yes."
> "Someone should have thought of daisies."
> "Yes."
> "Ah, well." (361)

The anonymity of the conversants indicates their status as generic mourners who are engaged in an act of remembrance that is neither grand nor dramatic. They are, rather, individuals who reflect upon the object of memory generally. The generic mourners are metonymical of the role that readers have in relation to the novel and its memorial structure, for readers, too, engage with the story of Daisy's life and the losses she suffers, considering her as a citizen of the century, rather than in a specifically personal way. Further, Shields suggests that language is fraught in its relation to remembrance, creating a tension between the desire to make concrete what is being mourned and the inability for language to provide that certainty. This tension is reflected in all aspects of the novel's engagement with memorializing, from the title to the final words, that provide less a finality to the novel than a petering out.

Contributing to the structuring of the novel as memorial text is the title, *The Stone Diaries*, which signals tension between memorializing and articulation. The first half of the novel's title, for example, suggests solidity—elemental and indeed monumental matters. There is a play on notions of gravestones, and the epitaphs commonly found on them, and the ways in which "stone" and language intertwine in remembrance through the artifact of the gravestone. The second half makes complex the solidity indicated in the first part: the notion of diaries is invoked as an uncertain category. The full title suggests resonances and tensions between notions of stones, as having monumental status and notions of autobiography, and suggests that a memorial and elegiac function is fundamental to the process of articulating the narrator and protagonist's self textually. Allusions to Laurence's canonical fictional autobiography, *The Stone Angel*, and Kroetsch's elegy, "Stone Hammer Poem," frame the Canadian literary historical roots of Shields's practice in her novel. Like Shields, Laurence and Kroetsch are interested in how the self can be articulated through autobiographical strategies and in how that articulation is implicated in elegiac acts of remembrance that stem from elegiac expression.

While Shields overtly structures her novel in ways to signal how text can serve to enact a work of mourning and become a memorial structure, exploration of the two main engagements with grief work indicates that Shields is skeptical about the success of textual constructions to fulfill the needs of her mourning characters. Just as her title suggests, the ambiguous nature of her literary enterprise (is it a set of diaries made of stone? diaries about stone? something else altogether?), Shields too takes a suspicious approach to the efficacy of memorializing. She establishes a remembrance structure to the novel and then undercuts it by the inadequacy of structures that her characters themselves implement or erect. Daisy writes the mother's body, and Cuyler builds a stone memorial, both taking on paradoxical qualities for Shields in their enactment of generic attributes of elegy while simultaneously working against them. The opening sequence, for example, operates like many elegies to figure textually the dead body, desiring to give it presence in language, and solidity in poetry (or narrative, as is the case in *The Stone Diaries*). In *The Rhetoric of Death*, Ronald

Schleifer points out that rhetorical structures of grieving, such as elegies, are intended to recover "voice in the face of" death (221), and conventional elegies, such as John Milton's "Lycidas" and Percy Bysshe Shelley's "Adonais," figure the body throughout as a means to resurrect the dead, ending in consolatory triumph as they elevate the dead to an imagined heavenly apotheosis. When Daisy figures her mother's death and body in the opening sequence of the novel, she does so only within the context of fictional invention, rather than in recuperation of memory. Her words are purely imaginative, as they cannot possibly be created out of any lived experience that Daisy has, given that the entirety of her mother's life and death occurs before and as she is born. The detailed figuration of the mother's body, while concretely established in the opening chapter, is undermined in the rest of the novel, thus serving not as the figurative elevation of the body of conventional elegy, but as testament to the impossibility of such textual resurrection. Shields remarks about Daisy that "much of what she has to say is speculative, exaggerated, wildly unlikely" (148), and yet, as she remarks, "hers is the only account there is, written on air, written with imagination's invisible ink" (149). The photo of her mother, Mercy, which appears toward the middle of the novel, bears no relation to the wild description Daisy conjures of her mother as a profligate eater who is perhaps to blame for the failure of her own body to survive the alimentary challenges that she inflicts on herself. Daisy describes Mercy's body as "a vault of" flesh with a "wide face" and "thick doughy neck" with "great loose breasts and [a] solid boulder of a stomach" (7), and yet the photo does not support the description.

After his wife's death, Cuyler Goodwill attempts to memorialize her, recognizing the inadequacy of language to repair loss, despite his monumental efforts to construct a permanent structure. He carves a gravestone, "but almost immediately he perceived that the monument was pitifully inadequate, too meagre and insubstantial for the creature who had been his sweetheart" (58). The inscription on the stone does no more than note the bare particulars of Mercy's life, which does not provide any sense of her presence. In response, Cuyler constructs a stone tower, laboring to create a tall stone structure in place of the gravestone: "Where my mother's solitary gravestone once sat, now rises a hollow tower some thirty feet in height and still growing" (63). Cuyler inscribes the stones "with elaborate cipher," yet this task is fraught with challenges to articulation and communication, for "Patterns incised on this mineral form seem to evade the eye....This impediment is part of the charm for him. What he carves will remain half-hidden, half-exposed" (63). As much as the tower is solid in its construction, it is evasive in its meaning, failing to commemorate his dead wife and failing to provide a narrative to others—or himself—that might create comfort. The experience of carving becomes a fully embodied experience to Cuyler as "the act of carving never ceases to be labor for him—the whole of his body bends into the effort" (65), but the physical labor offers no tangible connection to the dead. Cuyler's pyramid is deemed "a 'permanent memorial' to his life" (210–11), but its status is tenuous, as it is in danger of being bulldozed (221); so the nature of stone as eternal is undercut by the stone tower's tenuous and illusory status as a memorial structure. Johnson argues "That the tower in *The Stone Diaries* disintegrates is no reason to see it as a failed monument. We learn that not only do the natural forces of erosion—wind, water, time—wear away at the limestone's engraved surface and solidity; people, too, have their hand in pulling the piece of art apart" (223–24). However, the facts of the tower's incomprehensibility and lack of longevity support the idea of its failure as a memorial object. It fails to serve a community, functioning only in the private grief of Cuyler.

Likewise, for Daisy, the notion of her diaries as objects that will remain beyond herself fails as she approaches death. Initially, she seeks structure in the telling of a life: "All she's trying to do is keep things straight in her head. To keep the weight of her memories evenly distributed. To hold the chapters of her life in order" (340). Later, however, as she approaches her final moments, words are supplanted by stone, and she imagines her body becoming stone and *not* story: "Stone is how she finally sees herself" (358). In writing her protagonist's death in this fashion, Shields challenges the elegiac, for elegy has as its purpose (however unsatisfyingly) to memorialize the dead in text, in language. Even the most basic of memorials, such as a simple gravestone, conventionally contains language, but, for Shields, the body becomes stone in death: it is no longer the living body nor is it the signaling stone of the conventional memorial structure. She plays with the duality of her novel's title, for "stone" and "diaries" together might create the kind of memorial structure that is customary in elegiac texts, but Shields extends this contemplation of the elegiac to challenge the way in which we remember the dead and the role and power we ascribe to language in this endeavor. It is not a cynical gesture toward the complexities of grief, or toward the implacability of death, but is rather in keeping with her larger theoretical project of interrogating how fictional forms can address everyday life. As she suggests in "Open Every Question,

Every Possibility," she is interested in "the full potential" of narrative (129).

In the cases of Cuyler and Daisy the acts of grieving and remembrance result in failure to provide understanding, emotional support, and a sense of how narrative can provide consolatory power to those who grieve. Arianne Zwartjes, in *Detailing Trauma: A Poetic Anatomy*, articulates the problem that Shields identifies in her characters and more broadly in how her novel theorizes what the memorial purposes of language can be. For Zwartjes, language tries to do the impossible, attempts to fill absence, paradoxically existing only as itself, rather than what it hopes to inscribe, which is of course the dead person. She writes, recognizing the paradox inherent in her logic: "What then do we do with language (*believing that holes can be filled with language is dangerous*) if not use it to fill what is empty (*only space itself occupies empty space*). To define what is empty" (65). Her conclusion, which can be applied to Shields's approach in *The Stone Diaries*, is that "Perhaps this is the danger: we seek to believe in language because it gives us the illusion of control" (66). Zwartjes's conception of the impossibility of language is inherent in Shields's articulation of a text that claims to commemorate, to offer memorial power, but does not do so. From its title to its construction as a series of diaries that purport to depict the life of Daisy Goodwill and its effect on her progeny, to its articulation of "stone" as an artefact of remembrance, *The Stone Diaries* presents only *the illusion* of the power of language. In its treatment of memory work the novel asserts instead the inability of language to possess such a force. This, then, is part of the "agenda" (120), as articulated in her essay "Open Every Question," and is part of her desire to work against "the problem-solution story" (28) that she so forcefully expresses her disdain for in "Boxcars."

Many of Carol Shields's essays from *Startle and Illuminate: Carol Shields on Writing* provide useful avenues to define her theory of fiction writing, and *The Stone Diaries* provides a fruitful entrance to the complexity of the quotidian that she invigorates in her writing. Shields especially addresses memorializing in *The Stone Diaries* through the lens of her theory of fiction writing, confronting what John B. Vickery identifies as the potential "disintegration of...[the] role and purpose" of elegy in the face of the prevailing tumultuous and varied losses of the twentieth century (164). While it is tempting to read in Shields's treatment of loss in *The Stone Diaries* an affirmation of Vickery's conception of the decline of the elegiac, one might more productively return to the paradox of the title, which asserts simultaneous silence and articulation in presenting the challenges to remembrance as resistant to cohesive narrative. I began this chapter by considering how Shields looks to "narrative's full potential" ("Open" 129) to deploy a theory of fiction writing that looks forward, while also acknowledging the historical roots of literary expression. This duality is well expressed in her treatment of memorializing in *The Stone Diaries* as she works out not the grandeur of memorial work, as the literary history of elegy has it, but the limitations of remembrance in the twentieth century.

In her essay "Pacing, Passion and Tension" in *Startle and Illuminate*, Shields critiques "the need a writer feels to 'frame' the story….[I]nstead of simply telling the story, a scaffolding is set up, a way into and out of the story. The relationship between the teller and the tale is laboriously worked up and is almost always in clumps and interfering" (69–70). This distrust of the efficacy of overt framing devices is evident in how Shields approaches the construction of *The Stone Diaries* and its treatment of memorializing, for she asserts the necessity of memory work without making explicit her intentions, without the "clumps and interfering," as she puts it. I have argued in this chapter that Shields generates a theory of fiction writing in her essays that is evidenced in how she deals with loss and mourning, and her essays make it clear that her treatment of memorializing is concomitant with her understanding of fiction writing as an endeavor that pushes boundaries and extends the possible, while also attending to the quotidian.

If memorial work is ultimately ambiguous in *The Stone Diaries*, it is because it is a reflection of the limitations of what language can provide in response to loss. This is seen as Cuyler Goodwill lies dying and reflects upon the monument he has constructed and the box he buried under it, contemplating that its purpose is to address his losses: "He had imagined himself to be a man intent on making something" (278). Yet, when he worries that the "treasure" needs to be saved, he is unable to recall what is important about it. "What treasure was this?" (279), he asks. Language fails to account for memory or to make up for absence. Likewise, when Victoria considers how her "Great-aunt Daisy" would characterize "the story of her life," the response is mundane, lacking in the drama that makes a life memorable: "this is what happened, she would say…and this is what happened next" (279). What Shields gives, then, in *The Stone Diaries* is the kind of story that goes "sliding off the page, taking a chance, risking the subversion of the story, but suggesting some new pattern" ("Pacing" 78). This push to the new is what defines Shields's theory of fiction writing, and her approach to textual memorializing is indicative of this impulse. Her unconventionality reflects her desire to address the disjunction between narrative and experience, which she defines in a letter as "the human need for narrative, and how our available narratives don't always match our experience" ("Open" 115). Elegiac texts have hitherto not reflected the experience she refers to, and, instead, a new kind of memorial text is needed. This is, as *The Stone Diaries* shows, a kind of text that recognizes the limitations of remembrance.

NOTES

1. This essay is a slightly revised reprint of "Narrative Hunger and the Overflowing Cupboard", appearing in *Carol Shields: Narrative Hunger, and the Possibilities of Fiction*, Edited by Edward Eden and Dee Goertz, Toronto: UTP, 2003.
2. I discuss Kroetsch's engagement with elegy fully in "Stone Hammer Poem" in "Robert Kroetsch's *Stone Hammer Poem*: Elegy and Memorial."
3. Mandel's complex articulation of a long poem as memorial structure is discussed in my article, "Mourning, Memorial, and the Yizkor Books in Eli Mandel's *Out of Place*."
4. I give full consideration to how Laurence addresses the work of mourning in *Writing Grief: Margaret Laurence and the Work of Mourning.*
5. See my essay, "Writing Grief: The Fraught Work of Mourning in Fiction," for a discussion of Joy Kogawa's engagement with literary memorial structures.

WORKS CITED

Becker, Ernst. *The Denial of Death.* The Free Press, 1973.

Beckman Long, Brenda. *Carol Shields and the Writer-Critic.* University of Toronto Press, 2015.

Derrida, Jacques. *The Work of Mourning.* Edited and translated by Pascale-Anne Brault and Michael Naas, University of Chicago Press, 2001.

Foer, Jonathan Safran. *Extremely Loud & Incredibly Close.* Mariner Books, 2005.

Giardini, Anne, and Nichola Giardini, editors. *Startle and Illuminate: Carol Shields on Writing.* Toronto: Random House, 2006.

Gilbert, Sandra M. *Death's Door: Modern Dying and the Ways We Grieve: A Cultural Study.* W. W. Norton, 2006.

Gorer, Geoffrey. "The Pornography of Death". *Death, Grief, and Mourning.* Edited by Geoffrey Gorer. Doubleday, 1955, pp. 192–9.

Kroetsch, Robert. "Stone Hammer Poem." *Completed Field Notes*. University of Alberta Press, 2000.

Johnson, Lisa. "'She Enlarges Upon the Available Materials': A Postmodernism of Resistance in *The Stone Diaries*." *Carol Shields, Narrative Hunger, and the Possibilities of Fiction*. Edited by Edward Eden and Dee Goertz. University of Toronto Press, 2003, pp. 201–229.

Kogawa, Joy. *Obasan*. 1981. Penguin, 2017.

Mandel, Eli. *Out of Place*. Porcepic, 1977.

Milton, John. "Lycidas". *The Major Works*. Oxford University Press, 2008.

Ramazani, Jahan. *Poetry of Mourning: The Modern Elegy from Hardy to Heaney*. University of Chicago Press, 1994.

Riegel, Christian. "Mourning, Memorial, and the Yizkor Books in Eli Mandel's *Out of Place*." *Mosaic: An Interdisciplinary Critical Journal*, vol 50, iss. 2, 2017, pp. 187–204.

———. "Writing grief: The Fraught Work of Mourning in Fiction." *Exploring Grief*. Edited by Michael Hviid Jacobsen, and Anders Petersen, Routledge, 2020, pp. 104–122.

———. "Robert Kroetsch's *Stone Hammer Poem*: Elegy and Memorial." *Wild Words*. Edited by *George* Melnyk and Donna Coates. Athabasca University Press, 2008, pp. 47–60.

———. *Writing Grief: Margaret Laurence and the Work of Mourning*. University of Manitoba Press, 2003.

Roy, Wendy. "Autobiography as Critical Practice in *The Stone Diaries*." *Carol Shields, Narrative Hunger, and the Possibilities of Fiction*. Edited by Edward Eden and Dee Goertz. University of Toronto Press, 2003, pp. 113–146.

Schleifer, Ronald. *Rhetoric and Death: The Language of Modernism and Postmodernist Discourse Theory*. University of Illinois Press, 1990.

Shelley, Percy Bysshe. "Adonais." *The Major Works*. Oxford University Press, 2009.

Shields, Carol. "Narrative Hunger and the Overflowing Cupboard." *Carol Shields, Narrative Hunger, and the Possibilities of Fiction*, edited by Edward Eden and Dee Goertz. University of Toronto Press, 2003, pp. 19–38.

———. *The Stone Diaries*. Toronto: Random House, 1993.

———. "Boxcars, Coat Hangers and Other Devices." *Startle and Illuminate: Carol Shields on Writing*. Edited by Anne Giardini and Nicholas Giardini. Toronto: Random House, 2016a, pp. 23–30.

———. "To Write is to Raid." *Startle and Illuminate: Carol Shields on Writing*. Edited by Anne Giardini and Nicholas Giardini. Toronto: Random House, 2016b, pp. 31–36.

———. "Open Every Question, Every Possibility." *Startle and Illuminate: Carol Shields on Writing*. Edited by Anne Giardini and Nicholas Giardini. Toronto: Random House, 2016c, pp. 115–130.

———. "Pacing, Passion and Tension." *Startle and Illuminate: Carol Shields on Writing*. Edited by Anne Giardini and Nicholas Giardini. Toronto: Random House, 2016d, pp. 67–81.

———. "Writers are Readers First." *Startle and Illuminate: Carol Shields on Writing*. Edited by Anne Giardini and Nicholas Giardini. Toronto: Random House, 2016e, pp. 1–15.

Smythe, Karen E. *Figuring Grief: Gallant, Munro, and the Poetics of Elegy*. McGill-Queen's University Press, 1992.

Stovel, Nora. "Written in Stone: subverting the authoritative (auto)biographical voice—Carol Shields's *The Stone Diaries* and Margaret Laurence's *The Stone Angel*." *American Review of Canadian Studies*, vol. 46, no. 4, 2016, pp. 513–31.

Zeiger, Melissa F. *Beyond Consolation: Death, Sexuality, and the Changing Shapes of Elegy*. Cornell University Press, 1997.

Zwartjes, Arianne. *Detailing Trauma: A Poetic Anatomy*. University of Iowa Press, 2012. Eden, Edward and Dee Goertz, editors. *Carol Shields, Narrative Hunger, and the Possibilities of Fiction*. University of Toronto Press, 2003.

Man in the Maze: "Where Curiosity Leads" and *Larry's Party*

Warren Cariou

Whenever I was sick as a child (tonsilitis, strep throat, flu, sniffles), I got to stay home and do mazes. Mom had several books of supermarket pen-mazes stashed away for every occasion of illness, and if she brought them out in the morning before school started, it meant I was sick enough to stay home. I spent hours in bed with these maze books propped against my knees, squinting through the addled haze of my illness, tracing my pen back and forth along the incomprehensible route, as if to wend my way back to health. When I reached a dead end, I went back to the previous fork in the road and tried again. Eventually the goal would be attained,

"Man in the Maze: 'Where Curiosity Leads' and *Larry's Party*" is a substantially revised reprint of Warren Cariou's essay "Larry's Party: Man in the Maze" in *Carol Shields: The Arts of a Writing Life*, edited by Neil K. Besner for Winnipeg's Prairie Fire Press in 1995, pages 87–96.

W. Cariou (✉)
University of Manitoba, Winnipeg, MB, Canada

© The Author(s), under exclusive license to Springer Nature Switzerland AG 2023
N. F. Stovel (ed.), *Relating Carol Shields's Essays and Fiction*,
https://doi.org/10.1007/978-3-031-11480-9_10

and I would look back at the sorry record of my mistakes, trying to understand how there could possibly be so many.

I imagine Mom thought these games would simply take my mind off my symptoms—and they did. But they were also a depressing lesson in the pragmatics of free will and determinism. As my pen wandered those circuitous hallways, I came to see how arbitrary choices are, and how uncertain are rewards and punishments. I also learned that, while an action can be undone, it can never be fully erased: it leaves a path there for all to see.

However, one day as I doodled around the exit to an uncompleted puzzle, I stumbled upon the most crucial and empowering of my maze lessons: how to cheat. I discovered it was far easier to solve a maze if I began at the ending. I could zip right back through the various choices with nary a mistake. And to anyone viewing the pristine finished product, it was impossible to tell what direction I had taken.

"Hey Mom, take a look! Perfecto!"

All hail to the powers of hindsight.

Who would have believed that such a lesson would ever be useful again, but now I have been asked to write about Carol Shields's *Larry's Party*, which is all about mazes. And in approaching the maze that is *Larry's Party*, I've known from the start that I will follow my cheating instincts and begin with the finale. It's my only way to avoid getting lost, so forgive me. I could invoke the Kierkegaardian maxim that life is lived forward yet understood backward—but it would only be an excuse, and why would I need that? Who said critics were ever interested in playing by the rules?

So, beginning at the ending. Larry's party, the chapter: the culmination, the *goal* of the novel. What is it, this perilous dinner party that Larry throws? Who in their right mind would invite two ex-wives and a current girlfriend to a party? It is of course a recipe for all manner of disasters, especially when we consider what happened so many years earlier when Larry's poor mother, Dot, invited her in-laws over for dinner. The sudden demise of Mum Weller provides ample evidence in the novel that a dinner party can be a fatal mistake, can be murder. Even so, Larry tempts fate at his party by serving beans, the same "treasonous vegetable" (53) that killed his grandmother and made his mother's life a purgatory. It's as if he is purposely loading the dice against himself, as if he knows at an unconscious level that he must dance through the minefields of his past relationships if he is to reach his goal (more about that goal anon). This party is his most crucial test as a maze-man. If he can get through it unscathed, he might be a hero after all.

Yes: the party is itself a kind of interpersonal maze, a psychomachia maze, the barest grid of which is outlined in Larry's sketch of a seating plan (304). It is in the final chapter, "Larry's Party," Shields writes, that "Larry confronts the major maze of his life, the maze of love and being loved, of permanence, of wisdom, and, in a sense, of a return to a knowledge of his self" (*Startle* 90). *This is where they begin,* we tell ourselves, tracing the sight lines across the table, *but where will they end up?* The situation throbs with treacherous potential. Mistakes will certainly be made. And we know that Larry is the king of mistakes. But the only way to know what these mistakes will be is to follow the game through to the end.

In a sense every narrative is a journey through a maze. There is the branching of paths, the illusion of freedom, the irrevocability of actions once they have occurred. John Gardner in *The Art of Fiction* suggests that the plot of a novel should be both entirely surprising and entirely preordained. When we are reading through, it should seem that anything could happen, but when we look back from the end, every event should seem inevitable. That's what time is, I suppose: the transforming of the possible into the inevitable. And we try to capture this mystery of time whenever we recount a story or whenever we receive one. Gardner's characterization of fiction seemed right to me when I first read it, and I remember feeling a tremor of recognition a few years later when I reached the ending of David Adams Richards's *Nights Below Station Street*, where one of the main characters, Joe, thinks back on the events of the novel, "not knowing how this all had happened, only understanding that it was now irrevocable because it had" (225).

This prompts me to return to Kierkegaard's dictum that life is lived forward but understood backward. Living, by such a definition, is confusion. But confusion is not always a cousin of dementia and delirium, not always an occasion of crisis. As Shields illustrates in Larry's recollection of his first wanderings in the Hampton Court Maze, confusion can also be a balm, a revelation, an occasion of *ekstasis*:

> He has never been able to identify what happened to him during the hour
> he wandered lost and dazed and separated from the others, but he remem-
> bers he felt a joyous rising of spirit that was related in some way to the self's
> dimpled plasticity. He could move beyond what he was, the puzzling hedges
> seemed to announce. (217)

What an elated confusion this is for lost Larry, who says much later to Dorrie when recounting the incident, "I wanted to be lost" (335). For me such language perfectly describes what it's like to get lost in a story, a novel, a memoir. In them or through them we are able to slip beyond ourselves, to explore the wilds of otherness, the shaggy hedgerows of unreason. They are a pleasant madness, a holiday from selfhood, and as such they are indispensable.

Indeed, books and treed mazes are similar in many respects. Larry's one-time neighbor Lucy Warkentin explains to him, "A paged book was called a codex....the word comes from the Latin, meaning wood" (86)— which reminds one of Dante's dark wood, the entrance to the maze of the Christian universe. Similarly, the bizarre reversals and transformations of *A Midsummer Night's Dream* occur entirely in the labyrinth of a darkened wood. And it is not quite too much of a coincidence that in the medieval period, the word "wood" also once referred to a state of frenzied insanity.

As Larry eventually gains his expertise in maze-making, this knowledge does not exempt him from the confusion that is felt by those who simply muddle through the mazes of existence. He remains just like the rest of us. That is indeed one of Shields's primary points about Larry. He is normal, average, typical. And yet his work and his luck are extraordinary. By this analogy a writer is not, say, a diviner or a leader of men or some other variety of paragon, but rather a humble maze maker, a creator of structures which confuse and delight, structures which have only a tenuous relationship to the rest of the world. A maker of systems, not a seer into the life of things. I suspect this is how Carol Shields would characterize her own role as an author, mingling a postmodern view of the human subject and a refreshing aesthetic of humility.

So, Larry's party is a maze, and narratives are mazes, and writers are maze-makers, and this novel is a series of interconnected maze chapters. Even Larry's body is "an upright walking labyrinth" (269). I'm getting somewhere now, tracing my way back from the inevitable, covering my pen tracks.

But I'm left with another possibility, a road not taken that I wish I'd at least taken a peek down. It's about this party. I'm thinking the word itself, *party,* is a forking path, a place where two roads diverge in a wood. Larry's party is his celebration, yes, his attempt at domestic entertainment. But it is also his partiality, his side, his affiliation. Larry is not a joiner, but still he has inherited some affiliations, the most important one in this novel being his membership in "the company of men" (331). His party is his gender.

And I suppose it is also his race and his class and sexual orientation, though these aspects of Larry are given less attention in the novel. He is a white middle-class heterosexual male—stereotypically the most boring, yet most privileged and culpable, demographic on the planet. He is "a walking, head-scratching cliché" (165), as he himself is aware. He and his party have been blamed for much of the degradation, violence, abuse, and mendacity in the history of Western civilization. And what does he have to say for himself, for this great luck of having been born a privileged, powerful, imperialistic man?

Not too much. When one of his guests asks point blank, "What's it like being a man these days?" (315), Larry is conspicuously silent. He reflects, suddenly, that this is the first party he has ever hosted in his life, and this realization bespeaks a sea change in him, though it's one he hasn't begun to analyze. Midway along the path of his life, he has stepped into a darkened wood and has become Mrs. Dalloway. But he doesn't know this, of course, and doesn't have more than the slightest inkling of how significant this transformation might be. Because if Larry's dinner party is a maze for him to negotiate, then so is his other party. He really has little idea what it's like being a man. He is forever wandering the mirrored hallways of gender, understanding precious little about the roles of son and husband and brother and father, which he mimes.

In this too, he is average, typical. Men, the current TV stereotype goes, are the ones who don't ask for directions, who don't read the manual, who try to bully or bluster or fake their way through. And this is why they always get lost. But I wonder if the order of this progression might need to be reversed: perhaps the lostness is what comes first, and the bluffing and the acting out derive from it. When someone moves the shrubbery halfway through the maze (as Larry's wife Dorrie does with his Lipton Street effort), the result might well be a particularly overwhelming disorientation.

"Shields's essays illuminate the revisionist policies of her fiction," as Nora Foster Stovel states in her introduction to this edition. In her essay, "Where Curiosity Leads," Shields is candid about her struggles with writing from the male point of view in *Larry's Party*. Always interested in the *Other*, the title of her first collection of poetry, she acknowledges, "My 'other' was men" (*Startle* 87).[1] She recalls that she and her women friends started "wondering what it's like to be a man at the end of our century" and so "I started asking some of the men I knew this question, and I started writing a novel called *Larry's Party*" (87). She explains that her reflections on gender coincided with her interest in mazes: "While I was thinking of the problems of men and women, I was also pursuing my interest in mazes and labyrinths" (90). Thus, "it seemed natural to give Larry Weller my passion for mazes" (*Startle* 90).

Larry, with his dinner party, does something other than wander aimlessly in the ruined avenues of identity. While this dinner party is certainly a disaster waiting to happen, it is also in another sense a triumph, because it announces a change in his approach to gender roles, and specifically because it reveals Larry to be for the first time an *active* participant in those roles. Larry is not the uncommunicative couch potato that his own father was, nor is he the freewheeling tomcat of the masculine postmodern novel, nor the reactive backlasher of concern to feminists, nor the predator, nor the buffoon. He has become instead a man for whom there is as yet no available template, a man who is not effeminate but who also understands and deeply appreciates what the women in his life have meant to him: "Oh, these women, these beautiful women. He regards them with wonder. These women are separate selves, but also part of Larry's self" (330).

By placing himself in the social role of a Mrs. Dalloway figure, Larry unknowingly creates the maze of gender anew for himself. Or, in the metaphoric timbre of the novel's first chapter (steering now toward the entrance of the maze), this change in Larry is like the removal of an accidentally acquired garment. Late in the party, he recognizes this, or almost does, remembering a gesture from 20 years earlier that suddenly acquires new significance:

> Walking alone on a Winnipeg street, twenty-six years old, he'd seen, perhaps for the first time, the kind of man he could be. He'd felt the force of the wind, and impulsively he'd whipped off his tweed jacket, offering himself up to the moment he'd just discovered, letting it sweep him forward on its beguiling currents. (331)

It is worth remembering that the coat being described here is actually not Larry's own. He has accidentally picked it up as he left a party, and he only belatedly recognized that it was not his. In a sense, it represents the gendered identity he has picked up without even knowing it. And now, with this gesture of removing the jacket, it seems possible Larry is casting off the mantle of his forefathers, shucking received notions of maleness, opening himself to a new kind of masculinity that will evolve haphazardly and unconsciously in the coming years. And this new male self will only become clear to him in the moments before he solves his dinner party maze and reaches his heretofore unknown goal: a reunification with Dorrie, who has herself traveled a path of change in the intervening years.

I can't help feeling disappointed when Larry arrives at this goal, partly because finding the goal means that the confused pleasure of maze-wandering is at an end, but also because it seems to me that in the mazes of gender and other accoutrements of the self, there is no real place of arrival, of finality. It is rather a process, a continuing one. For me, Larry's joyous return into the arms of his first wife feels contrived. But then, I wonder, what is a maze but a contrivance? What is luck but the occurrence of the unlikely, the unbelievable? Larry has always been a lucky man. He makes all the right mistakes. That he should be blessed with a happy ending worthy of a Greek hero is perhaps perfectly appropriate. Dorrie and Larry: Ulysses and Penelope: Hera and Zeus: Titania and Oberon. All is well again in the world.

Still, it is important to delve a little more deeply into the problematics of contrivance here, because in many ways, the meanings of *Larry's Party* depend on our understanding of it. Postmodernism repeatedly reminds us that all art is contrivance, and yet most of us are painfully aware that in life, if not in art, a happy ending is highly unusual. Larry's journey in the novel needs to be situated somewhere between these two poles of referentiality: the contrived and the quotidian. The hedge mazes that Larry designs throughout his career provide an interesting case in point here, since, although they are composed of plants, these plants largely cease to signify their plant-ness and move toward a more or less blatant expression of the maze-maker's abstract conceptions.

Mazes, like topiary, advertise their own contrivance, and in fact part of their effect depends upon the absurdity of vegetable matter being made to take on the form of abstract representation. I am reminded of Saussure's famous diagram illustrating the arbitrariness of the sign, which consists of an image of a tree separated by a line from the word "arbor" (67). For Saussure, the signifier "arbor" is arbitrary (and the wordplay here seems intentional and appropriate), while the image of the tree stands in for an idea of the stolid presence of the signified. However, a hedge maze playfully explodes the distinction between signifier and signified, and I believe Carol Shields is well aware of this semiotic aspect of the novel's governing metaphor. The shrubs *are* the arbitrary pattern of the maze. The tree *is* the arbor. It is both natural and a contrivance.

What does this mean in relation to the politics of identity that the book attempts to grapple with? Is gender itself to be understood here as a comingling of the natural and the contrived? Perhaps Shields is also suggesting something about the role of the inauthentic in finding our way to the truth—a common enough postmodern trope. However, it is worth noting that even Shields herself was not satisfied with the ending of the novel, as she indicates in a 2003 conversation with Nora Foster Stovel:

> I regret concluding *Larry's Party* with the traditional "happy ending" of marriage. I wish I had ended it differently. I was enchanted with the idea of coming back to the place where you started. But I think that the published ending doesn't work because it hasn't been led up to. ("Excursions," 273)

This rare authorial admission of an error in the writing is especially illuminating in relation to a novel that is very much about mistakes, as Nora Foster Stovel explores in her article "'By Mistake.'" Shields's main regret is that the ending "hasn't been led up to," which is an interesting turn of phrase when applied to a novel about mazes—those structures which lead us, eventually, to the goal, even though we may make a number of mistakes along the way. Shields goes on to say that "the logical ending for Larry is a general misalignment with women and the contemporary world" (273), which suggests that her choice at the time to embrace the "happy ending" may have been an attempt at wish-fulfilment, a fantasy of gender harmony. Later, she seems to decide that this is not believable within the world of the novel and that a form of "misalignment" would be a more appropriate representation of Larry's place in the politics of gender.

In "Where Curiosity Leads," Shields reflects, "as I wrote *Larry's Party*, I thought often about the immense mysteries men keep from women. And the mysteries women keep from men" (87). These mysterious aspects of gendered identity, and the confusion that such mysteries inevitably create, comprise a crucial part of the novel itself, and it seems clear that Shields was attempting to address some of these mysteries through the process of writing. "I do think it's important that men try to write about women and women about men" (87), she writes. Writers, she adds, attempt "not just writing about the other sex, but speaking through its consciousness, as I tried to do in *Larry's Party*" (88). She goes on to lament the idea of "segregated" (88) identity-based literatures. In this context, *Larry's Party* can be seen as an experiment of sorts, an attempt to reach beyond her own gendered position and to genuinely engage with her other. Perhaps Larry's life is, for Shields, a kind of maze to navigate. She notes that she "didn't quite manage" to portray Larry with "dignity" in the first draft (89), but that the process of revision enabled her to "restor[e] him to himself and to my initial image of who he is" (89). While she was trying to portray Larry as "a good man," she also did not want him to appear a buffoon, and so she revised the portrait, taking "a small piece of sandpaper" to her final draft (89).

And yet, despite Shields's intention of bridging a gulf between men and women in her writing of *Larry's Party,* the novel is a study of misalignment in gender relations, even in spite of its harmonious ending. We can see this in the symbolism of Larry's first maze on Lipton Street and the discord it causes between him and Dorrie. In his obsession, he is oblivious to her feelings about the maze, and this is why he is utterly shocked when he learns she has begun the process of destroying it. But there are signs that both of them could have read before it came to this disastrous result, ways that both of them could have sought to bridge the mysteries that they are keeping from each other in relation to the maze. Larry's "maze madness" (91), as Dorrie calls it, also "drives her crazy" (92). In a sense, both Larry and Dorrie become "wood" (insane) within the wood of the maze that is also their home. Dorrie's reasons for destroying the maze are never articulated nor is much of Larry's response to this action. They are keeping mysteries from each other, and in a sense this creates their mutual form of insanity. Nonetheless, the fact that Dorrie only destroys half the maze and then continues to live with the other half is a wonderful symbol of an opening toward communication across gender boundaries. They can't rebuild the maze, but they can live in a way that exposes both the damage and the mysteries. The rest is left to the vagaries of luck and the compiling of uninformed choices that lead one along a path that eventually becomes a life.

I am left contemplating one of Carol Shields' enduring preoccupations: the blind happenstance that is the mother of superstition and that has so much weight in our lives, whether we want it to or not. One manifestation of this chimera for me was the unusual fact that the day I moved to Winnipeg was the day Carol Shields moved away. I was coming from Vancouver; she was going to Victoria. I learned about this changing of places about a week after it had occurred, when she and her husband were already long gone to the land of prairie retirements. I didn't know she was planning to move. She didn't know I existed. So, what meaning could there possibly be in our transcontinental crisscrossing? For most people, it would mean nothing at all. But for me, it had at least a pleasing symmetry. It was something that might have happened in a novel—especially a Carol Shields novel—and might have had significance there. And I suppose I wanted it to have some larger purport, to be some token of luck for me as a writer moving to a new place. I will admit I even hoped for some kind of transmigration of talent and determination and grace. Why not hope? Happenstance inspires it.

I never did meet Carol Shields, but often these days I feel that I inhabit her mazes. I write this in the Wolseley house that my partner Alison and I bought several years ago, only a couple of blocks away from Larry and Dorrie's fictional Lipton Street house, just down from the friendly bakery where everyone knows Larry's name (and mine). A few years ago, I drove out to the Tyndall stone quarry at Garson, Manitoba, and witnessed what must have been the inspiration for *The Stone Diaries*. This city has become for me an extension of her novels.

And not long after the first time I read *Larry's Party*, I found (or lost?) myself in London with Alison, on what was a kind of honeymoon, three months before our wedding. There, near the end of a mad week of galleries and theatres and charging through the clamoring, dustblown streets of the city, we took a brief detour out of town to visit Hampton Court Palace. After a tour of the royal gardens, resplendent with rhododendrons and lilacs and withering daffodils, we found our way to the goal. There, we paid our three pounds each, pushed through the turnstile, and entered the shrubby realm where so much of everything started for Larry Weller.

But our experience of the Hampton Court Maze was somewhat different from Larry's first visit there. For us, the greatest challenge of the maze was not the arrangement of the hedgerows, but rather the crush of our fellow humans. Larry in his first visit to this same maze, on his honeymoon, had "will[ed] himself to be lost, to be alone" (35), but for us the latter was impossible. We had chosen a Sunday afternoon, not the best time for maze exploration. Hundreds of people were jammed in there with us, filing up and down the pathways, talking and laughing and catcalling as they went. It was a thrumming, cacaphonous hive. One young couple wheeled a huge and ungainly pram down the narrow avenues, barely negotiating the hairpins, while their red-haired baby entertained us with his one-toothed grins. "Help me!" someone cried out, and there was a general outburst of hilarity.[2]

People called to each other through the foliage, and even reached through to clap hands with their compatriots. Yes, the maze was full of gaping holes, through which we could see the neighboring alleyways and sometimes even the ones beyond them. Strangely, this made it more difficult to find our way, since being able to see your goal—as we did several times through the fringes of ragged plant stock—can sometimes be more misleading than helpful. There was a wrought iron grate running down the middle of each hedgerow to prevent us from charging through to the goal prematurely.

Despite our best efforts to seek the contemplative mentality of aloneness, the quest became a collective effort. "Dead end!" someone would say, and we would all turn on our heels and follow each other back out. It was like an absurd dance routine, something from Charlie Chaplin, and I thought of Larry's characterization of mazes in one of his conversations with Beth: "A maze...is a kind of machine with people as its moving parts" (218). Often we didn't even see the dead ends ourselves; we just had to take someone's word for it. Certain leaders or would-be leaders distinguished themselves (mostly by their height) and they would charge ahead of a group, at which point the question became: to follow, or not? We wanted to maintain our own autonomy, to make our own mistakes, to have ownership over our confusion, so we tried not to follow. But then resolutely choosing the alternate path from the self-appointed leaders was in its way a relinquishment of choice too, so sometimes we did follow after all.

We tried to read the maze on the faces of the people going back the other way. Was that the disappointment of the blind alley visitor or the subtle elation of someone who had already found the prize and was on their way back out? It was hard to tell because almost everyone had a pleasant puzzlement in their features, as they bumped and jostled through the narrow tunnels of ragged shrubbery. The throng was almost indistinguishable from the crowded streets of London, or Toronto, or even the busy avenues of Winnipeg on crazy pre-Christmas days—except everyone was clearly *loving* this. I had never seen such happy lineups.

In the tiny courtyard at the center of the maze was another tumult. Children, mothers, octogenarians, folks in wheelchairs, and many other mazewalkers were gathered under the two big elms that marked the spot. At the base of one tree, three boys of about 14 were sitting, slouch caps pulled down over their foreheads, oblivious to the traffic around them as they passed a bottle of cheap champagne back and forth. At the base of the other tree, various tourists jockeyed for position, posing for the panoply of cameras that aimed at the scarred trunk. Its bark was torn away and the bare wood was riddled with initials.

The spectacle didn't feel like much of a goal to us, so we turned back quickly into the mazeway itself, wanting not to savor this feeling of dubious accomplishment but rather to share again the sense of common movement, of linked mistakes. And as we threaded our way back through a flow of human faces both new and already familiar, I arrived at what seemed like a labyrinthine epiphany. We are each other's mazes, I thought. The structure itself is hardly necessary. And I stood for a long minute at the entrance to a little cul-de-sac while my fellow denizens of the maze surged past me in both directions. Here, we were, all of us, a community of convolution, a single seething organism of recreation. I wondered at us all. And as I did, I thought of how Larry also wonders at almost everything in his life: his boy Ryan, "his two magnificent wives" (330), his amazing luck. I had believed this was a byproduct of his innocence, his prodigious confusion, but now for the first time I saw that it might instead be a genuine talent. Yes, I thought. Maybe Larry Weller's greatest gift is amazement.

NOTES

1. "Where Curiosity Leads" is derived from Shields's talk, "Gender Crossing," given in 1997, the year LP was published. She also uses the term "gender hopping" (*Startle* 88).
2. Marta Dvořák, in her essay "'Controlled Chaos' and Carol Shields's 'A View from the Edge of the Edge'" included in this volume, writes, "Shields's works seem to be designed according to the "controlled chaos and contrived panic" (*Larry's Party* 313) inherent in the art of the maze: that apparently random pattern which leads to a goal, prize, or destination—"what the puzzling, branching path is all about" (*LP* 149)."

WORKS CITED

Adams Richards, David. *Nights Below Station Street*. Toronto: McClelland & Stewart, 1988. Print.

Cariou, Warren. "Larry's Party: Man in the Maze." *Carol Shields: The Arts of a Writing Life*. Ed. Neil K. Besner. Winnipeg: Prairie Fire Press, 1995. 87–96. Print.

Dvořák, Marta. "'Controlled Chaos' and Carol Shields's 'A View from the Edge of the Edge'" Shields, Carol. *Larry's Party*. Toronto: Vintage, 1997. Print.

Shields, Carol. "Where Curiosity Leads." In Giardini, Anne and Nicholas, eds. *Startle and Illuminate: Carol Shields on Writing.* Toronto: Random House Canada, 2016. 82–91. Print.

Saussure, Ferdinand. *Course in General Linguistics.* Ed. Charles Bally et al. Trans. Wade Baskin. Toronto: McGraw-Hill, 1966. Print.

Stovel Foster, Nora. "By Mistake": Larry Weller as 'The Stone Guest' in Carol Shields' Novel *Larry's Party.*" In Carol Beran, ed., *Contemporary Canadian Fiction* (Hackensack, NJ: Salem Press, 2014), 152–166. Print.

———. "Excursions into the Sublime": A Personal Reminiscence of Carol Shields." *SCL/ÉSC* 38, 1 (December 2013): 267–280. Print.

Advice to Writers in Carol Shields's *Unless*

Wendy Roy

The posthumously published *Startle and Illuminate: Carol Shields on Writing* (2016) brings together a variety of advice Carol Shields gave to writers over the years, in a variety of forms. The collection includes several of her published speeches and essays on reading and writing; a number of previously unpublished talks and notes for presentations from the Shields fonds in Library and Archives Canada; a lecture on writing she presented in Germany; writing notes and an assignment for students in her creative-writing classes; and letters of advice she sent to some of those students.[1] In some chapters, editors Anne Giardini and Nicholas Giardini, Shields's daughter and grandson, bring together published and unpublished sources, juxtaposing them in such a way that convergences in Shields's pronouncements—how she elaborated on particular points about writing and reading over time, through different media—become evident. The Giardinis also intriguingly intersperse the edited versions of Shields's essays and speeches with quotations from her other published writings that reinforce or demonstrate the guidance about writing evident in the collection's source texts.[2] While a few of these quotations are excerpts

W. Roy (✉)
Department of English, University of Saskatchewan, Saskatoon, SK, Canada

© The Author(s), under exclusive license to Springer Nature
Switzerland AG 2023
N. F. Stovel (ed.), *Relating Carol Shields's Essays and Fiction*,
https://doi.org/10.1007/978-3-031-11480-9_11

from her 1987 novel *Swann* and short stories such as "Flitting Behavior" (1985) and "Segue" (2003), and several more come from her critical study of Jane Austen (2001), the majority are taken from the 2002 novel *Unless*. As these inserted quotations suggest, Carol Shields's most sustained and creative discussion of writing can be found not in her essays or speeches but in her final published novel.

The varied sources in *Startle and Illuminate* exemplify Shields's long history of writing and speaking about what it means to be a writer. Her ideas on this subject are evident in her interviews over many years with academics and journalists such as Harvey de Roo and Eleanor Wachtel. To de Roo, for example, she said in 1988 that writers like her need to think not about plot but instead about "interesting ways of providing that tension that avoid the old, artificial rhythms of convergence, catastrophe and reconciliation" ("A Little" 47). In the last of many interviews with CBC journalist Eleanor Wachtel shortly before her death in 2002, Shields similarly discussed the process of writing—in particular "sometimes letting the novel go in different directions than we find in traditional novels" (*Random Illuminations* 165). While in these interviews Shields focuses on plot, in many of her speeches she talks about the writer's relationship to readers. One such discussion is in her 1996 address to students and staff at her *alma mater*, Hanover College in Indiana, published in 2003 as "Narrative Hunger and the Overflowing Cupboard" (and, as with several of her essays on reading and writing, republished in an edited form in *Startle and Illuminate*). In this speech, Shields argues that characteristics of the novel include "a texture that approximates the world as we know it; characters who in their struggle for the world resemble ourselves; dilemmas which remind us of our own predicaments; scenes that trigger our memories or tap into our yearnings; and conclusions that shorten the distance between what is privately felt and universally known" ("Narrative Hunger" 22). Remarkable in this advice is the way that Shields relates writing to reading, by linking the writer of novels to the "we" and "us" of the readers who encounter them.

From the start, much of Shields's fiction has explored how writers do their work. This focus began as early as her first, unpublished novel, *The Vortex*, a melodramatic mystery about the female editor of a well-respected literary journal; the 1973 manuscript can only be found in Shields's papers in Library and Archives Canada, but the plot revolves around a poem and how it is read. Much of Shields's subsequent published fiction focuses on writers and the ways they overcome the obstacles that prevent them from expressing, through the written word, their ideas, knowledge, and creative energy. These include the biographer and poet sister-protagonists of *Small Ceremonies* and *The Box Garden*, published in 1976 and 1977, as well as the historian of *Happenstance* (1980), the titular poet and her biographer and critics in *Swann* (1987), the folklorist of *The Republic of Love* (1992), and the popular novelist of the short stories "Flitting Behaviour" and "Block Out" from 1985 and 1989, as well as the husband-novelist and wife-poet of the 2003 story "Segue." In addition, as demonstrated in Christl Verduyn's discussion in this volume of the essay-like aspects of the short story "Eros," Shields has long used her fiction to make personal and polemical pronouncements, as well as didactic and argumentative statements, on a number of subjects.

I have argued elsewhere that *Unless* is Shields's most overtly feminist novel, one that purposefully "ties together feminist threads" from her previous fiction, and that unambiguously names concerns and strategies related to gender relations in our contemporary social world (Roy, "*Unless*" 126). In that 2003 essay-review, I also pointed out that the novel focuses in particular on unraveling the mystery of why the eldest daughter of protagonist and narrator Reta Winters has chosen to drop out of her life and sit on a street corner in downtown Toronto with a cardboard sign around her neck reading "GOODNESS" (Shields, *Unless* 12, 18). In the years since publication of that paper, other literary commentators have focused on the exploration of the concept of *goodness* (Steffler 2009, 2014; Heath 2014), as well as various related aspects of *Unless*, including its approach toward loss (Staels 2004); metafiction and translation (Stovel 2006, 2013); representation of mother–daughter relationships in a post-colonial context (Boehmer 2009); presentation of work as transcendent (Guenther 2010); use of discursive frames and technological mediations (McGregor 2013); relationship to the transnational gothic (Melikoğlu 2015); employment of meta-autobiography (Beckman-Long 2015); and representation of public space (Rosenthal 2011; Melikoğlu 2020). As Smaro Kamboureli's essay in this volume demonstrates, a concern in a number of these essays and chapters is the racialization or *othering* of a Muslim woman whose death Reta's daughter witnesses (Boehmer 2009; McGregor 2013; Steffler 2009; Ramon 2008), in what Kamboureli concludes is an example of "negotiating the imperative to pursue anti-racist critiques but often doing so in the name of the proverbial Canadian civility" (215). This sustained critical attention is essential to an understanding of *Unless*. Few of these previous commentators, however, address the novel's focus on writing, except briefly Nora Foster Stovel, who in her analysis of metafiction in *Unless* notes that among the intertexts in *Unless* are the novels that character Reta writes (64–68), and Bethany Guenther, whose discussion of several of Shields's novels highlights Reta's writing as creative work that allows *Unless* to broach the concept of transcendence (148, 159–61).

I argue that, in addition to the other work it does, *Unless* is Shields's most explicit fictional commentary on writing, one that consciously unites approaches to writing expressed over the preceding quarter century in her essays, talks, interviews, and works of fiction, and that deliberately identifies strategies related to the techniques and importance of writing.[3] Thus, the early pages of *Unless* feature a discussion of "a novel's architecture" (13), and the later pages a statement that the "remaking" of the world "through the nib of a pen" matters a great deal (208). Advice about writing in this novel consists of the general as well as the specific, often through how first-person narrator Reta considers her work of writing in the past, present, and future, as well as how she responds to a particular critic: the new editor assigned by her publishing house. The novel concludes with advice, both explicit and implicit, that writers must tackle subjects they consider crucial: in the case of both Reta Winters and Carol Shields, an exploration of women's tenuous place in their social and political worlds.

In Reta's opening listing of her writings, which includes her translations from the French of works by Danielle Westerman (modeled on Simone de Beauvoir, *Random Illuminations* 160) and her book on flowers in Shakespeare, Reta mentions short stories she has written and planned. She criticizes their whimsicality and the fact that she is unable to explain why anyone should care about the protagonists (9). The problem Reta identifies is that she had really wanted to write a novel, "About something happening. About characters moving against a 'there'" (11). A novel, she implies through this statement, can focus more than can a short story on characters traveling through time. Reta's advice to herself is to realize that she does not first have to do apprentice work writing short stories, but instead can simply tackle a novel. This echoes guidance Shields gives in both her interview with de Roo ("A Little" 39) and the paper "Myths that Keep You from Writing," published in *Startle and Illuminate* (18). In that paper, Shields "seriously question[s]" the notion that short fiction is only "an apprenticeship" for a novel that one hopes to write (18).

In *Unless*, one aspect essential to writing is emphasized: the importance of individual words. Reta meditates on the definition of the word *goodness*,[4] the relationship between *time* and *thyme*, and especially the functions of those "little chips of grammar" (313)—conjunctions, prepositions, adverbs—that connect, locate, and modify and thus are critical for communication. Each chapter in Shields's book carries one or two of these functional words as its title, as does the novel itself. As Shields much earlier told de Roo, "Language has been important to me from the beginning; every phrase has mattered, its shape and balance and resonance" ("A Little" 48). *Unless* in particular is highlighted as a word that matters, appearing as the title of both a chapter and of the novel itself. Its role as conjunction is to question the validity of a statement or state of being—in this case what the novel and wider world would look like if the solution to 19-year-old Norah's despair were never revealed, and, more broadly, if women's limited place in their social world were never challenged. In the novel, Reta calls *unless* a "worry word" (224), but Shields herself calls it "a hopeful word," one with "possibilities" to bring about change (*Random Illuminations* 149).

Another pivotal word in *Unless* is *novel*.[5] Reta thinks that she understands "something of a novel's architecture, the lovely slope of predicament, the tendrils of surface detail, the calculated curving upward into inevitability, yet allowing spells of incorrigibility, and then the ending, a corruption of cause and effect and the gathering together of all the characters into a framed operatic circle of consolation and ecstasy" (13). This passage provides a complex and evocative description of the trajectory of a novel of the kind that both Reta Winters and Carol Shields would advise others to write: it is rich in surface detail, it is predictable and yet at times resists the apparent inevitability of plot, and its conclusion upturns cause and effect as it gathers the characters together in joy and comfort. Reta is somewhat embarrassed about winning the Offenden Prize for her first novel, *My Thyme Is Up*, but is not really embarrassed about what the prize celebrates: "holding the reader in mind," avoiding playing games, resisting throwing "a mask of noir over every event" (82). While Shields resists comparison to Reta (*Random Illuminations* 171), Shields's writing, too, was initially dismissed as too focused on the feminine and the domestic, and she, too, wants to break down these classifications.

In *Unless*, Reta represents life itself as narrative. As she tries to understand why Norah has chosen to live on the street, she asks, "How did this part of the narrative happen? We know it didn't rise out of the ordinary plot lines of a life story" (13). While she is trying to figure out what happened to derail her daughter's life plot, Reta is at the same time working out the plot of her second novel, *Thyme in Bloom*. As the narrator of *Unless*, she repeatedly describes how she is considering structuring that narrative. Details have to be worked through, such as what the apartment of her narrator, Alicia, looks like and what kind of car Alicia's fiancé, Roman, drives (111). The concerns of the characters of this imbedded novel, and even their conversations, become part of the narrative of *Unless*.

Reta is working on a particular kind of novel: a popular sequel, something that Shields herself clearly considered when she published her companion novels *Small Ceremonies* and *The Box Garden* in 1976 and 1977 and *Happenstance* and *A Fairly Conventional Woman* in 1980 and 1982.[6] Reta understands the conventions of literary sequels: the title she has chosen echoes that of the first book, and she has considered a third title "in the event [she] decide[s] to go for a trilogy" (140). She knows that the sequel must reiterate the setting, characters, and situations of the first book (243), and that narration must be in the first person because the precursor novel "employed the first person, and a sequel must be consistent in such matters" (205–06). Her musings are good advice for anyone writing a sequel.

As *Unless* progresses, however, its imbedded commentary on writing takes a step beyond the sequel novel Reta is writing to invite readers to consider novel-writing in general. In her opening commentary in the chapter "Thereof," Reta says, "There is a problem all fiction writers must face if they want to create unique and substantial characters. Characters, at least those personages who are going to be important to the developing narrative, require context. They can't simply be flung onto the page as though they had metamorphosed from warm mud" (139). But how much context is necessary, Reta asks herself, and asks us as her implied auditors. She concludes that "Only a few vital family traces are required, the sense that the character isn't self-invented or arbitrary" (140). She initially describes the context she plans to provide for Alicia and Roman, but then slides into a discussion of her husband's childhood, and her own, as well as that of her daughter, Norah. Both because of the broad nature of this chapter's statements about writing—"There is a problem all fiction writers must face"—and the move into Reta's own family situation, readers are compelled to apply what Reta is saying about character development not just to the book she is writing, but also to the book Shields has written, the one we hold in our hands. What happens in *Unless* is not exactly what happens in Margaret Laurence's 1974 novel *The Diviners*, in which the novel the protagonist Morag Gunn is writing throughout is implicitly identified on the final pages as the one we are reading. *Unless* does demonstrate, however, that Shields is showing readers the importance of context in a novel both through how Reta plans her characters and how Shields, in the outer part of the nesting box, presents hers, including Reta.[7]

Another piece of advice Reta as writer-narrator in *Unless* provides is that the work of the primary characters in a novel must be shown. Shields has said in both early and late interviews, "I like to write about work … and wonder why we don't see more of it in our fictions" ("A Little" 44), and "I like to think of characters in novels having jobs and actually seeing them working" (*Random Illuminations* 165). In *Unless*, Reta states even more categorically, "I passionately believe a novelist must give her characters work to do. Fictional men and women tend, in my view, to collapse unless they're observed doing their work, *engaged* with their work, the architect seen in a state of concentration at the drafting table, the dancer thinking each step as it's performed" (264).[8] That is "the great joy of detective fiction," Reta tells her readers: "watching the working hero being busy every minute with work" (264). Thus, Reta investigates and provides information about her characters' work lives. But so, too, does Shields, since the protagonist of *Unless* is a writer, and we are reading about her work, the primary activity of writing a novel.

While, as noted earlier, many of Shields's other literary works demonstrate the labor of writing, a particularly good example is Judith Gill working in *Small Ceremonies* on her biography of Susanna Moodie and on her own failed novel. Shields's first published novel, like her last, is written through the first-person voice of a writer. In it, Shields describes Judith's biographical research in libraries and archives (33, 154), and how she writes the pages of her biography, sitting at the card table in the corner of her bedroom and using tools, including index cards and a portable typewriter (5, 8). As Judith meditates on the process of writing, she also provides advice for writers of biography, some of it ironic: "The task of the biographer is to enlarge on available data," she says, and then she provides an implicit critique of the shreds of information that can be found in metaphoric cupboards, medicine cabinets, bookshelves, and bank accounts (35).

Judith's attempts to write fiction also encompass advice she might give and has received, both good and bad. She surreptitiously reads another failed writer's unpublished novels and writer's diary (37–39), and then writes one of each herself (55, 72). She notices the "lust after other people's stories" that is part of her children's lives, as well as her own (45), and she affirms that developing a fictional plot involves selection: "It's the arrangement of events which makes the stories. It's throwing away, compressing, underlining" (51). Judith compares biography to fiction, finding some similarities but some differences, the most obvious being that, "unlike biography, where a profusion of material makes it possible and even necessary to be selective, novel writing requires a complex mesh of details which has to be spun out of simple air" (66).

More detailed and sometimes contradictory advice about writing is evident in Judith's description of her experiences as a student in a creative-writing seminar taught by her friend, novelist Furlong Eberhardt. She writes about the warm-up exercises, "in which we were to describe such things as the experience of ecstasy or the effect of ennui" (68); the term project of a short novel (69); the way in which her fellow students listened politely as she read her contributions aloud, "and never ventured any remarks except perhaps, very deferentially, that my sentences were a bit too structured or that my situations seemed a little, well, conventional and contrived" (68). When Judith hits a writer's block that causes her to drop out of the seminar, advice from Furlong is simply to let "your mind go free" and then get back to class and to work on writing (70). She overcomes her block in an inadvisable way: by borrowing the plot of one of the unpublished novels that she has clandestinely read. While she soon thinks better of her act and withdraws the manuscript, she later discovers that Furlong has, in turn, stolen her plot for his own very successful next novel (105). When confronted about his action, Furlong declares that there are only seven possible plots and that "Writers don't steal ideas. They abstract them from wherever they can," and then enhance and develop them (131). As this discussion indicates, Shields sometimes critiques clichéd and faulty advice about writing, both implicit and explicit, through the experiences of the writer-narrator of her first, as well as her last published novel.

"[T]he comfort of printed pages" in *Small Ceremonies* (108)[9] is contrasted with "the poison of the printed page" in *Unless* (16). Shields has said that in this passage from her final novel, she was referring to "dangerous places, where you only live off the printed page" (*Random Illuminations* 168). She was also, perhaps, pointing to the potential pitfalls of metafictionality. In Reta's embedded novel *Thyme in Bloom*, Alicia's work is also as an author: she writes for a fashion magazine. When Reta tells readers that she is "aware of being in incestuous waters, a woman writer who is writing about a woman writer who is writing" (208), it is clear that Shields is also aware that she has plunged even more deeply into these waters.[10] The reason Reta provides for her choice of profession for

Alicia is related to the importance of writing: "This matters, the remaking of an untenable world through the nib of a pen; it matters so much I can't stop doing it" (208). For Carol Shields, as well as Reta Winters, writing, and describing the process of writing, is so important that it must be done again and again. "I know perfectly well that I ought to be writing about dentists and bus drivers and manicurists and those folks who design the drainage beds for eight-lane highways," Reta says, adding that she writes about authors because theirs is "the richest territory" she can conceive (208). Shields told Wachtel that while she believes it is important to give characters professions other than that of author, with *Unless*, "I wanted to write about what was terribly interesting to me, and that was writing a novel: how you write a novel, how you *make* a novel" (*Random Illuminations* 165). For that reason, Reta had to be a "novel-maker" who was working out how to construct her own extended work of fiction.

As well as showing the work of writing, *Unless*, like *Small Ceremonies*, describes what it is like to give and receive criticism about written work. In a 1990 lecture in Trier, Germany, titled "Be a Little Crazy: Astonish Me" and later published in *Startle and Illuminate*, Shields commented that her description of the creative-writing class in *Small Ceremonies* got some things right but not others (40–41). While the "class exercises" and "vaguely worded student criticism" were accurate, Shields said she was wrong about the boldness of student expression: "Creative writing students are often painfully guarded; it is one of the great problems of teaching" (41). In *Unless*, Shields revisits such a gathering, not through a class, but through Reta's writing group. Like students in her earlier fictional seminar, the group's members offer only encouragement and tentative suggestions—"critical crumbs," such as, "I think you're maybe one draft from being finished," or "Doesn't character X enter the scene a little too late?" (92). These fictional budding writers clearly understand how much of themselves they are revealing through their writing and thus are reluctant to potentially destroy others through active criticism.

Unless explores the pitfalls and perils of definitive writing advice through the character of Reta's new editor, Arthur Springer, who has no qualms about telling her exactly how she should be writing and what she should be writing about. When they meet in person, he asks a provocative question: should a novelist "Provide closure for the reader? Or open the narrative to the ether?" (277). This is an important question, as Shields herself outlines in "Myths that Keep You from Writing," when she notes that "The feeling of completion, however imperfect, is what makes art"

(*Startle and Illuminate* 19). In *Unless*, Arthur interrupts Reta's thought-ful reply to his question, as he does repeatedly throughout their conversa-tion. Fortunately, as the narrator of *Unless*, Reta is able to resume her response by telling readers several chapters later that, in *Thyme in Bloom*, "Everything is neatly wrapped up at the end, since tidy conclusions are a convention of comic fiction." She then interrogates this decision in a way her editor has not allowed her to do; she says, "I have bundled up each of the loose narrative strands, but what does such fastidiousness mean? It doesn't mean that all will be well forever and ever, amen; it means that for five minutes a balance has been achieved at the margin of the novel's thin textual plane; make that five seconds; make that the millionth part of a nanosecond" (318).[11] Through Reta, Shields expresses her understand-ing that tidy conclusions are only a literary convention, since, as Shields has noted elsewhere, "Anyone who lives an ordinary life" knows that "those knots aren't going to stay done for more than two minutes" (*Random Illuminations* 173).

Earlier, in their conversation in her home, Reta's editor has dictated what he thinks should be her central concern—namely, "the pursuit of identity" (279). Although Reta clearly disagrees, Arthur again refuses to listen to her response. He tells Reta that she should focus on the identity of the character whom he perceives as capable of "greatness"—her male character Roman. In his opinion, her own central character, Alicia, cannot be "the moral centre of this book" (285) because her identity is insignifi-cant and her life trivial: "She writes fashion articles. She talks to her cat. She does yoga. She makes rice casseroles." He then adds several more disjointed but unambiguous judgements: "She is unable to make a claim to— She is undisciplined in her— She can't focus the way Roman— She changes her mind about— She lacks—" (286). Reta sums up and then provides a brief but astute analysis of his critique: in his opinion, a female character cannot be "the decisive fulcrum of a serious work of art" simply "Because she's a woman" (286). When Arthur objects to her interpreta-tion, Reta repeats it three times: "Because she's a woman" (286, 287). Again, some time after this conversation has abruptly ended with the dis-covery of Norah in hospital, Reta as writer explicitly rejects Arthur's bad advice, insisting that readers simply accept that her female protagonist is "intelligent and inventive and capable of moral resolution, the same quali-ties we presume, without demonstration, in a male hero" (320). Reta knows that women's lives are not trivial and that women are as important to the functioning of the world as are men.

Reta's advice to herself in *Unless*, and her active repudiation of the misguided recommendations of her editor, together constitute a summation and reconsideration of the guidance Shields presented to other writers throughout her career. The final chapter of *Unless*, "Not Yet," indicates that such guidance will always be needed, and concludes by reiterating several pieces of advice implicit earlier in the novel: think about what words mean to you (313), form your own "coherent narrative" (313), tie up "the loose narrative strands" (318), and take your own work seriously (320). Most significantly, the text as a whole directs authors to write about what is important to them: in the case of *Unless*, to explore the pervasive silencing of women that is "enforced by cross-cultural gender codes" (Roy, "*Unless*" 132). Reta has earlier argued that the world is divided into those who "are handed power at birth"—men—and all the rest—women— "who fall into the uncoded otherness in which the power to assert ourselves and claim our lives has been displaced by a compulsion to shut down our bodies and seal our mouths and be as nothing against the fireworks and streaking stars and blinding light of the Big Bang" (270).[12] She notes that while this statement is "excessive, blowsy, loose, womanish," she is willing to be brave, to unseal her mouth and "blurt it all out" (270). Shields, too, demonstrates in her final novel that she is willing to "blurt it all out," both about women's lives and about how to write about them. *Unless* can be read in conjunction with her essays, interviews, and letters, and with some of her previous works of fiction, as encouragement in the craft and politics of writing. This encouragement is of value both to writers of fiction and to writers of academic studies, including people like me who study Shields's fiction.

I conclude this essay with a short detour into the world of adaptation. I am fascinated by adaptations, and so I watched with some interest and some trepidation the 2016 film adaptation of *Unless*, written and directed by Irish filmmaker Alan Gilsenan and starring American actor Catherine Keener. While the portrayal of Reta by Keener is moving, I found problematic the filmmaker's decision to order events chronologically, beginning with a snapshot of the Winters family before they discover Norah on a Toronto street corner. This simplified chronology blunts the force of Reta's opening despair about her daughter and undoes the nuanced way in which the past and present are entangled in the novel. Also vulnerable to critique is the graphic and prolonged nature of the scene near the film's conclusion that shows Norah's intervention in the much greater suffering of another woman. Most striking, however, is what the adaptation does with the activity of writing. While the film maintains Reta's occupation as a writer and translator, almost every detail of her hard work of writing, and all of her advice about writing, are excised. It is as though Gilsenan chose not to see, or chose not to represent, that the novel is not just a kind of mystery about the events of one particular young woman's life and its effects on her family, but is also about a writer's life, and about how that writer actively theorizes her craft. The film does not follow Shields's advice: it does not show a writer doing her work, or talking about that work for the benefit of both herself and others. And the film is less effective because of this omission.

NOTES

1. As the editors of *Startle and Illuminate* note (149–50), Shields's theories about writing are also evident in her letters to her friend, writer Blanche Howard, published as *A Memoir of Friendship* (2007).
2. I would argue that the least successful parts of *Startle and Illuminate* are the sections at the end of each chapter that pluck out and summarize Shields's presumed advice to writers, in order to turn the collection into a type of writing manual.
3. Shields is not the only writer who provides advice about writing in fiction. In his study of Don DeLillo's writings, R. Mac Jones argues that in DeLillo's interviews and essays, as well as in some fiction, he provides advice to writers to counter "a contemporary culture that falls most readily into patterns of mass consumption, assimilation, and waste" by working "to find the smallest moments of the individual life" (182).
4. See essays by Margaret Steffler and Tim Heath for detailed discussions of this meditation.
5. As Heath points out, the name that Reta gives one of the characters in her own imbedded novel, Roman, is the word for *novel* in several languages other than English (167).
6. See my essay "Revisiting the Sequel: Carol Shields's Companion Novels" for a more detailed discussion of Shields's conception and exemplification of the companion novel.
7. I borrow the term "nesting box" from Shields's description of the structure of her best-known novel, *The Stone Diaries* (1993; *Startle and Illuminate* 26).
8. In her discussion of work as transcendent, Guenther points to this pivotal passage in *Unless* (148).
9. The passage refers to the way in which Judith's daughter, Meredith, finds solace in reading.

10. Shields told Wachtel that, while she knew she should not be entering these "incestuous waters," she decided, "just for once, I'm going to allow myself to do it" (*Random Illuminations* 168).
11. Here, Reta rephrases and counters female mystic Julian of Norwich's c. 1393 comment, "All shall be well, and all shall be well, and all manner of thing shall be well."
12. This passage echoes the diction of her epigraph from George Eliot, about "that roar which lies on the other side of silence" (*Unless*, np).

WORKS CITED

Beckman-Long, Brenda. *Carol Shields and the Writer Critic.* U of Toronto P, 2015.

Boehmer, Elleke. *Stories of Women: Gender and Narrative in the Postcolonial Nation.* Manchester UP, 2009.

Guenther, Bethany. "Carol Shields and Simone de Beauvoir: Immanence, Transcendence, and Women's Work in *A Fairly Conventional Woman, The Stone Diaries,* and *Unless.*" *Studies in Canadian Literature,* vol. 35, no. 1, 2010, pp. 147–64.

Heath, Tim. "Narrative Pragmatism: Goodness in Carol Shields's *Unless.*" Staines, pp. 161–75. 2014

Jones, R. Mac. "'Fiction is the Final Draft': Don DeLillo's Advice to Fiction Writers." *New Writing,* vol. 10, no. 2, 2013, pp. 182–87, https://doi.org/1 0.1080/14790726.2012.753910.

Laurence, Margaret. *The Diviners.* McClelland and Stewart, 1974.

McGregor, Hannah. "Reading Closely: Discursive Frames and Technological Mediations in Carol Shields' *Unless.*" *Canadian Literature,* vol. 217, 2013, pp. 35–52.

Melikoğlu, Esra. "Public Space as Inspiration for the Writer: Writing the Diverse Nation and the Threat of Privatisation in Carol Shields's *Unless.*" *British Journal of Canadian Studies,* vol. 32, no. 1–2, 2020, pp. 43–63.

———. "*Unless:* A Covert Post-Colonial and Transnational Gothic Novel, or the Haunted House (of Fiction) Is Falling Apart." *Studies in Canadian Literature,* vol. 40. no. 2, 2015, pp. 211–25.

Ramon, Alex. *Liminal Spaces: The Double Art of Carol Shields.* Cambridge Scholars, 2008.

Rosenthal, Caroline. "Specular Images: Sub/Urban Spaces and 'Echoes of Art' in Carol Shields's *Unless.*" *New York and Toronto Novels After Postmodernism,* Camden House, 2011, pp. 169–214.

Roy, Wendy. "*Unless* the World Changes: Carol Shields on Women's Silencing in Contemporary Culture." *Carol Shields: The Arts of a Writing Life,* edited by Neil Besner, Prairie Fire, 2003, pp. 125–32.

———. "Revisiting the Sequel: Carol Shields's Companion Novels." Staines pp. 63–79.

Shields, Carol. "Block Out." *The Orange Fish*. Vintage Books, 1989, pp. 90–109.
———. *The Box Garden*. 1977. Vintage Books, 1994.
———. *A Fairly Conventional Woman*. 1982. Rpt. as *Happenstance: The Wife's Story* in combined volume. Vintage Books, 1994.
———. "Flitting Behavior." *Various Miracles*. Vintage Books, 1985, pp. 48–61.
———. *Happenstance*. 1980. Rpt. as *Happenstance: The Husband's Story* in combined volume. Vintage Books, 1994.
———. *Jane Austen*. Penguin, 2001.
———. "A Little Like Flying: An Interview with Carol Shields." By Harvey De Roo. *West Coast Review*, vol. 23, no. 3, 1988, pp. 38–56.
———. "Narrative Hunger and the Overflowing Cupboard." *Carol Shields, Narrative Hunger, and the Possibilities of Fiction*, edited by Edward Eden and Dee Goertz, U of Toronto Press, 2003, pp. 19–36.
———. *Random Illuminations: Conversations with Carol Shields*. Interviews with and edited by Eleanor Wachtel, Goose Lane, 2007.
———. *The Republic of Love*. 1992. Vintage Books, 1994.
———. "Segue." 2003. *Carol Shields: The Collected Stories*. Toronto: Random House Canada, 2004, pp. 1–20.
———. *Small Ceremonies*. 1976. Vintage Books, 1995.
———. *Startle and Illuminate: Carol Shields on Writing*, edited by Anne Giardini and Nicholas Giardini. Toronto: Random House Canada, 2016.
———. *Swann*. Vintage Books, 1987.
———. *Unless*. Toronto: Random House Canada, 2002.
———. (Polly Pen). *The Vortex*. Manuscripts of unpublished novel. 1973. Ms. coll. Shields acc. 1, box 23, files 1–14, Library and Archives Canada, Ottawa.
Shields, Carol, and Blanche Howard. *A Memoir of Friendship: The Letters Between Carol Shields and Blanche Howard*, edited by Blanche Howard and Allison Howard, Viking Canada, 2007.
Staels, Hilde. "Verbalisation of Loss in Carol Shields' *The Stone Diaries and Unless*." *Zeitschrift für Kanada-Studien*, vol. 24, no. 2, 2004, pp. 118–31.
Staines, David, editor. *The Worlds of Carol Shields*. U of Ottawa P, 2014.
Steffler, Margaret. "A Human Conversation about Goodness: Carol Shields's *Unless*." *Studies in Canadian Literature*, vol. 34, no. 2, 2009, pp. 223–44.
———. "'To Be Faithful to the Idea of Being Good': The Expansion to Goodness in Carol Shields's *Unless*." Staines pp. 143–60. 2014.
Stovel, Nora Foster. "'Because She's a Woman': Myth and Metafiction in Carol Shields's *Unless*." *English Studies in Canada*, vol. 32, no. 4, 2006, pp. 51–73.
———. "Written in 'Women's Ink': French Translation and Female Power in Carol Shields's *Unless*. *Canada and Beyond*, vol. 3, no. 1–2, 2013, pp. 219–41.
Unless. Film adaptation. Written and directed by Alan Gilsenan, performance by Catherine Keener, Media Pro et al., 2016.

In/visibility, Race-Baiting, and the Author Function in Carol Shields's *Unless*

Smaro Kamboureli

Startle and Illuminate: Carol Shields on Writing, edited posthumously by Anne Giardini and Nicholas Giardini, reads like life writing: life writing as a genre encompassing autobiography or memoir, but also conceived at once in broader and more specific terms, that is, as a narrative by a writer reflecting on the importance of writing and her own writing process at the same time. This compilation of talks, essays already published, letters, and excerpts from her books reveals at once the intricacies of Shields's vision about literature and life and her approach to "the craft of writing" (*Startle* 181). As the title of this collection makes it abundantly clear—indeed, as Nora Foster Stovel states in her Introduction to this volume—Shields's non-fiction writing reveals elements of her fictional creations that may otherwise remain

---

I wish to express my appreciation to the City, Urban Cultures and Sustainable Literatures project, lead by Eva Darias Beautell (La Laguna University, Spain), whose vibrant conversations served as the original inspiration for this chapter.

S. Kamboureli (✉)
Avie Bennett Chair in Canadian Literature, University of Toronto,
Toronto, ON, Canada

N. F. Stovel (ed.), *Relating Carol Shields's Essays and Fiction*,
https://doi.org/10.1007/978-3-031-11480-9_12

193

undisclosed to the reader. "Shields's essays," Stovel writes, "clarify her icon-oclastic approach to rules of narrative and illuminate her revisionist poli-cies" (3). This is certainly the case, but it is also important to note that the relationship between Shields's fiction and essay writing is not necessarily a one-way reading trajectory. Her essay writing itself is also "illuminated" by her fiction. For example, many of her reflections are punctuated by excerpts from Reta Winters's own ruminations about her life as well as about her literary career in *Unless*. The result of the editorial discernment that the col-lection's two editors display when they pair Shields's "ideas about the pro-cess of writing" with her fiction (*Startle*, Anne Giardini xv),[1] the echo effect that emerges serves as an invitation to the reader to approach these two authors—Carol Shields and Reta Winters—via each other.

Reta, the protagonist of *Unless*, the last novel Shields published before her death, is a translator and an author of comic romances who tries to come to terms with the crisis in her life not only by writing but also by reflecting on the function of writing. A self-reflexive novel, *Unless* per-forms many of Shields's ideas about writing and gender—"Writing is per-formance," Shields says (*Startle* 16)—thus tempting the reader to view Reta as Shields's other. Reta may be the kind of writer who is "familiar with bread-baking terminology," the tongue-in-cheek term Shields employs when talking about how to render "actual experience" in fiction (*Startle* 17), and her first-person narrative may be categorized as what Shields calls "domestic fiction"—a novel "that reflect[s] the daily life of ordinary people" (*Startle* 104)—but her identification as a writer with Shields the author ends here. Although Reta Winters and Carol Shields are, to quote the latter, each "a person with a self as slippery as your own [the reader's]" (*Startle* 57), they are very different "persons."

Shields writes that fiction "allows us to be the other, to touch and taste the other, to sense the shock and satisfaction of otherness" (*Startle* 14), a statement that accounts, as Marta Dvořák's chapter in this volume demon-strates, for many of Shields's central thematic as well as formal concerns. In *Unless*, however, otherness, specifically the otherness of racialized sub-jects, is not as eagerly welcomed. It is circumscribed by the ideological, cultural, and social tensions embedded in the urban space as it is produced by Reta's field and range of vision. It is only the evanescent figure of the Muslim woman in the text that has compelled critics to ask probing ques-tions about the representation of cultural otherness in the novel.[2] Nevertheless, although the Muslim woman operates as a salient cue that guides us to view *Unless* through a racial critical lens, most interpretations of this figure address her problematic depiction, yet circumvent the question of racism. One reason for this, I believe, is that critics insist on reading the Muslim woman in ways that fit the canonical status of the historical author as a humanist and feminist writer.[3]

Carol Shields, writes David Staines, was "compassionate and forever human and humane" (2). This sentiment, along with Shields's own emphasis on gender, underscores much of her critical reception, irrespective of the particular methods employed by her readers. Whether she is referenced as the actual or reconstituted author, her writing about writing and women has shaped how her fiction has been read. In a lecture she gave in 1997, Shields said that

> Toni Morrison talks…about the split of consciousness of most Americans, and the fact that this splitting is caused by an ever-present consciousness of race, the guilty and haunting sense of 'the other.'
> But my 'other' was men. What they were, who they were or what they wanted, despite having a father, a brother, a husband, a son, and a few—not a lot but a few—men friends. And as I wrote *Larry's Party* I thought often of the immense mysteries men keep from women. And the mysteries women keep from men. (*Startle* 87)

This statement, which echoes her view that "serious literature" is not meant to engage with "war or race relations" (Anderson 143), might explain why some of the readers of *Unless* are reluctant to engage with how "race" is inscribed in the novel. The fact that the other in *Unless* is a Muslim woman and not a male character, and that this other is treated as an expendable figure, lays out the focus of my argument here. By paying attention not to the actual author but to how the author function operates in the text, I intend to address the complex concatenations of otherness in this novel. In *Unless*, otherness is constructed as a result of the mutual relationship between Reta's acts of seeing and looking. Reta's range of vision is bounded by the social and familial values she embraces, a vision that blurs, and ultimately evacuates from her narrative, the differences between white and racialized subjects. The governmentality Reta exercises through her acts of seeing and looking, evident in the ways she monitors her wayward daughter Norah and references the Muslim woman, is crucial to understanding the interplay between visibility and invisibility that constitutes marginality in the novel. A brief account, then, of these two key concepts that frame my argument is in order here.

* * *

The difference between seeing and looking is one of awareness and atten-tiveness. The act of looking targets a particular visual field, turning seeing into a conscious act that focuses on a specific scene or object, in effect rendering what falls beyond its range invisible or inconsequential. Seeing, in contrast, does not require the heedfulness that characterizes looking; a sensory performance, it occurs involuntarily because we have eyes that acknowledge visual stimuli. We see our city as the location of our daily life, but we do not always notice what marks it as a "social space involving subjectivities and identities differentiated by class and race, gender and age, education and religion" (Huyssen 3). In other words, not everything we see merits our attention. According to John Berger, "[t]he way we see things is affected by what we know or what we believe" (8). Although the "reciprocal nature of vision" (Berger 9) materializes via the spectator's agency, it remains shaped by the ideological apparatus that determines gaze conduct. Material and social visibilities are not necessarily coincident nor is the invisible always contingent on the visible.

As Rey Chow demonstrates, "visibility is not to be confused with visible objects" ("Postcolonial" 66). Chow's argument about visibility as a func-tion of entrapment, especially in the post 9/11 context, relies on Foucault's theory of visibility. Foucault has been instrumental in developing a notion of the visible that, although associated with restraint and detention, is the product of light. The operating principle of his panopticon relies precisely on its ability to hold its subjects within its sphere of illumination, i.e., sur-veillance, while rendering the observation point opaque: the detainee seen but not seeing, the guard seeing but not seen. Yet if "[v]isibility is a trap" (Foucault, *Discipline* 200), it is a trap that also entraps the guard, for the panopticon is not just an assemblage of different acts of seeing and look-ing. Not only does the subject observed become her own guard since she does not know when she is being watched, but the discursive relationship between what the observer can see and the observed cannot disperses the authority of the former.

This point, in tandem with Foucault's attention to how the process of making visible involves an emphasis on articulation and its relationship to in/visibility, is at the core of Chow's critique of readings that employ vis-ibility as metaphor. Chow disputes the assumption that visibility is "con-tinuous and equitable to, or analogous with, the non-visible" and, by extension, "with verbal language, in particular: what you 'see' *is* (or is like) what you speak about" ("Postcolonial" 65). She shows, instead, that visi-bility cannot "be treated as the secure opposite of what is hidden...Rather, visibility is…caught up in the shifting relations of political sovereignty and in the discontinuities among different representational orders" ("Postcolonial" 64). Releasing visibility from its metaphorical function challenges its association with articulation whereby it has less to do with the actual sense of seeing and more to do with critiques of hegemony. When not considered to be a transparent sign or a metaphor of power relations, visibility maintains an irreducible relationship with articulation. The articulable and the visible belong to the same "circuits of communication" (Foucault, *Discipline* 217) in that the former shapes the latter but they are not equivalent to each other. Understanding the visible and the articulable as two domains that define and are themselves defined by their points of contact but also by the gaps between them invites us to remain attentive to the web of connectivities and disjunctions generated as much by their mutuality as by their irreducibility.

My reading of *Unless* revolves around this tension between the visible and the invisible. As I hope to show, Reta's conduct as a first-person narrator exemplifies the reciprocal and conflictual relationships that exist between what she looks at and what she does not see, as well as between what she sees and what she articulates or leaves unsaid. While Shields's choice of first-person narration may imply that what Reta sees and what she represents in her narrative are analogous to each other, the technologies of visuality and control that comprise the story she tells suggest otherwise. Moreover, I argue, the irony that often punctuates the treatment of Reta's acts of seeing and looking is an authorial ruse that at once questions and upholds the narrator's representation of otherness, and does so in relation to the critical field of the novel's reception. Because the ideological implications embodied in Reta's acts of visuality are most prominent when she visits Toronto, the space where both Norah and the Muslim woman are situated, I begin my close reading of the text by first examining how her narrative constructs Toronto's urban imaginary.

* * *

"Here's," the title of the novel's opening chapter (1), situates Reta's life "in the prosperous rolling hills of Ontario, only an hour's drive north of Toronto" (2). As she drives toward her house in the countryside, going through "Orangetown, down its calm, old-fashioned main street," her scanning gaze sees Toronto in the distance, "monumental and lonely," its "outskirts… ragged, though its numbered exits pretend at a kind of order"

(25). The Canadian metropolis is in the periphery of her world but remains within the reach of her vision. Cast as a "there" to her "here," Toronto is visualized as a space that spawns Reta's resistance to it. Orangetown, writes Caroline Rosenthal, "resonates with the garrison mentality; it is... an idyllic anti-metropolitan community for ex-Torontonians who seek a cleaner, safer, and decidedly 'waspisher' rendition of the metropolis as well as an escape route from the complexity of multiculturalism" (177). Rosenthal is right to evoke what has been a central trope in the formation of Canadian literature, but it is important to note the two meanings Northrop Frye attaches to the garrison: a retreat from an inhospitable wilderness, an alien environment that threatens settler consciousness, and, inversely, "as society gets more complicated and more in control of its environment," a domesticated nature in response to the disorderliness of the metropolis (Frye 346). Firmly ensconced in her neatly circumscribed environs, a garrison in the second sense of the trope, Reta delivers her narrative in a fashion that replicates the humanistic paradigm of nature/culture. Although Reta's garrison mentality is modulated by her frequent forays into the city, its binary construction reveals the ideological foundation of her resistance to urbanism.

Interestingly, it is not so much her proximity to the natural world that Reta foregrounds but rather Orangetown's simultaneous distance from and contiguity with urban space. Her movement in and out of Orangetown casts it as a transitional zone between Toronto and her house that lies "five miles out of town" (43). Orangetown may emerge as a third space but the way in which it is configured in Reta's narration rejects the incommensurability Homi Bhabha and Ed Soja ascribe to this concept.[4] As an in-between realm, Orangetown both epitomizes the inherited dichotomy between countryside and city and rescripts it in terms that evoke a desire for space which, though bearing urban markers, is safe and hospitable to a measure of diversity. Lynn, one of Reta's close friends, may not lock her bike "'Because this is Orangetown'" (76), but this small town is far from embodying the kind of homogeneity implied in conventional configurations of the garrison mentality. Lynn "was born and educated in North Wales" (75), while another close friend, Annette, came to Orangetown, via Toronto, from Jamaica. Yet, while Reta comments on Lynn's "strong Welsh accent" (115) and provides a detailed description of Annette's "slim-waisted" body (75), she refrains from identifying the latter as a Black woman. This omission may not carry any significance in this passage where Reta goes into considerable detail about her women friends' physical appearance, but it becomes important when encountered later in the text in the context of how "race" signifies, an issue I discuss below. To quote Shields again, "the right detail in the right place" (*Startle* x).

Orangetown as the third space that results from Reta's depiction of her geographical and social habitat is thus delimited by the moral order of her humanism. Abundantly evident in the novel, Reta's humanism is advanced as a tested perspective, the result of her having considered and subsequently rejected poststructuralism—"Too much Derrida might be the problem" (4). Against the death of the subject and textuality—"They published my 'text,' such a cold, jellied word" (7)—Reta privileges a paradigm of the human that refracts urban heterogeneity as a cultural formation marked by instability and disorder. Accordingly, she constructs Orangetown and her house as a regulated zone that is immune to the presumed contagion of the city. The horizontal movement of her frequent shuttling to and from Toronto—"The drive is...repetitive, the colour of cement" (179)—enacts the governmentality she wields over the spaces that she both traverses and inhabits.

If, despite her resistance to Toronto, Reta glides in and out of it with ease, it is not only because her weekly visits to the city are transitory. Knowing that she can always return to the domestic stability of her gentrified house, she manages to thwart what she finds undesirable about the city. The details she provides about the house's architectural style and furnishings emphasize its material role as refuge but also accentuate its construction as the ideological edifice of her value system: the house "in *excess* of its primary function as artificial shelter," a structure encapsulating "the dialectic that emerges between these two impulses: shelter and identity" (Smyth and Croft 13). This double function of her house becomes apparent when Reta admits that she is "obsess[ed]" (61) with cleaning: "I dust and polish this house of mine so that I'll be able to seal it from damage" (62). The emotional equilibrium she achieves through her house cleaning performs a catachrestic instance of the garrison mentality, but also goes beyond it.

While the domestic has always been employed by Shields as an important emancipatory trope in relation to her female characters,[5] no matter how ironized in this novel, it also functions as a trope that frames, a means of entrapment. The lyricism that characterizes Reta's accounts of her cleaning—"dusting, waxing, and polishing offer rewards...I especially love the manoeuvring of my dust mop over the old oak floors" (61)—may border on satire, but satire's predilection for role-playing does not cancel out the performativity of her domestic activities. Whether she looks for dirt "under the sink" (61) or "glance[s] at the oak banister" that requires polishing (62), Reta's cleaning entails an intensified engagement with both seeing and looking that is analogous to the transparency panopticism requires. Her desire to keep out "whatever presents threat or disorder" (61) reifies the binary opposition between inside and outside and manifests her need for mastery and containment. Her cleaning, then, acts as a form of governmentality, that is, a habitual practice individuals employ to exercise disciplinary power and regulate the disbursement of power to others. She associates her cleaning with caring—"If I commit myself to its [the house's] meticulous care, I will claim back my daughter" (62)—but her caring is also a corollary of territorial control, of how things should be. Dusting as sealing is thus a trope that admits to and negates the porousness of her house. This dialectic betrays Reta's aversion to otherness, an "intolerance," to echo Wendy Brown, that "articulates" a "'native'…response to difference" (183). Casting as menacing or rendering invisible what is not consonant with Reta's views configures her extended narrative about her house as a parable about subjectivity and subjectification: the house as a panopticon, an assemblage of the articulable and the visible that operates as a disciplinary apparatus that both controls and is controlled by Reta. Facilitated by her scrutinizing gaze, her obsessive cleaning positions her as her house's guard on the lookout for what might disrupt the harmony in her family, a guard, however, who is herself subjected to her gaze's structural surveillance.

In both senses of the word as sight and worldview, Reta's vision determines what and whom she sees when she visits Toronto at the start of the novel. What precipitates this particular foray into the city, indeed what occasions the entire narrative, is the sudden turn of events in her oldest daughter's life. Nineteen-years old, Norah abandons her studies at the University of Toronto, her boyfriend and the basement apartment they share, and disassociates herself from the comfort of her middle-class family to panhandle, becoming a constant and silent presence at the intersection of Bathurst and Bloor streets in downtown Toronto. It is not uncommon to see panhandlers, mostly homeless people, along that stretch of the city's core. Norah's oversized "old gardening gloves" (41), "matted" hair, "torn jeans," and the "cardboard sign on her chest," with its "single word printed in black marker—GOODNESS" (12), complete her image as a street person at that corner, a familiar, albeit abject, figure. She stands for the kind of urban malady, usually linked with criminality or mental illness, generally viewed as an assault to the city's attempt at decorum and containment. At the same time that Norah appears in Reta's narrative as a sore sight that represents the socio-economic reality meant to stay invisible in the city, she also throws into stark relief what her mother's narratorial gaze remains oblivious to, thus visualizing the discrepant elements that Reta's family regime strives to hold at bay.

Because Norah does not bear the stereotypical signs of youth rebellion—"tattoos and pierced tongue" (12)—Reta fails to recognize her daughter's behavior as a protest against her own but also urban governmentality; instead, she pathologizes her. Norah, we read, has gone "off the track" (13); "[t]here's nothing natural" (13) about her "demented" state" (105). To Reta's eyes, Norah embodies a disease that goes counter to the Winters family economy, a psychological malady and not part of a social ill. Reta's diagnosis may reflect her motherly despair and hope but also misreads the signs of civic dissent evident in Norah's actions. Norah's squatting on the pavement, a practice evoking Theodor Adorno's "micrological activity" (28)—bringing to the foreground minor phenomena, what the logic of master narratives renders inconspicuous and irrelevant—affords her a visual perspective from below that is absent in Reta's ways of seeing and looking. The micrological proximity produced by Norah's gaze unsettles the logic of identity and identification generated by Reta's binary vision. Because mother and daughter practice different modalities of the gaze, Reta remains blind to the implications of Norah's desire "to belong to the whole world" (166). Not only does she reject her daughter's perspective—Norah "is doomed to miniaturism" (249)—she also fails to consider that the need Norah feels "'to find where I fit in'" (132) might be a rejection of her family's liberal values.

To Reta, Norah's behavior reflects a regression to adolescent immaturity, the reason why she declares that Norah "can't" and "won't" "belong to the whole world" (166). These negative imperatives are revelatory as much about Reta's insular perspective as about Norah's existential discomfort. Norah's seemingly passive figure denotes an aporetic condition that troubles her mother's ordered world: her relinquishment of her middle-class life; the city corner she chooses; her silence; and her panhandling—these are elements that stand for what Foucault calls "'counter-conduct,'" a "struggle against the processes implemented for conducting others" (*Security* 201). Her street presence is the kind of "constant, everyday event" typifying the tactics of counter-conduct that "modify relations" by their "conceptual movement from ideology to practice" (Demetriou

222). Norah's counter-conduct causes a seismic change in her family, albeit one the sociopolitical implications of which go unheeded by Reta. The single viable reason Reta considers for Norah's behavior is that she "half knows the big female secret of wanting and not getting" (98). Privileging gender as the most plausible reason for Norah's transformation brackets the possibility of also considering class, "race," or empathy for marginalized people as factors that might have caused Norah to change the course of her life.

It is not, then, surprising that, bearing witness exclusively to her daughter's precarity, the solipsism of Reta's act of looking obliterates from her vision field not only the city's detritus but also the present tense Norah inhabits. It is her younger daughters who notice that "there are about four other [panhandling] guys" at the same corner (161). Reta's overdetermined "voyeurism...blot[s...] out" the Norah of the present with the Norah of her memories: "Norah sitting at the kitchen table studying for exams"; "Norah trying on new school shoes; Norah sleeping, safe" (26). These recollections that situate Norah within the family domain do not merely reflect Reta's nostalgia for the way things were before Norah's "self-renunciation" (42); they also evince her exercise of disciplinary power, her calculated gaze that decidedly resists and is resisted by the alternative optics generated by Norah. When Reta "look[s] back," she remembers that "Norah had been a good, docile baby and then she became a good, obedient little girl. Now,... she's so brimming with goodness that she sits on a Toronto street corner, which has its own textual archaeology, though Norah probably doesn't know about that" (11). Reta's ideological blindness prevents her from finding a correspondence between the goodness of docile Norah and the "GOODNESS" Norah calls for in the present. While the former is synonymous with acquiescence in the sovereignty of the family and its complicity with the state apparatus, the latter enunciates the desire for what Carl Death calls "'not being like that,'" "the production and performance of alternative subjectivities through processes of ethical self-reflection" (202). Norah's apparent lack of action brings into material and affective relief the gap that separates the Winters household from Toronto's heterogeneity at the same time that it speaks back to her disciplined upbringing, thus signifying both interpellation and subversion.

Reta's effusive representations of the life of plenty her daughter has renounced—"abundant, bustling, but with peaceful intervals, islands of furniture, books, music, soft cushions to lean into, food in the fridge, more in the freezer" (44)—differ sharply from the life of poverty Norah embraces at present. "I don't need any money. That's what's so astonishing," Norah states (130) shortly before she becomes a street person. Reta, however, does not dwell on this comment. Her worldview renders scarcity invisible as a social condition, a disturbing image she deflects: "all my living perfume washed off because my oldest daughter has gone off to live a life of virtue. Her self-renunciation has even made her choose a corner of Toronto where the pickings are slim" (42). It is ironic that, despite her sorrow, Reta cannot help but register her daughter's earnings, but this remark is also an instance of ironic inversion that turns Reta's self-irony about her "living perfume" into a critique of her middle-class smugness.

* * *

No matter the irony that some critics find in Shields's treatment of Reta, the novel cannot be reduced entirely to a parody of the protagonist's ideologies.[6] Instead, irony operates as a protective economy; it is a ruse that enables the text's "'author' as a function of discourse" (Foucault, *Language* 124) to express what Reta's gaze eliminates or what she leaves unsaid. While the ironic tenor that often accompanies Reta's articulations undermines some of her views, it also creates fissures in the narrative that illuminate the role of the author, textual moments that materialize the distinction between Reta's regime of visuality and the "author [who] explains the presence of certain events within a text, as well as their transformations, distortions, and their various modifications" (Foucault, *Language* 128). This understanding of the author is not to be confused with the person behind the author's name: it is a "'second self' whose similarity to the author is never fixed," a discursive formation arising "in the division and distance of the two" (Foucault, *Language* 129).

Interestingly, Shields also employs the same phrase—"second self"—to distinguish between the author and the writerly figure inscribed in an author's text: "when a writer picks up a pen, a second self comes out," she writes in *Startle*. She qualifies this "second self" as "[t]hat which *seems unguarded*" precisely because it expresses the author's "unspoken reserves of thought" (64, 63). There is, then, a distance between this second self, the author function, in *Unless* and the novel's actual writer, but the distance between the author[7] inscribed in the text and the narrator often collapses so that Reta's views and those of the author blend, becoming congruent.[8] Deployed both as shield and ammunition, the irony that oftentimes imbues

Reta's articulations and actions exposes her social myopia but also allows her to speak on behalf of the author. For example, Reta's aversion to post-structuralism enables the author to express her own misgivings against this approach. Such instances of textual ventriloquism highlight the permeable boundary between character and author. Yet, since one of the actions the author as a function of discourse performs is to "neutralize the contradictions" (Foucault, *Language* 128) in a text and thus also control the ambivalence the proliferation of meaning generates, this ventriloquism posits the author as a figure who now critiques, now upholds Reta's biases, thus revealing the text's otherwise concealed ideological apparatus. If *Unless* is the author's own panoptical construct, then these textual and ideological strategies position the author as guard, a guard who is not seen but who herself can be detected within these textual fissures: to appropriate Shields's own terms, the author as the *unguarded* second self. Consequently, what is omitted in what Reta sees or looks at is not necessarily an inadvertent oversight; one of the functions of the author figure, Foucault says, is to regulate "nonaccidental omissions" (*Language* 135).

One notable example of the strategic occurrence of omission is Reta's description of the spot where Norah panhandles at "a nervous, feverish corner of the city" (179). This comment echoes Reta's own nervousness about finding herself in a neighborhood that has long been socio-economically and culturally mixed. This is why her initial account of that location presents it only in terms that are familiar to her as a writer: "the poet Ed Lewinski hanged himself in 1955 and... Margherita Tolles burst out of the subway exit into the sunshine of her adopted country and decided to write a great play" (11). Reading that corner via (fictitious) literary history produces what Rob Shields calls "empirical space," a space "complacently understood" because it "excludes important cultural and cognitive issues from consideration" (187). By subtracting from that locality's complexity what is not relevant to her, Reta reads this cityscape only through her literary identity and cultural capital.

Reta does not simply overlook something that is familiar to her. Because her act of seeing edits out what categorically resists invisibility in 2000, the year the novel's action unfolds, this omission is yet another manifestation of the author function. Norah, as Reta concedes half way through her narrative (179–80), sits across from Honest Ed's, the legendary discount department store that was the main shopping stop for generations of immigrants and discount seekers. Frequently featured in Canadian fiction, e.g., Austin Clarke's *Nine Men Who Laughed* (1986) and M.G. Vassanji's

No New Land (1997), it was built by the entertainment mogul Ed Mirvish (1914–2007). Spanning an entire block, it was a city landmark since it opened in 1948 and until it was demolished in 2016 in the name of urban development. At the start of the new millennium when Norah sits right across from Honest Ed's, its façade, along both sides of the entire block at Bloor and Bathurst streets, was illuminated day and night by 23,000 light bulbs and adorned by slogans ("Welcome, don't faint at our low prices, there's no place to lie down").[9] That Honest Ed's up-your-face spectacle is entirely absent in Reta's narrative suggests that her translation of the store's social history and lurid aesthetics into literary history is equivalent to her censoring act of dusting, an instance of how the articulable and the in/visible, what she says and renders visible or absent in her account, function simultaneously within the city's same vector without, however, being subsumed into one another.

Had the reader not been expected to visualize Honest Ed's, the store's and street names would have been fictionalized. Thus, while Reta's account obfuscates this location's social history early in the narrative, the author's function is to draw attention to it. Serving as the boundary line between the west side of The Annex neighborhood and the east side of Koreatown, the area around the Bloor and Bathurst intersection was the center of the Jewish community until the Second World War and subsequently became known as a Hispanic and Hungarian enclave, a history alluded to by Reta through her references to the Jewish suicide poet and the Hispanic playwright. Still, when she registers the "rowdy" and "cheap" milieu of that same location and references Honest Ed's later in the novel as "an eccentric" store (179), she does so by attributing her earlier omission to "Norah's posture [that] excludes everything around her" (180), in effect implying that she sees that corner through her daughter's eyes; but she doesn't. Employing a rhetoric of visuality that demarcates spatially her social difference and monitoring role, Reta "observe[s]" Norah from a distance, "remain[ing] unseen," a "comforting," as she admits, position (180). This scene captures Reta's affect—her "steady, resolute, useless anxiety" (180)—but also materializes the incongruence between Norah's and her own fields of vision. While for Reta her daughter's "embodie[d] invisibility" is a consequence of Norah living the life of an "outcast" (12), her own invisibility behind a shop window dramatizes her practice of surveillance. Although in this scene mother and daughter inhabit the same city field, their relationships to it, what their acts of seeing and looking attest to, are radically different precisely because their positions are marked by their different gaze modalities. This tension between the in/visible and the in/articulable that ultimately constitutes Norah as an inscrutable character can be deciphered by paying attention to the author function and the Muslim woman.

* * *

As far as Reta is concerned, Norah's condition becomes legible only after she catches pneumonia and is hospitalized, and the truth about her scarred hands is finally made "visible" (263): they bear the burning marks of her accidental encounter outside Honest Ed's with a woman who immolated herself. This revelation, although recounted in the last few pages of the novel, constitutes the pivotal part of Reta's narrative:

> [A] young Muslim woman (or so it would appear from her dress)...poured gasoline over her veil and gown, and set herself alight....Without thinking, and before the news teams arrived, Norah had rushed forward to stifle the flames. The dish rack [that she has just bought at Honest Ed's] became a second fire, and it and the plastic bag in which it was carried burned themselves to Norah's flesh. She pulled back. Stop, she screamed, or something to that effect, and then her fingers sank into the woman's melting flesh—the woman was never identified—her arms, her lungs, and abdomen. These pieces gave away. The smoke, the smell, was terrible. Two firemen pulled Norah away, lifting her bodily in a single arc, then strapped her into a restraining device and drove her to Emergency, where she was given first aid. A few minutes later, though, she disappeared without giving her name. (314–15)

The details furnished by Reta's account not only abet her fear of the social ills lurking in Toronto and their assumed infectiousness but also provide the most probable reason for Norah's behavior "post-traumatic shock" (263). This same passage has also provided ample fodder for critical arguments about the extent to which *Unless* engages with racialized others or tests the limits of white subjects' empathy. Notwithstanding the compelling interpretations this sketchily described woman has given rise to, I read this scene as belonging to the same panoptical pattern Reta's narrative constructs, a paradigm that is ultimately sustained and instrumentalized by the author function.

The circumstances of the Muslim woman's self-immolation are highly mediated via newspaper reports discussed between Reta and her friends

(41, 117–118), "Honest Ed's exterior security video" submitted to the police (315), and Reta's own remediation of these accounts in the narrative we read. Configured as a product of intermediality, the Muslim woman emerges as an always-already figure lacking ontological presence. As Andrzej Warminski writes about this concept, the "*always-already* points at...an absolute past and passivity that can never be fully reactivated and awakened to presence" (xi). That this Muslim woman becomes the subject of different articulations at the same time that she is rendered entirely inarticulate; that this transference from the inarticulate to the articulate is initiated at the moment of her death, namely when she reaches visibility degree zero; that her self-immolation takes place in a public site the visuality of which Reta has already tailored in ways that mirror her values; and that her textual presence is formed by means of deferral and belatedness— all these elements suggest that this figure never attains the stature of a fleshed out character. Although the effacement characterizing the always-already figure "leaves a mark, a signature that is retraced in the very thing from which it is withdrawn" (Warminski xi), such a mark cannot become equivalent to a character or a subject, even one understood as subaltern.

Considering the Muslim woman as a character who facilitates cross-cultural exchanges (Roy, Stovel); whose agency is denied or curtailed (Boehmer, McGregor); whose self-immolation stands for "the urge to immolate women's *false I* with the aim to free their *real ones*" (Moreno-Álvarez 101); or whose "Orientalist" representation enables the novel "to promote its own feminist agenda" (Steffler 227)—these interpretations exemplify the prevalent critical desire in Canadian literary studies to redeem the subaltern by creating space for her presence and voice. But this Muslim woman cannot possibly have her absence restored or have a voice in *Unless*. Her self-immolation, along with her constructedness, speaks loudly that, as long as Reta's governmentality remains intact, there can be no critical intervention either from inside or outside the text, "no politics that is not always already based on subaltern negation" (Moreiras 123). Margaret Steffler is right when she states that "Shields...wants the reader to wrestle with the lack of attention given to the absence of an 'after' for the 'young Muslim woman'" (228). But taking on this challenge also demands that we ask in what terms the text encourages this attention and why this figure is treated this way in the first place. As I hope to show in what follows, Reta may be blind to "race" matters, but the author is not.

As an always-already figure whose anonymity is never overcome, one without kin and thus outside Reta's homogeneous notion of the Canadian family, the Muslim woman exists only as an object of reference. At the level at which the author operates, however, the Muslim woman is granted a paramount role, one that reveals how racialized subjects and cultural differences are at once inscribed and invisibilized in the text. I thus consider her appearances and disappearances in the text to be calculated, manifestations of the author function's agency. Reta's first-person narrative may show disinterest in the Muslim woman, but this minimalist telling, precisely what has intrigued readers, is complemented by the ways in which the author function maximizes the significance of Reta's narrative economy. In other words, the Muslim woman is designed not only to convey the author's views on diversity but also lure the reader's attention to her fleeting appearances.

The Muslim woman is thus an instrument employed by the author to provoke the kind of argument Alex Ramon makes against Rana Dasgupta's response to the text. Although Ramon finds Dasgupta's concerns about *Unless* "valid," namely that "'[w]e do not need to know the name of [the Muslim] woman…or her biography…for it is a complete image in itself of all the repugnant things 'we' already know about Islam and women'" (Dasgupta qtd. in *Liminal* 172),[10] he nevertheless goes ahead to acquit the text from any charges of prejudice. He reads the Muslim woman's representation as "a reflection of…an attempt to highlight the nature of silence imposed upon ethnic voices, rather than a simple participation in that silencing" (*Liminal* 172). Moreover, by noting that Dasgupta reads *Unless* as an American text, thus "disregard[ing] the very diverse histories of immigration and assimilation" in Canada and the United States ("Domestic" 30), Ramon endorses the colonial benevolence that typifies the master narratives of Canada as a settler and multicultural nation-state, which advance the notion that Canada's brand of subtle racism is innocuous compared, say, to that in the United States. Nevertheless, simply pointing to the silencing of the other is hardly a gesture of political import, as Ramon suggests, especially at the start of the millennium, the novel's temporal frame. If, despite her intermittent, truncated, and mostly casual depiction, the Muslim woman has become the object of critical attention, it is because readers, especially politically minded ones, cannot help but notice her deliberately, at least in my mind, problematic representation. The Muslim woman, I contend, is best read as an authorial ruse, a cunning artifice that both raises and problematizes matters of "race."

It is this cunning trope that presents the Muslim woman in paradoxical terms, that is, at once as a non-character and as the focus of critical attention. This same trope also contests and preserves the moral order of Reta's gatekeeping, an order marked by her whiteness. If her response toward the Muslim woman is marked by an insensibility symptomatic of the ideology characterizing her acts of seeing and looking, the author instrumentalizes that insensibility by playing the racial card in a way that incites critical apprehension about Reta's views while also disclosing her own symptoms of multicultural fatigue. Implicitly gesturing toward the anti-racist, decolonial, and ethical turns in Canadian literary studies, the author instantiates in the text a provocative case of race-baiting and its reversal, a double strategy apostrophizing the reader. Race-baiting works at Reta's expense, but its main purpose as it is enacted by the author's deployment of the Muslim woman is to deflect any charges of racism against the novel, hence its reversal. This strategy, however, backfires, for it becomes an alibi for a different kind of racism. Reta does not overtly express racist views. Instead, the regulatory ideology that imbues her acts of seeing and looking emblematizes post-racialism. "[P]ost-racial ideology," David Chariandy states, "contributes directly to a renewal and/or production of racism" (13). While its prefix post- points to a movement beyond a particular historical moment, it simultaneously reflects the residual, indeed persistent, presence of racializing and racist ideologies it purports to have overcome. The novel's post-racial sensibility echoes Paul Gilroy's notion of "New Racism" which, although "openly uncomfortable with the idea that 'race' could be biologically based," is characterized by "its strong culturalist and nationalist inclinations." At issue here is the conversion process racialized subjects undergo from being identified "as inferior" to being considered "out of place" (Gilroy 32). Remaining complicit with the very ideologies it seeks to supersede, this shift in racial relations does not make space for the racialized other to speak; rather, it speaks on behalf of those already empowered to do so. Hence, the Muslim woman's deafening silence in the text.

Reta's acts of seeing and looking, along with what she registers or omits, are redolent of this differently coded yet equally harmful view of otherness. This is abundantly obvious in the extended account she offers of one of her regular meetings with her women friends in Orangetown. On this occasion, they talk about women's lives in Africa and the Muslim woman. While, as I suggested earlier, Reta refrains from identifying Annette's racial identity at this point in the narrative, she tells us that Annette is "black" later in the text (252). In a way that echoes the strategic omissions in the representation of Honest Ed's and the deferral strategies of the Muslim woman's representation—as Shields writes in *Startle*, "[c]ertain themes require slower revelation (x)—in this scene, too, "race" remains unarticulated yet inferred by Annette's Jamaican origins, a case of the author's explanatory interventions in the text. The delayed manner in which Annette's in/visible origins are disclosed instrumental-izes her character at the same time that it is offered as evidence of Reta's post-racial liberalism. This instance of how the discursiveness of the articu-lable is embedded in the non-discursiveness of the in/visible validates the circumscribed world produced by Reta's acts of seeing and looking. To put it bluntly, the author is signaling to the reader that, since Reta does not register her friend's blackness, she cannot possibly be a racist. Reta's color-blindness, however, is not innocent; it is a manifestation of her post-racial attitude.

Read in this context, that Annette is assigned the task of voicing con-cerns about the limits of empathic response to subaltern women is not a coincidence; instead, it underscores her character's role in the text:

> "All I'm saying…is, what did we do about that [an African woman giving birth on a tree because of flooding]? Such a terrible thing, and did we send money to help the flood victims in Mozambique? Did we transform our shock into goodness, did we do anything that represented the goodness of our feelings? I didn't."
> "No," I [Reta] said. "I didn't do anything." (117)

The first-person plural of Annette's utterance expresses a version of humanitarian concern that is akin to Reta's own liberalism but also sub-sumes her identity difference into a collective "we." Having a Black woman legitimize Reta's white liberalism is meant to cancel out the text's race-baiting. That during the course of these friends' conversation about subaltern women Reta is "toying with the plastic flowers in the middle of the table… [and] observing the dog hairs on [her] dark blue sleeve" (118) is an ironic evocation of Shields's fascination with the mundane. But these seemingly unimportant details operate as yet another deliberate bait, one intended to foment a critical response from readers who may find Reta's comportment at this point to be callous. These would be precisely the kind of readers Reta disapproves of, "advocate[s] of a diverse new out-pouring of Canadian voices, the post-colonial cry of blaming anguish" (32). Their "pious opinions about the literature of the Great North" (31), i.e., Indigenous and Inuit voices, are represented in the novel by the male literary critic who interviews Reta about one of her publications. Incensed by his gender biases and his view that what threatens "the authentic national voice that rose from the landscape itself" is literature about "middle-class people living in cities"—a view that both echoes Reta's binary conception of space and undervalues her first novel, *My Thyme Is Up*, which is set in a city "the size of Toronto" (13, 14)—she constructs a scathing image of him (31–35), an image that, implicitly, caricatures post-colonial critics.

Reta's talk with her friends ends with an exchange among them that references the Muslim woman—"Was she a Saudi?" (117); did she wear a "chador," a "veil," "a burka" (118)?—yet most of these questions are not attributed to specific interlocutors. The interchangeability suggested by having these friends' individual identities edited out at this point in their dialogue reinforces the assimilationist character of Reta's governmentality. A version of Annette's first-person plural utterance, the erasure of the speakers' identities is an act of racial ventriloquism, a purposeful conflation of white and Black voices, yet another instance of authorial intervention. Cast as a character whose racial difference is at once implied and suspended, Annette serves to both sanction and revoke Reta's whitening ways, in effect becoming the Black equivalent of the Muslim woman. If Annette is de-racialized at the same time that her blackness serves to assuage any doubts about Reta's post-racial attitudes, the Muslim woman's racial and cultural identity is simultaneously diluted and reified. The repeated references to and amplification of her garment—veil, burka, chador—erase her cultural particularity, thus operating as a synecdochal gesture of identification that further reduces her to a function. Her disembodied figure echoes those Western, including Canadian, master narratives that have constructed her Islamic garment marker as a vexing, if not insurmountable, cultural and religious difference that is at best tolerated, at worst legally outlawed.

While these women's collective utterances construct the Muslim woman as a totalized sign, her self-immolation, addressed by Reta only insofar as it affects Norah, is simply referenced as an "incident" (309), a "this" (316), an "event" (309, 310, 313). An event does not exist in and by itself. As Reta says in the beginning of the novel's last chapter, "Not Yet,"

A life is full of isolated events, but these events, if they are to form a coherent narrative, require odd pieces of language to cement them together, little chips of grammar (mostly adverbs or prepositions) that are hard to define, since they are abstractions of location or relative position, words like *there-fore, else, other, also, thereof, theretofore, instead, otherwise, despite, already,* and *not yet.* (313)

Despite her emphasis on these "chips of grammar," many of which serve as the titles of the novel's chapters, her list includes a word that is neither an adverb nor a conjunction, one that is, instead, both noun and adjective: "*other.*" This "*other*" constitutes a significant instance of the author inter-vening in the narrative, a textual gesture that disrupts the logic of Reta's grammar. It creates a caesura that stands for the excess of otherness Reta's narrative cannot accommodate. Appearing where it does not belong syn-tactically, that is, in keeping with the ways in which the author adumbrates the narrative, this "*other*" at once hails and elides difference.

Reading this "*other*" as a textual event in its own right illuminates the Muslim woman and her self-immolation as an event the depiction of which remains at once incomplete and in excess of what transpired. Reta may acknowledge the complex structure of an event, but her account of what happened to her daughter closes off the different temporal registers that the self-immolation encompasses. The epistemological break signaled by the intrusion of the "*other*" is immediately suspended by the lyrical medi-tation she offers on the very word that grants the novel its title, "*unless.*" "The conjunction and (sometimes) adverb *unless*," Reta muses, "with its elegiac undertones, is a…word breathed by the hopeful or by writers of fiction wanting to prise open the crusted world and reveal another plane of being, which is similar in its geographical particulars and peopled by those who resemble ourselves" (313–14). In Reta's view, "*unless*" does not usher in a different world; it reaches out toward alternatives, may even seek to establish relationality, but does so only within familiar (and famil-ial) parameters, thus bolstering the governmentality she exercises both as mother and narrator.

It was "a coincidence that Norah was standing on the corner where Honest Ed's is situated when [the] young Muslim woman…set herself alight" (314), but it is not a coincidence that both Reta and the author evacuate from the narrative the possible meanings of the Muslim woman's act. Self-immolation, as a public spectacle that has a long and diverse, as well as highly contested, history, is usually an act of self-sacrifice for reli-gious reasons, or an act of martyrdom for the sake of a political cause, oftentimes associated with terrorism.[11] Yet Reta remains resolutely indif-ferent to what might have compelled the Muslim woman to sacrifice herself. It is the shock value of the violence of the self-immolation's visuality that holds her attention. The casual repetition of this decontextualized image-event throughout the novel ultimately operates as catachresis. The Muslim woman instantiates catachresis as "the representational mode suffered by the beleaguered human rights object" (Huehls 52), a trope that erases difference and "only sees objects" (Huehls 57). Her literal disintegration—"her melting flesh," "her arms, her lungs, and abdomen…gave way" (315)—shows that she exists in Reta's narrative as an entirely non-salvageable figure. That the author does not intervene to alter or contextualize this generalized image of Islam testifies to the fact that Reta's governmentality, instrumentalized as it is by the author, extends beyond her immediate environment to interpellate the reader. It is precisely the catachrestic representation of the Muslim woman's inflamed body that has animated critical interest. Its narrative incommensurability persists as the main crisis point in the text, transferring the responsibility to speak about it to the reader.

At the very end of the novel, with Norah back home a year after she walked out, and thus safely away from the dangers of the city, Reta promises her daughter that she "can put this behind" her, that the family will "remember it" on her behalf, "*a memory of a memory*…Unless we ask questions" (316; my emphasis), but they never do, at least not in the text we read. Like other crucial elements in the novel, asking questions about what happened to Norah, and presumably the Muslim woman, is deferred. Maintaining her position as a "voyeur" (301), Reta places herself at the center of Norah's experience, usurping any desire Norah might have to deal with her encounter with the Muslim woman in her own terms. As "a memory of a memory" the Muslim woman recedes even further, beyond the urban space which she momentarily claims, in effect turning into a non-event that is meant to be of no lasting concern. Having served her catalytic role in Reta's view of what precipitated Norah's condition, she has now reached the telos of Reta's linear and progressive time. Her complete erasure guarantees the novel its comedic resolution, restoring Norah back into the family fold, an ending consistent with Reta's own comic fiction.

This restoration is punctuated by a representation of the city that lies safely away, "[i]n the obscuring distance, *melting* into sunsets and handsome limestone buildings and asphalt streets and traffic lights" (310; my emphasis), an image of Toronto that bears traces of the Muslim woman's dissolved body. This charged image, which also echoes the trope of riding off into the sunset, a motif in the Western genre that invariably follows death, renders the novel, as some critics have argued, "ambivalent" (e.g., Beckman-Long 122). There is no doubt a lot of ambivalence in the novel, but I don't think there is anything ambivalent about the function of the Muslim woman. The additional deferral she undergoes at the novel's end suggests that, beyond not having a past in the text, she will not have a future either, except insofar as she is to become the focus of critical debate.

* * *

If *Unless* strains to draw attention, in overt and convert ways, to the Canadian politics of difference, it is because the author seeks to convey her frustration with how discourses of "race" and racism have evolved in Canada. The white protagonist's post-racial attitude both displays and subverts the "prohibition against racism" (Ahmed) that Canada, like most nation-states, promotes. Reta's characterization enables the author to submit to the reader the idea that this injunction has become a dominant discourse in its own right, and thus a discourse that demands a "refusal of [its] orthodoxy" (Ahmed). This is not a position that most Canadian critics would endorse. One way of reconciling the disavowal of racism prevalent in Canadian literary studies with the various arguments that rationalize the treatment of the Muslim woman without, however, attending to the overall inscriptions of "race" in the novel, or that attempt, as Ramon's does, to rescue the novel from charges of discursive racism, is by resorting, again, to a statement the historical author makes.

The closest Shields comes to acknowledge the complex racial politics in Canada is in her essay "Writing from the Edge." Following her matter-of-fact statement that "there is [a] divide between the dominant culture and the marginal culture" (*Startle* 133), she highlights the fact that the Canadian literary canon has been diversified so that it now includes "immigrant writers." If she uses the rather neutral term "immigrant writers" as opposed, say, to writers of color, it is because she finds this shift to be "risky." "Canadians, these days," she writes, "are directing serious attention to that very seething, smoking, chaotic, multicultural muddle which is, in fact, our reality. This is risky; one almost wants to whisper—un-Canadian" (*Startle* 23). Shields does not spell out what exactly these risks entail and the negative terms in which she references multiculturalism are ambivalent at best, virtually echoing Reta's own binary logic of order versus chaos. Perhaps what Shields has in mind is "the spectre of political correctness [that] has...plac[ed] limits on our available narrative field, restraining even the possibilities of observation, let alone development" (*Startle* 127). Political correctness, no matter some of its chilling effects in Canada, can hardly be the reason why the Muslim woman is presented at once as a tantalizing and disconcerting figure. Shields's view that multicultural politics is "un-Canadian" is an explicit reference to the civility that has been a foundational concept and practice in the formation of Canada and its literary tradition. Canadian civility, Daniel Coleman writes, "operates like a trance that insulates us from the realities in our midst" (26); it "shepherds people onto the path of progress because it names a future ideal as if it were a present norm"; what's more, it "operates as a mode of internal management: the subjects of the civil order discipline their conduct in order to participate in the civil realm, and they themselves gain or lose legitimacy in an internally striated civil society depending on the degrees to which they conform to its ideals" (29). Shields's writing, including *Unless*, exemplifies this civility, but this novel, as I hope to have demonstrated, puts civility to the test. One has to uncouple the novel from its historical author in order to unscramble what Reta's coupling of "a memory of a memory" advocates. If the critical responses the Muslim woman has elicited so far address subalternity but leave it at the comfortable level of ambivalence, it is because Canadian literary studies remains caught in a quandary: negotiating the imperative to pursue anti-racist critiques but often doing so in the name of the proverbial Canadian civility.

NOTES

1. Virtually all of the essays in this collection are interspersed with excerpts from Shields's books which, selected by the two editors, are designed to further illuminate and reinforce Shields's points.
2. See, for example, Ramon (2008) and McGregor, as well as the other critics I reference below.
3. Lest I be misunderstood, my intention here is not to devalue either the importance of reading *Unless* from a feminist perspective or the particular feminist readings that the novel has elicited. Rather, my point is that gender and "race" are contingent and interconnected when it comes to interrogating marginalized others.
4. Coming to this term from different directions—Bhabha via postcolonialism, Soja via urbanism and Henri Lefebvre—they both posit third space as a departure from dualisms: a radical re-conceptualization of bounded space, it produces an in-betweenness that enables marginalized subjects to

reconstitute dominant notions of space and power relations. See Bhabha (36–9), Soja (248–9).

5. See, for example, Guenther.

6. Beckman-Long writes that Shields's "portrayal of Reta as a supposedly representative subject is parodic and her parody is subversive" (110).

7. To avoid cumbersome formulations, in what follows "author" refers to the author function, unless otherwise indicated.

8. Employing the concept of implied author, Beckman-Long makes a similar point, but her reading privileges the meta-autobiographical and feminist elements in the text (8–9, 109–26).

9. See http://honesteds.sites.toronto.com/history.html; http://www.mirvish.com/aboutus; and https://toronto.citynews.ca/2007/07/11/think-you-know-mirvish-some-honest-ed-facts-that-may-surprise-you/. Accessed August 22, 2018.

10. The URL reference to Dasgupta's article, "Readings in Contemporary American Fiction" (2005), no longer exists, and I have been unable to locate his article otherwise.

11. For an analysis of the different meanings of self-immolation, see Kitts.

Works Cited

Adorno, Theodor W. *Negative Dialectics*. Translated by E.B. Ashton, Routledge, 1990.

Ahmed, Sarah. "'Liberal Multiculturalism is the Hegemony—Its [*sic*] an Empirical Fact'—A response to Slavoj Žižek." *darkmatter*. February 18, 2008. http://www.darkmatter101.org/site/2008/02/19/'liberal-multiculturalism-is-the-hegemony—-its-an-empirical-fact'-a-response-to-slavoj-zizek/. Accessed August 17, 2018.

Anderson, Marjorie. "Interview with Carol Shields." *Prairie Fire*, vol. 16, no. 1, spring 1995, pp. 139–50.

Beckman-Long, Brenda. *Carol Shields and the Writer-Critic*. U of Toronto P, 2015.

Berger, John. *Ways of Seeing*. British Broadcasting Corporation and Penguin Books, 1972.

Bhabha, Homi K. *The Location of Culture*. Routledge, 2004.

Boehmer, Elleke. *Stories of Women: Gender and Narrative in the Postcolonial Nation*. Manchester UP, 2005.

Brown, Wendy. *Regulating Aversion: Tolerance in the Age of Identity and Empire*. Princeton UP, 2006.

Chariandy, David. "Black Canadian Literature: Fieldwork and 'Post-Race.'" *The Oxford Handbook of Canadian Literature*, edited by Cynthia Sugars, Oxford UP, 2016. https://doi.org/10.1093/oxfordhb/9780199941865.001.0001.

Chow, Rey. "Postcolonial Visibilities: Questions Inspired by Deleuze's Method." *Deleuze and the Postcolonial*, edited by Simone Bignall and Paul Patton, Edinburgh UP, 2010, pp. 62–77.

_____. *Entanglements, or Transmedial Thinking about Capture*. Duke UP, 2012.

Coleman, Daniel. "From Canadian Trans to TransCanada: White Civility to Wry Civility in the CanLit Project." *Trans.Can.Lit: Resituating the Study of Canadian Literature*, edited by Smaro Kamboureli and Roy Miki, Wilfrid Laurier UP, 2007, pp. 25–43.

Death, Carl. "Counter-Conducts as a Mode of Resistance: Ways of 'Not Being Like That' in South Africa." *Global Society*, vol. 30, no. 2, 2016, pp. 201–17.

Demetriou, Olga. "Counter-Conduct and the Everyday: Anthropological Engagements with Philosophy." *Global Society*, vol. 30, no. 2, 2016, pp. 218–37.

Foucault, Michel. *Discipline and Punish*. Translated by Alan Sheridan, Vintage, 1979.

_____. *Security, Territory, Population: Lectures at the Collège de France 1977–1978*, edited by Michel Senellart, translated by Graham Burchell, Palgrave Macmillan, 2007.

_____. "What Is an Author?" *Language, Counter-Memory, Practice: Selected Essays and Interviews by Michel Foucault*, edited by Donald F. Bouchard, translated by Donald F. Bouchard and Sherry Simon, Cornell UP, 1977, pp. 113–38.

Frye, Northrop. "Conclusion." *Literary History of Canada*, 2nd ed., edited by Carl F. Klinck, U of Toronto P, 1976, pp. 333–61.

Gilroy, Paul. *Against Race: Imagining Political Culture beyond the Color Line*. Belknap P of Harvard UP, 2000.

Guenther, Bethany. "Carol Shields and Simone de Beauvoir: Immanence, Transcendence, and Women's Work in *A Fairly Conventional Woman, The Stone Diaries*, and *Unless*." *Studies in Canadian Literature*, vol. 35, no. 1, 2010, pp. 147–64.

Huehls, Mitchum. *After Critique: Twenty-First-Century Fiction in a Neoliberal Age*. Oxford UP, 2016.

Huysen, Andreas. "Introduction: World Cultures, World Cities." *Other Cities, Other Worlds: Urban Imaginaries in a Globalizing Age*, edited by Andreas Huysen, Duke UP, 2008, pp. 1–32.

Kitts, Margo, editor. *Martyrdom, Self-Sacrifice, and Self-Immolation: Religious Perspectives on Suicide*. Oxford UP, 2018.

McGregor, Hannah. "Reading Closely: Discursive Frames and Technological Mediations in Carol Shields' *Unless*." *Canadian Literature*, vol. 217, Summer 2013, pp. 35–52.

Moreiras, Alberto. *The Exhaustion of Difference: The Politics of Latin American Cultural Studies*. Duke UP, 2001.

Moreno-Álvarez, Alejandra. "The Empowerment of Women's Silences in *Unless* by Carol Shields." *Representing Minorities: Studies in Literature and Criticism*, edited by Larbi Tonaf and Soumin Boutkhil, Cambridge Scholars, 2006, pp. 98–105.

Ramon, Alex. *Liminal Spaces: The Double Art of Carol Shields.* Cambridge Scholars, 2008.

———. "Domestic Violence? A Reassessment of the Fiction of Carol Shields." *Visions of Canada / Visions du Canada,* edited by Catherine Bates et. al., Canadian Studies in Europe, vol. 6, The Central European Association for Canadian Studies, 2007, pp. 19–34.

Rosenthal, Caroline. "Textual and Urban Spaces in Carol Shields' *Unless.*" *Reading(s) from a Distance: European Perspectives on Canadian Women's Writing,* edited by Charlotte Sturgess and Martin Kuester, Wissner-Verlag, 2008, pp. 175–86.

Roy, Wendy. "Unless the World Changes: Carol Shields on Women's Silencing in Contemporary Culture." *Carol Shields: The Arts of a Writing Life,* edited by Neil K. Besner, Prairie Fire P, 2003, pp. 125–32.

Shields, Carol. "Carol Shields." *22 Provocative Canadians: In the Spirit of Bob Edwards,* edited by Keith Longpré and Margaret Dickson, Bayeux Arts, 1999, pp. 26–31.

———. *Startle and Illuminate: Carol Shields on Writing,* edited by Anne Giardini and Nicholas Giardini. Toronto: Random House, 2017.

———. *Unless.* Toronto: Random House, 2002.

———. "A View from the Edge of the Edge." *Carol Shields and the Extra-Ordinary,* edited by Marta Dvořák and Manina Jones, McGill-Queen's UP, 2007, pp. 17–29.

Shields, Rob. "Spatial Stress and Resistance: Social Meanings of Spatialization." *Space and Social Theory: Interpreting Modernity and Postmodernity,* edited by Georges Benko and Ulf Strohmayer, Blackwell, 1997, pp. 186–202.

Smyth, Gerry, and Jo Croft. "Introduction: Culture and Domestic Space." *Our House: The Representation of Domestic Space in Modern Culture,* edited by Gerry Smyth and Jo Croft, Rodopi, 2006, pp. 1–26.

Soja, Ed. "Planning in/for Postmodernity." *Space and Social Theory: Interpreting Modernity and Postmodernity,* edited by Georges Benko and Ulf Strohmayer, Blackwell, 1997, pp. 236–49.

Staines, David. "Introduction." *The Worlds of Carol Shields,* edited by David Staines, U of Ottawa P, 2014, pp. 1–3.

Steffler, Margaret. "A Human Conversation about Goodness: Carol Shields' *Unless.*" *Studies in Canadian Literature,* vol. 34, no. 2, 2009, pp. 223–44.

Stovel, Nora Foster. "'Because She's a Woman': Myth and Metafiction in Carol Shields's *Unless.*" *English Studies in Canada,* vol. 32, no. 4, 2006, pp. 51–73.

Warminski, Andrzej. *Readings in Interpretation: Hölderlin, Hegel, Heidegger.* U of Minnesota P, 1987.

Afterword: "Little Shocks of Recognition": Carol Shields's Book Reviews

Alex Ramon

"I find it hard to separate my life as a reader from that as a writer," Carol Shields claims in "Writers Are Readers First" (in Giardini 2016, 40). The book reviews that Shields wrote throughout her career testify to that vital interrelation. Yet these reviews have thus far received scant attention within Shields studies, and their importance has perhaps been undervalued even by the author herself. "I love having written reviews, but feel a good deal of anxiety while in the midst of writing them," Shields confessed to Blanche Howard in an email message dated June 16, 1997 and published in the collection of their correspondence *A Memoir of Friendship* (2007). "I don't quite understand this but it makes me reluctant to take on too many" (Shields in Howard 2007, 363). In fact, belying the modesty of her own assessment, Shields amassed a significant body of book reviews during her literary career. Published between the late 1970s and the early 2000s, these critiques were initially written for specialist academic journals and then, later, commissioned for national and international publications such as *The Globe and Mail*, *The New York Times Book Review*, and *The Times Literary Supplement*, as Shields's own literary

A. Ramon (✉)
University of Lodz, Lodz, Poland

N. F. Stovel (ed.), *Relating Carol Shields's Essays and Fiction*,
https://doi.org/10.1007/978-3-031-11480-9_13

celebrity increased. I first discovered the reviews while researching in the Shields fonds in Library and Archives Canada in Ottawa and was immediately struck by the ways in which they reflected and refracted the concerns of Shields's fiction through a direct dialogic engagement with the writing of some of her contemporaries. With the renewed emphasis on Shields's non-fiction inspired by the publications of Beckman-Long's study *Carol Shields and the Writer-Critic* (2015) and the Giardinis' edition *Startle and Illuminate: Carol Shields on Writing* (2016), now seems a particularly appropriate moment for further reflection on Shields's reviews and their place within her wider literary production.

"A Delicate Balancing Act": Approaches, Style, and Development in Shields's Reviews

The sharing of recommendations of particular books, the pleasure of discovering new writers and of commenting on the evolving work of established favorites, was always an important part of Shields's experience, as her correspondence with Howard, for one, attests. While Shields's private judgments on literary texts could be both acerbic and unorthodox—letters find her briskly dismissing *The Double Hook* as "dreadful imitation Faulkner" (Shields in Howard 2007, 10), *The English Patient* as "awfully studied, terribly solemn, taking itself incredibly seriously" (274) and *The Blind Assassin* as "a long dull read" (474)—her published reviews generally lack such sharpness of tone, indulging in few outright "pans" or sweeping dismissals. [1] This is certainly not to suggest that Shields avoids negative judgment in her reviews: her pieces on Rachel Ingalls's *The End of Tragedy*, Whitney Otto's *How to Make an American Quilt* and, as will be discussed here, Erica Jong's *Fear of Fifty: A Midlife Memoir* offer critical perspectives on aspects of each of these works. However, the texts' perceived shortcomings are examined in an even-handed way, with a sense of disappointment at opportunities missed, reflecting the spirit of open-minded inquiry in which Shields's reviews are generally conducted. "Reviewers do have power," Shields acknowledged in a piece reflecting on the craft of reviewing: "Book-reviewing is a delicate balancing act requiring not obsequiousness or scorn, but respect," she avers; "And, if in doubt, a little humility never goes amiss." [2] Overall, the belief expressed in *Swann* "that books, particularly fiction, form a valuable core of experience" (Shields 1987, 178) radiates throughout Shields's reviews, and when she finds a book that she likes—be it Angela Carter's *Artificial Fire*, Alice Munro's *Friend of my Youth*, Toni Morrison's *Paradise*, or Cynthia Ozick's *The Puttermesser Papers*—she writes about it with a sense of celebration.

With occasional forays into poetry and non-fiction, Shields primarily reviewed prose fiction (novels or short story collections), and work by British and North American women writers predominates; indeed, it appears that Shields was often tasked with reviewing texts by authors with whom her own writing shared perceived stylistic or thematic affinities. (The by-line attached to her review of Otto's *How to Make an American Quilt* makes the connection explicit by including the detail that Shields's *A Fairly Conventional Woman* "takes place at a quilters' convention"— although, as noted, Shields disliked Otto's novel.)

Varying in length, the reviews cover the expected elements of each text, paying attention to plot, form, structure, language, and characterization; also notable is Shields's ability to combine such detail with a summary of the particular qualities of a writer in an economical, epigrammatic phrase. "Anita Brookner's greatest gift ... is to combine a rare sophistication and felicity of language with an even rarer innocence of vision" is Shields's opening salvo in her review of Brookner's *Lewis Percy* (Shields 1990, "Innocence...", n.p). Of Anne Tyler's *A Patchwork Planet* she avers: "Tyler has always been a warmly compassionate recorder of middle-class America, yet one who is wide open to the riffs, the reverberations, the trajectories of the dislocated" (Shields 1998, "Odd Jobs," 12). Of Morrison's *Paradise*, she notes, "as in all [Morrison's] novels, the mythic and the colloquial share the same breathing space" (Shields 1998, n.p). The reviews also demonstrate a novelist's gift for evocation through figurative language and include many appealing, lyrical turns of phrase. Tyler, Shields writes, "extends towards [her characters] a corona of sympathy" (Shields 1998, "Odd Jobs," 12). The protagonists of Kate Jennings's *Snake* are described as living "lives that throb with emptiness" (Shields 1997, "Scenes..." 11). The chapter endings and beginnings in Peter Carey's *The Unusual Life of Tristam Smith* "bite down on each other like sets of teeth" (Shields, "Vorstand...", 1995, n.p). Such observations demonstrate that Shields brought to reviewing the same care and attention to phrase-making that distinguish her fiction.

Indeed, to read the reviews in sequence is to bear witness to the development of Shields's critical voice, which grows in assurance, particularly when it comes to making connections and placing texts within broader contexts. One of her first published pieces, on Janis Rapoport's *Winter*

Flowers, begins with two simple statement of value—"There are some fine poems in this collection. At her best Janis Rapoport can be lyrical and reflective, witty and precise"—and then proceeds to a close textual analysis of a selection of the poems (Shields 1979, 79); there is no attempt here, however, to consider the collection in a wider framework related to Rapoport's earlier work or contemporary Canadian poetry. Later reviews, in contrast, tend more toward expansiveness, contextualizing the text in question with references to wider themes or including a reflection upon relevant issues. For instance, Shields's *TLS* omnibus review of four Eudora Welty-associated texts offers a thorough appraisal of the concept of Southern writing and the value (or limitation) of viewing writers in terms of regional affiliations, while her response to Richard Bausch's *Rare & Endangered Species* begins with a commentary on the status of domesticity in fiction. Similarly, her piece on John Irving's *A Widow for One Year* commences with a (self-implicating) reflection on novelists' creations of writer protagonists: "We know we shouldn't do it…but we can't help ourselves. We fiction writers love to write about writers" (Shields, " Writing…", 1998, D16). The combination of a wry, ironic tone ("We should be writing about dentists and manicurists, *of course* we should," D16) with a clear self-defense ("If writers don't write about writers, and the brimming satisfaction of putting words to paper, who will?", D16) is evidently inspired by Shields's own work and reflects her tendency to create writer protagonists in her novels and short stories, from *Small Ceremonies* through *Swann* to *Unless.*

Such self-referentiality indicates that, as attentive as she was to the particulars of individual authorial voices, Shields also used reviewing as an opportunity for reflection upon her own practices and preoccupations as a writer, and, more broadly, as a means to formulate and develop her vision of what literary fiction might be. Her review of Bausch's book remains emblematic in this sense, as Shields commends Bausch for what she identifies as his "unfashionable" focus on the quotidian and the domestic:

> While many of his male counterparts in the 1970's and 1980's were busy writing dense or elliptical fictions ignited by cross-cultural gunpowder or linguistic gamesmanship, Mr. Bausch consistently offered readers the intimate particulars of contemporary human beings who were trapped, and also exhilarated, by their domestic arrangements.
>
> Domestic fiction, of course, has stirred its share of suspicion in the second half of our century. But it is an undeniable fact that every man, woman

and child possesses a domestic life. People, real and imaginary, live for the most part in that highly specific—and richly allegorical—place they persist in calling home. And they are ineluctably *at home* with their wallpaper, cereal bowls and magazine subscriptions, their underwear and check stubs, their birthdays, their vitamin pills, their brilliantly functioning lawn sprinklers, their nights of despair and moments of redemption. (Shields, "The Life You Lead...," 1994, 6)

As Anne Giardini notes in her "Foreword" to this volume, Shields was consistently drawn to "vital material that had been overlooked, minimized, and marginalized" (Giardini, xx). Echoing ideas explored in a range of her essays, from "Arriving Late, Starting Over" and "Narrative Hunger and the Overflowing Cupboard" to the aforementioned "Writers Are Readers First," Shields's defense of domesticity in fiction connects here with the idea of "redemption," a key concept in much of her critical writing and a word that recurs with notable frequency throughout her reviews. Another early piece, a review of Don Coles's poetry collection *The Prinzhorn Collection*, praises the volume in the following terms:

> Coles is clearly drawn to those who slip through the net of history, leaving behind no word, not even a photograph ... These shadowy figures ...nevertheless led lives of incident and resonance and ... for all we know, may have powerfully affected others.
> Coles tracks more than the neglected person; he seeks out those elusive moments which, though unrecorded, he feels must have existed. (Shields 1983, 42–3)

Written between the publication of the *Happenstance* novels, with their subversive inquiries into what constitutes a "historical sense," Shields's remarks about Coles's poetry clearly echo and anticipate some of the abiding concerns of her fiction: namely, her preoccupation with the fallibility and selectivity of auto/biographical and historiographical processes, and her concern with whose stories are "recorded," and how. These concerns, central to *Swann*, and her two "auto/biografictions" *The Stone Diaries* and *Larry's Party*, indicate that, for Shields, the function served by fiction is fundamentally (counter-)historical, offering the opportunity for a detailed examination of the lives that "slip through the net of history": a redemption of "the neglected person" and "those elusive moments" deemed insignificant within conventional "Maps and Chaps" approaches to historiography. Such patriarchal approaches have "carried forward only the sketchiest outline of society," Shields argues in "To Write Is to Raid" (in Giardini 2016, 61); and in the essay "History and the Novel" she indicates how literary fiction might serve to fill the gaps:

> [w]e can … read Jane Austen and Dickens and George Eliot and F. Scott Fitzgerald and Hemingway and Margaret Atwood and find out what people ate, what they spent their money on, how people thought, what they did when they were alone in a room, the jokes they told, the forces that tormented them, in short the real history of their times and how that history is inevitably no more than one individual's take on the world. (Shields, "History and the Novel," CSF1, Box 63, f.11)

In their diverse ways, the writers to whom Shields responds most profoundly in her reviews provide such accounts: "a history of the human being to which we are blinded by the traditional histories of flashing, dramatic events" to use Stanley Cavell's phrase (Cavell 1984, 190–1). Importantly, however, the focus on the daily reality of characters that Shields advocates does not preclude or negate an engagement with the fantastical; on the contrary, these aspects may be viewed as deeply interrelated. In her review of *The Puttermesser Papers*, for instance, Shields commends Ozick for "playing with our notions of 'reality,' reminding us that the chronicles of our lives must expand so that they contain not just a series of registered events, but the fantastic and elaborate threads of daydream and desire, a mingling of longing and metaphor" (Shields, "Faux Biography," 1997, D16). This remark clearly evokes the imaginative transformations of personal history undertaken by Daisy Goodwill Flett throughout *The Stone Diaries*, "the supplementing, modifying," the "marching straight into the machinery of invention" (Shields 1993, 282, 311) with which the protagonist is engaged as she "thinks" her life story and the interwoven stories of acquaintances, friends, and family members. This is precisely the approach that Shields's essay "The New New New Fiction" sees as broadly characteristic of literature after postmodernism: "A return to realism, yes, but a reality that is enormously expanded so that those private areas of human consciousness have found a way into our fictions" (Shields in Giardini 2016, 127).

To develop such "expanded chronicles" of human lives is, for Shields, one of the great opportunities that fiction offers, and this perspective makes the relatively rare occasions on which she reviews *non-fiction* texts particularly compelling. Shields's reviews of three diverse examples of life-writing—Annie Dillard's *An American Childhood,* Erica Jong's *Fear of Fifty: A Midlife Memoir,* and Ruby Side Thompson's diaries, collected by Bonnie Thompson Glaser and Ann Martin Worster in *Ruby: An Ordinary Woman,* published in 1987, 1994, and 1995 respectively—are especially illuminating in this regard. These three texts by American women authors prompt contrasting responses that serve to illuminate some of the issues around auto/biographical discourses with which Shields so consistently engaged, further exemplifying the connections that Beckman-Long has highlighted between Shields's practices as writer and critic.

"METICULOUS MAPPING OF THE HOME TERRITORY": ANNIE DILLARD'S *AN AMERICAN CHILDHOOD*

In "Double Happiness," her essay about the shared reading experiences that formed an integral part of her communication with her mother, Anne Giardini notes that "an important book in our discussions was Annie Dillard's ... *An American Childhood*" (Giardini 2003, 19). Shields also reviewed Dillard's book for *The Globe and Mail* upon its publication in 1987, and her enthusiastic response to it further reveals how significant the text was for her in its precise and detailed evocation of "the interior life of a child who is arriving at awareness" (Shields 1987, "What it's like....," n.p). Shields begins her review by referring rather pointedly to the context in which Dillard presents this coming to consciousness: the suburbs of Pittsburgh, P.A., where, as Shields wryly notes in her introductory paragraph, "middle-class values rule and kill." The context is significant, recalling Shields's remarks about her own suburban American background and her gradual growth in confidence in its value in terms of providing material for her writing: "I ... came to see that all human relationships were complex, even those in that risky literary territory known as the suburban middleclass, which has been too often neglected in our fiction" (Shields in Giardini 2016, 35). Similarly, from the allegedly limited and limiting context of the Pittsburgh suburbs, Shields argues, Dillard develops a rich and revelatory text that is "exhilarating ...to read... because it extends the range of what on this planet can be loved" (Shields 1987).

"I saw that I could become a writer if I paid attention, if I was careful, if I observed the rules, and then, just as carefully, broke them," Shields notes in "Writers Are Readers First" (Shields in Giardini 2016, 40). Dillard's memoir offers a sustained meditation on the necessity of being

alert, of "paying attention": "Even at 10 [Dillard] knows that real engagement with the world lies in the passion for discovery and in a patient,
meticulous mapping of the home territory" (Shields 1987). What such
engagement entails is, once again, a focus on the details of dailiness, the
diverse contours of which may, if properly attended to, result in moments
of epiphanic vision: the kind of "random illuminations" that Shields herself identified as a route to meaning. "This is the way a child stays awake,
Dillard writes, by being alert to such moments, by remembering everything and by shutting off the debilitating egoism that keeps experience at
a distance" (Shields 1987).

The best literature, Shields argues in "Writers Are Readers First,"
"shortens the distance we must travel to discover that our most private
perceptions are universally felt" (Shields in Giardini, 34), a perspective
given verbatim to Frederic Cruzzi's friend Mimi in *Swann* (Shields 1987,
179). Dillard's book provides precisely this sense of connection, which
Shields figures as "countless little shocks of recognition" (Shields 1987)
between reader and writer. Written in language that Shields describes as
"fuller, more exuberant than the sometimes nibbled-seeming prose of
[Dillard's 1974 nonfiction] *Pilgrim at Tinker Creek*," the "enchantment"
of *An American Childhood* lies, for her, in its charting of such moments,
and Shields's review identifies some of Dillard's affections through one of
her own favorite methods: the list. Dillard, she writes, loves

> bugs, books, rocks, jokes, backyard fences, the elasticity of human skin, the
> cadence of certain Biblical passages (though not God), and she especially
> loves the mysterious, unknowable cleft between children and adults.
> (Shields 1987)

It is difficult not to read this review without recalling the fragmentary
flashbacks in the "Illness and Decline" chapter of *The Stone Diaries* in
which random scenes of Daisy's girlhood are figured as "[p]ictures that fly
into her head" (337): a series of vivid sense memories that range from
snap dragons to pancakes, the "dazzling iridescence" of oil spilled on the
road to the experience of "falling backward into a pile of leaves" (337–9).
In this way, Shields's review makes explicit an intertextual dialogue
between *The Stone Diaries* and Dillard's memoir as portraits of girls'
"arriving at awareness" through a close attention to details that suggest
the world's interwoven mystery and mundanity: "'The trick of reason,'

Dillard writes, 'is to get the imagination to seize the actual world'" (Shields 1987).

In addition, Shields's review also anticipates aspects of her unfinished final novel *Segue*, in which the narrator, the 67-year-old poet Jane Sexton, possesses a notebook in which she lists "new and possible subjects" for her poetry. These subjects include "the smell of taxis, the texture of bread, sleep, chewing gum, Picasso, flints and arrowheads, the cello, the shape of coastal islands and the children who are born on islands, cabbage, shingle beaches, feet, Styrofoam, photographs of the newborn [and] a medieval wooden Christ image" (Shields 2004, 5). The list suggests a direct homage to Dillard, whose "gift for redemption," Shields concludes, "makes her one of the most wide awake writers in America" (Shields 1987). The eclectic nature of *Segue*'s litany reflects a similarly democratic interest in the variety of elements which comprise the world, and a conviction that, for the "wide awake writer," each of these elements are worthy of attention in poetry or prose.

"Unrevised Ramblings": Erica Jong's *Fear of Fifty: A Midlife Memoir*

An American Childhood provides, for Shields, an exemplary incidence of a writer using her intimate experiences to fashion a highly literary, philosophical, and relatable text that invites the reader into close participation and engagement. By contrast, Shields presents Erica Jong's *Fear of Fifty* as precisely the opposite kind of memoir: "a sprawling, voyeuristic *People*'s magazine profile that has mysteriously gone from writer to reader unedited" (Shields, "Terrified...," 1994, n.p). While Shields strives to find some praiseworthy qualities in *Fear of Fifty*, her review of Jong's book is notable as one of the most negative of all her published reviews, and is therefore highly instructive in outlining what Shields perceived to be some of the pitfalls of life-writing as a genre, notably its failure to do justice to the complexities of "the arc of a human life" (Shields in Giardini 2016, 55). [3]

Shields begins the review by expressing some admiration for Jong's seminal first novel *Fear of Flying*, which, published in the context of second-wave feminism some 20 years before the memoir, "set... the tone for the early seventies [and] with a stroke redefined our sense of the heroine in fiction" (Shields 1994). In Isadora Wing, Shields notes, Jong created a protagonist who "knew what she wanted" and "what she wanted she got." However, it becomes apparent that Shields views Jong's approach in her memoir, with its focus on failed relationships, financial woes, and addictions, as much more problematic. The text's subtitle, Shields suggests, might have been "How I Didn't Get What I Wanted After All," as she identifies in Jong's writing a deep sense of dissatisfaction that is superficially catalogued yet never truly explored: "This is a sad book, particularly sad, because Jong herself doesn't appear to recognize the depth of its sadness" (Shields 1994).

Indeed, superficiality and an apparent lack of perceptiveness are among Shields's main complaints about *Fear of Fifty*. The text, she contends, only skims the surface of the midlife malaise it purports to explore: "[t]he problems are real. What feels stunted in this book is the level of emotional response" (Shields 1994). Where Dillard's accounts of her youthful experiences in *An American Childhood* are marked by an attentiveness that creates "little shocks of recognition" for the reader, Jong's writing exhibits "carelessness" that prohibits such connection. Quoting examples of "banalities" and "tossed off absurdities," Shields contends that *Fear of Fifty* is comprised of "unrevised ramblings," and challenges Jong's claims to universality in the text: "Jong believes her life experience is not very different from that of other women, but most women reaching the half-century have long since dealt with what she is belatedly questioning" (Shields 1994). This rebuke is particularly significant since Shields elsewhere identified herself precisely as she identifies Jong here: namely, as a woman born between the two feminist movements.

Shields also highlights what she views as pretentiousness and an air of flaunted privilege in Jong's approach: "the unabashed name-dropping, place-dropping, the endless self- absorption, the allying herself with Colette, with George Sand" (Shields 1994). Self-absorption, in particular, is the aspect of *Fear of Fifty* that most stirs Shields's skepticism. If Dillard's text advocates a "shutting off [of] the debilitating egoism that keeps experience at a distance," then Jong's memoir too frequently indulges in precisely this kind of limiting self-focus.

Shields's review acknowledges some strengths in the work: "[w]hen Jong takes her time…the writing is rich in insight and attentive to its internal rhythms." Notably, though, it is Jong's focus on a humble object, rather than her cataloguing of signifiers of privilege, such as "parties, restaurants [and] rented houses in Italy," that Shields admires most: "an early poem about the lowly onion, reprinted in this book, makes one want to weep for so much lost promise" (Shields 1994). As an iconic writer of second-wave feminism, Jong's perspective remains valuable, nonetheless. Written "with candour as well as carelessness," her memoir reveals what Shields identifies as "a problem that has plagued women from the beginning of the feminist movement—the desire, and also the impossibility, of having it all." Shields closes the review by wondering about the "next instalment" of Jong's memoirs—"when she reaches 60? 70?"—and whether they will disclose "the choice she ultimately makes." [4] Thus, the mostly negative review concludes in an open-ended manner, advocating a view of life-writing as an ongoing process for the female subject.

"Found Treasure": *Ruby: An Ordinary Woman*

Despite their perceived differences in terms of affect and approach, Dillard's and Jong's memoirs are both texts by acclaimed authors who are writing for established readerships. *Ruby: An Ordinary Woman* is a very different kind of text, however: a collection of diaries which were never intended for publication, but which, collated and edited some 25 years after their final entry, constitute, in Shields's view, "an important cultural artefact ... a found treasure" (Shields, "Her letters...," 1995). Ruby Thompson (1884–1970) was a New Jersey housewife whose journals—no less than 42 handwritten books written between the years 1909 and 1969—were discovered by her granddaughter, Bonnie Thompson Glaser. Together with the historian Ann Martin Worster, Thompson Glaser edited her grandmother's journals into a volume which was published in 1995. Shields's extremely positive response to the text, which she reviewed for the *Boston Globe*, must be read in the context of her concern with the ways in which the experiences of "ordinary" women have been erased from the historical record, an erasure which the belated publication of diaries such as Ruby's challenges and at least partially redeems. "Think of the loss to history if we fail to record the full and authentic lives of people, their private lives, their domestic lives," Shields notes in "To Write Is to Raid" (in Giardini 2016, 61). Ruby's diary provides one such "record" of the kind of life more usually "lost to history."

Shields's review opens by drawing attention precisely to questions of anonymity and identity in relation to the authorial subject: "Who *is* Ruby Side Thompson? Who indeed?" (Shields, "Her letters...," 1995). Perhaps unsurprisingly, Shields proceeds to highlight the text's subtitle and to deconstruct its implications: "the word ordinary is troubling in itself, for surely we are all ordinary, or else none of us is." The review continues in an inquiring mode, as Shields wonders, "What can be done with this teasing conundrum, and how do we place a value on those elements that make up the ordinary?" (Shields 1995).

Ruby's diary provides one answer, revealing the existential anxiety of its subject through her detailed recording of her everyday experiences. The book's value, for Shields, lies in its vivid account of Ruby's daily struggles, which include a "tumultuous marriage," frustrated, unfulfilled ambitions to write fiction, and her experience of motherhood to seven sons. If "most of [Ruby's] diary entries are cries of frustration" about her lot, Shields also draws attention to the shifts in Ruby's attitudes, vacillations which point to wider dilemmas and patterns: "Daily she struggles between guilt and duty, between defeat and resolution, again and again vowing to take control of her life, and then letting her courage slip away, eroded by fatigue or else interrupted by a shining moment of joy" (Shields 1995).

In highlighting Ruby's vexed negotiations between her social roles and her inner desires, Shields's review echoes her piece on *An American Childhood* by once again establishing an intertextual dialogue with *The Stone Diaries*. Like Daisy, Ruby is "a 20th century woman" and Shields makes a case for her marginality too: "[N]either rich nor poor, [h]er education was adequate... but not as good as such an intelligent woman deserved.... Socially middle-class and aesthetically middle-brow, she was a woman who ought to have ended up in the middle of her society; instead she lived her life at the margins." The formulation explicitly evokes Warren's remarks in his "theory" about Daisy's depression in the "Sorrow" chapter of *The Stone Diaries*: "My mother is a middle-aged woman, a middle-class woman, a woman of moderate intelligence and medium-sized ego and average good luck, so that you would expect her to land somewhere near the middle of the world. Instead she's over there at the edge. The least vibration could knock her off" (Shields 1993, 252). However, where Daisy abandons "the practice of keeping a private journal," following the loss of her travel diary (Shields 1993, 156), and instead *(re-)thinks* her life experience, Ruby compulsively puts pen to paper; she is "an indefatigable diarist... asking questions, rejoicing, or else howling her disappointment—and writing it all down" (Shields 1995). A clear contrast becomes apparent here, for if *The Stone Diaries* posits autobiographical practice as an interwoven act of self-effacement and self-expression, in which the borders between self and other are continually destabilized, then *Ruby: An Ordinary Woman* is "without question, Ruby's book," a text in which "[t]he consciousness that might so easily have been erased is ... present in all its irascible and passionate splendour" (Shields 1995).

Still, Shields also highlights "a number of baffling gaps in Ruby's diary, a month a year, sometimes even several years" (Shields 1995). These "unexplained ellipses" evoke the "dark voids and unbridgeable gaps" of Daisy's life story (Shields 1993, 76) and inspire Shields to speculate whether these gaps "represent times of happiness for [Ruby], or moments when she is too exhausted and discouraged to lift up her pen" (Shields 1995). Beginning by placing a question mark over Ruby's identity, Shields suggests that the diaries offer their own, necessarily multifaceted, definitions. Ruby is a "swooning sensualist," "a feminist ahead of her time," and also a fine prose stylist, writing with "lyrical and elliptical elegance": "brilliant passages in this diary ... point to the compelling literary voice that might have been" (Shields 1995). Thus, the review critiques the notion of stable selfhood in relation to literary production as thoroughly as Shields's fiction does. "[W]hen a writer picks up a pen, a second self comes out, and this [also] applies ... to letters and even personal diaries," Shields argues in the essay "What You Use and What You Protect" (83). *Ruby: An Ordinary Woman* proves the case.

Indeed, a wider reflection upon the purpose and function of the diary form, particularly as employed by women writers, is also central to the *Ruby* review, as Shields wonders, "what is a diary for and [to] whom is it addressed?" The potential for "foolishness and self-indulgence" is acknowledged, and an echo of her critique of Jong's text is evident when she refers sharply to "Anais Nin and her marathon of self-absorption" (Shields 1995). However, references to Virginia Woolf and Lucy Maud Montgomery's journals are warmer, and, in Ruby's case, Shields presents the journal as both a necessary outlet for Ruby's creative urges and a way for her to overcome feelings of isolation and oppression. Ruby, Shields argues, "sees her diary as her only intimate," confiding in 1909, "I need to make a friend out of something even if it is only paper." "I will not pour out my troubles to anyone," Ruby writes: "What I must speak, I will write here." In this way, the diary form may provide for the "ordinary" woman an important vehicle for catharsis and creativity. As Ruby herself acknowledges: "This writing out, this writing down, is purgative... I know it's absurd, but I also know it works." It is in its vivid evocation of the existential anxieties woven into the texture of the quotidian, its attention to the seldom-documented realms of intimate female experience that *Ruby: An Ordinary Woman* establishes its importance as a cultural and historical artefact. By "enrich[ing] what we are able to understand about the private life of women in our era" (Shields 1995), the book is an example of life-writing that accomplishes what has been most often been the province of fiction, and is thus a text that speaks directly to Shields own literary project to challenge middle-class women's historical marginality and erasure in her work: her sustained commitment to "writing away the invisibility of women's lives" (Giardini 105–6).

Conclusion

Writing to Howard about Eudora Welty's book reviews, collected in the volume *A Writer's Eye*, Shields notes that "[a]t first I thought a collection of book reviews was of no interest to anyone, but, in fact, it provides a most compelling profile of her life" (Shields 2007, 302). To view Shields's reviews as adding up to a "profile of her life" may be to overstate the case. However, these critical pieces do offer a compelling, if necessarily partial, profile of Shields's *reading* life over 20 years, shedding light upon some key aspects of her own work and providing another perspective upon its profound intertextuality. As such, the reviews constitute an important, and thus far undervalued, part of Shields's literary output, one that may be productively placed between the discourses of the longer essays that she produced and her own literary fiction. The reviews speak to Shields's abiding preoccupations as a novelist and, in particular, as argued here, fruitfully extend her fiction's rigorous critique of auto/biographical practices, offering, as Christl Verduyn states of Shields's essays themselves in this volume, "another highly flexible mode of writing to reflect on and explore connections and contradictions in human experience" (Verduyn, 22). "I imagine the reader-writer relationship as a joint venture in the world," Shields remarked to Marjorie Anderson (Shields in Anderson 1995, 150). Appreciative and occasionally adversarial, revealing both expected and sometimes surprising intertexts and inspirations, the reviews administer their own "little shocks of recognition" to those who know Shields's fiction well, and serve to further illuminate her deeply interwoven identities as reader, writer, and critic.

NOTES

1. Shields's concern about not being tough enough as a reviewer was confided to Howard, in relation to Catherine Schine's *The Love Letter*, a novel that Shields confessed to finding "ditzy and dumb" and full of "thudding clichés." "I ended up writing 'around' the book rather than 'at' it," Shields admits. "I seem to lack the courage for demolishment, knowing how it feels I suppose" (Shields in Howard 2007, 319).

2. Carol Shields, "Writing Book Reviews," Carol Shields Fonds, 1st Accession, Box 62 [n.d., n.p]. Further references to fonds materials are cited in the text as "CSF1."

3. "I loved your Erica Jong review [and] couldn't help but think of those critics who accuse you of too much niceness," writes Blanche Howard to Shields, praising the piece for making its critical points "without ever indulging in the kind of hostility that goes under the name of reviewing. Acerbic but restrained, and subtle" (Howard 2007, 304).

4. In fact, the next instalment of Jong's memoir, *Seducing the Demon: Writing for my Life* was published 12 years later, when Jong was age sixty-six. The text was reviewed in *The New York Times* by Ron Powers in terms that unmistakably echo some of Shields's remarks about *Fear of Fifty*. Powers describes the book as a "headlong, disheveled memoir... an honest account of a life lies half-smothered between its pages" (Powers, "How to Save Your Own Life," *New York Times Book Review*, April 23, 2006). http://www.nytimes.com/2006/04/23/books/review/how-to-save-your-own-life.html

WORKS CITED

Anderson, Marjorie. "Interview with Carol Shields." *Prairie Fire* 16.1 (Spring 1995): 139–50.

Beckman-Long, Brenda. *Carol Shields and the Writer-Critic*. Toronto: University of Toronto Press, 2015.

Besner, Neil. *Carol Shields. The Arts of a Writing Life* (Winnipeg: Prairie Fire, 2003).

Cavell, Stanley. "The Ordinary as the Uneventful: A Note on the 'Annales Historians.'" In *Themes Out of School*. San Francisco: North PointPress, 1984: 184–94.

Eden, Edward and Dee Goertz (eds). *Narrative Hunger, and the Possibilities of Fiction*. Toronto: University of Toronto Press, 2003: 19–36.

Giardini, Anne. "Double Happiness." In *Carol Shields. The Arts of a Writing Life*. Besner, Neil (ed.) (Winnipeg: Prairie Fire, 2003): 15–22.

————, and Nicholas Giardini (eds). *Sparkle and Illuminate: Carol Shields on Writing*. Toronto: Random House Canada, 2016.

Howard, Blanche, and Allison Howard (eds), *A Memoir of Friendship: The Letters Between Carol Shields and Blanche Howard* (Toronto: Penguin Canada), 2007.

Powers, Ron. "How to Save Your Own Life." *New York Times Book Review* (23 April 2006) http://www.nytimes.com/2006/04/23/books/review/how-to-save-your-own-life.html Accessed: 8 September 2017.

Shields, Carol. "Arriving Late, Starting Over." In *How Stories Mean*. John Metcalf and J.R. (Tim) Struthers (eds). (Ontario: Porcupine's Quill, 1993a): 244–251.

———— "The Bleakest Vision: Review of *The End of Tragedy* by Rachel Ingalls" *The Globe and Mail* (28 March 1989): n.p.

————. *Collected Stories*. London: Harper Perennial, 2004.

———— "Erica Jong: 'Terrified' at 50: Review of *Fear of Flying* by Erica Jong." *The Globe and Mail* (30 July 1994a):

————. "Faux Biography is Extravagant, Daring Fiction: Review of *The Puttermesser Papers*." *The Globe and Mail* (14 June 1997a): D16.

————. "Her letters to the world, that never wrote to her: Review of *Ruby: An Ordinary Woman*." *Boston Globe* (30 April 1995a): B15, B18.

————. "Innocence in a State of Grace: Review of *Lewis Percy* by Anita Brookner." *The Globe and Mail* (7 April 1990): n.p.

————. "In Ontario: Review of *Friend of My Youth*." *London Review of Books* (7 February 1991a): 22–23.

————. "The Life You Lead May Be Your Own: Review of *Rare & Endangered Species* by Richard Bausch." *The New York Times Book Review* (14 August 1994b): 6.

————. "Lives of Unlikely Saints: Review of *Saint Maybe*." *The Globe and Mail* (31 August 1991b): D12.

————. "Lush Words and Loving Syntax: Review of Angela Carter's *Artificial Fire*." *The Globe and Mail* (23 March 1988): D17.

————. "Narrative Hunger and the Overflowing Cupboard." In *Carol Shields, Hunger, and the Possibilities of Fiction*. Eden, Edward and Dee Goertz (eds). *Narrative* Toronto: University of Toronto Press, 2003: 19–36.

————. "Odd Jobs: Review of *A Patchwork Planet* by Anne Tyler." *The New York Times Book Review* (19 April 1998a): 12–14.

————. "A Patchwork Effect: Review of *How to Make an American Quilt* by Whitney Otto. *The Globe and Mail* (6 April 1991c).

————. "Review of *Paradise* by Toni Morrison." *The Washington Post* (11 January 1998b): n.p.

————. "Review of *The Prinzhorn Collection* by Don Coles." *Contemporary Verse II: A Magazine of Contemporary Poetry Criticism* 7:3 (1983), 42–43.

————. "Review of *Winter Flowers* by Janis Rapoport." 1979: 79–80.

———— "Scenes from a Mismarriage: Review of *Snake* by Kate Jennings." The New York Times Book Review (5 November 1997b), 11.

————. *The Stone Diaries*. London: Fourth Estate, 1993b.

————. *Swann*. 1987. London: Fourth Estate, 2000.

————. "To Write is to Raid." in Giardini, *Sparkle and Illuminate: Carol Shields on Writing*. Toronto: Random House Canada, 2016a.I: 31–36.

———— "Voorstand, Go Home!: Review of *The Unusual Life of Tristan Smith* by Peter Carey." The New York Times Book Review (12 February 1995b): n.p.

———— "Wafts of the South: Review of Eudora Welty's *A Writer's Eye, The Optimist's Daughter, Losing Battles*, and Paul Binding's *The Still Moment: Eudora Welty: Portrait of a Writer*." *Times Literary Supplement*, 12 August 1994c): 20–21.

————. "Writers are Readers First." in Giardini, *Sparkle and Illuminate: Carol Shields on Writing*. Toronto: Random House Canada, 2016b.I: 1–15.

————. "What it's like to be awake: Review of *An American Childhood* by Annie Dillard" *The Globe and Mail*, f.6

————. "Writing Book Reviews." Carol Shields Fonds, National Library and Archives Canada, 1st Accession, Box 62 [n.d., n.p]

————. "Writing the Writer's Life: Review of *A Widow for One Year* by John Irving." *The Globe and Mail* (2 May 1998c): D16, D18.

Epilogue: Etching on Glass: Carol Shields's Re-vision

Aritha Van Herk

While I hesitate to wax anecdotal, as those who brag about encountering writers are apt to do, Carol Shields said to me once, in that light, fine-drawn voice that dispensed great wisdom with an elfin generosity: "Oh, I love the second to last edit, when you go through your work, and perform that final etching, buff the details to include small, intricate gestures." The rather domiciliary aspect of "buffing" as an act of polishing prose evokes both brisk efficacy and the near-nakedness of style that made Shields's writing so immodestly modest, layering this declaration as both personal appellant and writerly practice. The buffing image certainly delineates "Carol Shields," to the extent that she might be considered a construct of that charming sobriquet: she was an artistic buffer. Although we were acquaintances, I did not know Shields well in terms of intimate "real life," but I do believe I know her as a fictional character. "Carol Shields" would certainly buff her nails to a pearly gloss, and her shoes would wear the sheen of someone intolerant of scuffs.

A. Van Herk (✉)
University of Calgary, Calgary, AB, Canada

© The Author(s), under exclusive license to Springer Nature
Switzerland AG 2023
N. F. Stovel (ed.), *Relating Carol Shields's Essays and Fiction*,
https://doi.org/10.1007/978-3-031-11480-9_14

The sagacity of Carol Shields's precise "etching" is but one element of the many facets that make her work distinctive, her ambidextrous approach to writing effectively underlined in Nora Foster Stovel's Introduction, where she highlights "Crossing Borders and Breaking Rules," and in Christl Verduyn's analysis of how Shields deployed the essay's "freedom and opportunity." Most tellingly, "etching" speaks to writing that abjures carelessness, writing not driven by plot or action, the crass urgency of grist, but concerned with the rich effulgence of one of the lists included in her essay "Boxcars, Coat Hangers and Other Devices" in *Startle and Illuminate: Carol Shields on Writing*: "wallpaper ..., cereal bowls, cupboards, cousins, buses, local elections, head colds, cramps" (Giardini 28). The "lint trap[s]" (Giardini 32) that Shields notes in her essay "To Write is to Raid" and that contribute to the texture and taste of the worlds that she creates demand an attention that writers must both practice and cherish.

But the space for this "domestic" attention is often attenuated, and within an academic rubric for the teaching and learning of creative writing it accentuates a fascinating lacuna, the gap between the self-conscious deliberation of "writing" and "criticism," alongside the terrible intimacy of material and how that material comes alive on the page. The essays by Coral Anne Howells and Warren Cariou both address how Shields engages with the temptations of invisible dailiness and the terrorism of domesticity. As with the defining moments that Shields illuminates in her editing of *Dropped Threads*, as a writer, she highlights most the importance of paying attention to what might seem irrelevant: the gap in a sagging hem, the woman who has not had time to refresh her hair dye, the irritating—Sarah Maloney "irritates *herself*" (Giardini xxi)—twitch of an impatient colleague's foot. Shields said that her novel *Swann* was about "Appearance and Reality" (Giardini xx), but in that suggestion is the evidence that all writing tackles, the luminous and difficult, if occasionally liminal, boundary between what is seen and what is hidden, between what is wished for and what is attained. This probing of "appearance," as both Marta Dvořák's and Smaro Kamboureli's essays so assiduously delineate, performs that most effective of all Shields's sleights of hand, the importance of what is unimportant, the quotidian veneer that hides the momentous. This conundrum, this brilliant, and seemingly inconsequential legerdemain is what takes Shields's writing far beyond the conspiracy of plot or character, event, or sequelae.

Shields's ability to evade thematics in favor of fugitive asperity flints new writers in search of this elusive spark too. I once had a student in a Creative Writing class who every week argued insistently and with truly horribly passive aggressive courtesy ("May I make a point, Professor van Herk?" making me want to snarl, "NO, SHUT UP!") that all story needs a plot, complaining in his Ichabod Crane voice that his fellow students' stories had insufficient plot, and asking me, as the instructor, over and over again, how to work with plot effectively. My impatience with his desperate attachment to event—that Hemingwayesque preoccupation—grew apace, and finally, in a fit of long-suffering exasperation, I burst out, "Plot does not matter. Consequence does." It was my most Shieldsian moment ever, the revelation and the knowledge appearing with the actual speaking—consequence—and I wish only that I could relate that story to her, because I am certain she would relish it.

My revisited pleasure in her many apposite observations in *Startle and Illuminate* endorses my own perverse resistance to plottedness. Shields notes, "I'm comforted by something that Patrick White, the Australian novelist, once said: that he never worried about plot. What he wrote was life going on toward death" (Giardini 29). Only of course, a consequence of living, death, that is. Insufficient plot, or the appearance of insufficient plot—for can any event in any life be "insufficient"?—is akin to insufficient pain. As writers, we must be aware that every character suffers pain, each in her own inimitable way, whether that be the pain of a life lived carefully or the pain of improvidence and dissolution, heartbreak, and grief.

As a writing character then, although too uninteresting to appear in a Carol Shields story (I do not color-code my nightgowns with candles, as a woman says she does in Shields's essay "What You Use and What You Protect" (Giardini 51)—in fact, I own no nightgowns but sleep in long, loose cotton t-shirts), how do I etch plot avoidance in the already uneventful life of a writer and academic domestically attuned to the fine grains of consequence but certainly not much tortured or deprived. Shields makes some fine points about how little writing concerns itself with the suburban world, about how much contempt is coded into what is read as the safe, "bridge-and-tunnel" (yes that is a real description of suburban commuters) people. Hidden behind that designation is the realm of the middle-class woman, so seldom written about enthusiastically, yet almost always present as the reader of narratives that chronicle the etchings of unhappiness.

Shields argues that security and happiness are not excuses to avoid writing or to claim that one lacks a subject. Her recommended method of etching, her own development of how women writing "could make up in accuracy for what [we] lacked in scope, getting the details right, dividing every experience into its various shades and levels of anticipation," as she explains in her essay "Myths That Keep You from Writing" (Giardini 12–13), directly contradicts the general inclinations of contemporary fiction. While there is a trend toward issue-driven writing, and misery earns an avalanche of street credibility now, the illuminations of finely etched details should not be ignored, for often it is modesty that satisfies best, and quiet habitude becomes an important way to understand the news from another country. From Shields I have learned to cherish such satisfactions: how people air their laundry in Croatia; how Sunday afternoon after mass is the traditional time when northern Spaniards take vermouth together; how surprising to discover my sixth grade teacher's first name, pace Carol Shields's remarking, "how we loved to ferret out our teachers' first names." Such secluded, almost recondite information is reckless with possibility and clamors for story. Names, for example, first names and how they convey the tone of time (think of Mildred and Helen), and how they were treated as almost sexually private. Now first names are used as casually as if they wielded no authority, and my students think nothing of referring to me without title or surname. But yes, Carol Shields would appreciate my sixth-grade teacher's name, Clara Brady. We did not know her name was Clara; she was Mrs. Brady to us, and we said her name with a throb of fear and respect. Only later—last year, in fact, did I learn that before she became a teacher, Clara Brady defied her conservative father and set off to travel around Europe alone. I cannot resist etching that story, and although I have no biographical basis for these details, I imagine her scandalously roaming bohemian Europe all through the 1930s, finally running out of money and returning to Alberta, reduced to teaching in a mouse-infested one-room schoolhouse before marrying the most useless (although charming) of wastrel farmers, and turning into our fearsome grade six teacher at Edberg School. She was the one who chewed snuff and who slammed the leather strap down on her desk when she wanted to frighten us—gang of uncouth prairie rabble that we were—into silence. Her adventurous youth and "the arc" (Giardini 29) of her life are powerfully intriguing, although the plot points are mere ports of call. Consequence, all consequence, which accidentally coincided with my impudent curiosity.

Because, in life as in art, "There is a great deal of moving people around, and listening to what they are saying" (16) before any understanding of their motivations or sorrows arrives. This process entails, as Shields says, "the unsorted debris of existence" (Giardini 23) and how to translate it, make it work in a new dish, not as leftovers, but a whole new recipe, despite its original provenance. As Shields claims, "like my mother, who never threw out two tablespoons of leftover peas if she could help it" (Giardini 24), this becomes the garnish, the etched detail that turns the repast into a banquet or a condemned prisoner's last meal on earth, which traditionally has no peas—yes, the tradition is real—and if the prisoner has made no special request, he is given steak and eggs. I cannot help but wonder at the metaphor of Texas murderer James Edward Smith's last meal request for a lump of dirt, which he was denied. He had to settle for a cup of yogurt. That is the kind of detail that Carol Shields would relish, and the etching, the leap from two tablespoons of leftover peas to a final meal of a cup of yogurt would earn her attention, that alert tilt of the head that signaled her curiosity and private note-taking. We would both marvel at the murderer who asked for a single unpitted black olive, and how many prisoners choose pizza for their last meal. Wouldn't we ask for *coq au vin*?

Most telling too are Carol Shields's observations about the various shapes of fiction that inform her practice, as her practice informs her observations. The nine boxcars that she mentions as her structural sequence for *Small Ceremonies* (Giardini 24), or "the seven wire hangers on a coat rack" that position *The Box Garden* (Giardini 25), take on the wonderfully insistent symbolism of botanical scapes, those stems or stalks that come directly from a root, and form peduncles. (Ah, the very word, the sweet and useful language of biology, irresistible!) Typically, a scape takes the form of a long, leafless flowering stem rising directly from a bulb or rhizome, but here is the nub: it is the scapes of scallions, chives, garlic chives, and garlic that we use as flavor and garnish, potential etchings to the engraving art of cooking. Cooking and food are everywhere in Shields's oeuvre, precise as metronomes and yet as unusual as that Malvern pudding that Mercy Stone Goodwill is making before she dies in childbirth. In fact, it is the careful rendition of that particular dish that makes Mercy's death so effective, underlining the appalling immediacy of "the arc of a human life" (Giardini 29) and death awaiting all—consequence again. Shields's seemingly whimsical observation that Freytag's triangle looks "like nothing so much as a bent spatula" (Giardini 27) is a significant critique of the diagrammed plot that has so long cursed fiction: the "gently inclined line representing the rising action, then a sudden escalatory peak, followed by a steep plunge that demonstrates the denouement, and then the resolution... The novel as boxed kit, as scientific demonstration" (Giardini 27). Neither the diagram nor the architecture of its trajectory can encompass small acts of revenge, or the bandages that assuage hurt feelings, or how, in our individual and consequence-ridden lives, we seek to make the balance balance, or deliberately put a finger on the scale to imbalance the balance.

Contemporary fiction and critique would demand to know who "we" represents and how dare it pretend to encompass any "us," and what about the constructed nature of "the arc of a life" (Giardini 29), and what kind of lock closes the door to that house? Those unfathomable abstractions, those "linguistic skepticisms" that Shields notes in "What We've Discovered—So Far" (Giardini 109) do indeed belong to juiceless postmodernism: "a far too forgiving mode" (Giardini 109). Shields's astute observation about the etching of "absent narratives, the negative element of a photographic print—the dark void or unbridgeable gap, shadows, and mirages, the vivid dream that fades by morning, the missed bus, the men we didn't marry, the unconceived child, the confession murmured to a priest, or *not* murmured to a priest... This narrative lint refuses to collect itself" (Giardini 126–127), and so becomes the most compelling of narratives, and instead of plot the obstacles that drive a story forward become consequence.

In *Startle and Illuminate,* three sentences in particular characterize the inimitable affect of Carol Shields as a writer and creative thinker. They are casual, almost off-hand, but they recite the sagacity of one who invested her words with the intelligence and respect of significance, without making obeisance to plot-driven "great ideas" now translated as "big thinking"—our sizeism surely part of why the world is now in its current mess. Small but telling, observational rather than pronunciative, they are for all that, etchings of profound wisdom. The first is a metaphor, a warning about the "inferior fiction" (Giardini 95) of badly written love scenes, where Shields makes reference to "the beaten meringue of the Harlequin universe" (Giardini 95). Has there ever been so apt an encapsulation of the deceptive love story? Never. But only someone who has actually managed to whip a perfectly peaked meringue can understand this aptness.

The second is in the Letters section of *Startle and Illuminate: Carol Shields on Writing* (149–79), when Shields praises the use of irony in the writing she is responding to: "A feels that she is unworthy of a handsome man, for instance" (Giardini 177). The comment on the character and the writing is straightforward enough, but then Shields parenthetically adds one of those zinger curveballs that etch their own memorability: "(Someone out there gets the handsome men)" (Giardini 177). As a writer, I stop at that line, know that it speaks to the entire trajectory and consequence of a world desperate for connection, swiping through Tinder or Match, and hunting for the antidote to loneliness if not the appurtenances of casual sex. "Someone out there gets the handsome men," but not necessarily the happiness that we attribute to handsomeness. Ah, were I to host an imaginary dinner party, I would put Carol Shields right next to George Clooney and watch her seduce him.

Reading Carol Shields on writing coalesces a domino effect of discomfiting comfort for anyone who wants to believe in the writing miracle, anyone who has the desire and the dedication to attend to the consequence of inventing worlds with words. There is, as Anne Giardini's introduction to *Startle and Illuminate* reminds the reader, no perfect time or place to write (Giardini xxv), no perfect space, no inspiring trick that will put the wheels in motion and outdo plots in order to arrive at consequence. But there, tossed between a list of suggestions that are both organic and self-evident, is a quotidian but brilliant liturgical escutcheon, as useful as a spatula, but as transcendent as azure. "Read one page of the dictionary to settle your mind" (Giardini 142), Shields advises in "Be Bold All the Way Through." How brilliant an etching, how sensible an application, how marvelously retro, and yet how lexically farsighted. "Read one page of a dictionary to settle your mind." Illumination then. Even in a world without books, where we can hunt up any word on Google, keep this one indispensable manual and let it etch our practice: a dictionary, replete with promise, no plot at all but alphabet, and every word a consequence.

To practice what Carol Shields suggests, and to implement her advice in the most direct and personal way, I make myself one of her characters, a character becoming subject and student and writer at one and the same time. I gather the images that offer that "crinkly feeling" (Giardini 4) that Shields identifies in her essay "Writers Are Readers First": I puzzle over Toronto and its symmetry of Os, how everyone stands in the middle O to take the iconic "I-was-here" photograph. I wonder why Chantal Hébert so determinedly refuses to comb her messy hair. I revel in "domesticity, the shaggy beast that eats up fifty percent of our lives" (Giardini 28), where significance is carried by a clean window, a wilting plant, a perfect load of laundry, the dinner party that turned into a divorce. I notice that shops in airports are now stocked with funny socks, covered in messages or odd images. Have we taken to socks as political statements? Is geography really destiny, as Shields says that Eleanor Wachtel insists (Giardini 56) and if so, what am I doing here, on the selvage between prairie and foothills and nowhere? Is writing like that desire for the perfect haircut or is it about delicious revenge, the better taken for being hidden in a thicket of words? What "distant parts of myself" (Giardini 105)—as Shields quotes Alice Munro in her essay "The Short Story (and Women Writers)"—do I woo with this reading, this interest in whether or not people can die of bloat? Consequence and fumigation? Or simply my own unraveling patience with one old friendship that was falling apart because it was overreliant on plot? Ah, who can know, the writer, the reader, or the page, what indeed does startle and illuminate?

Works Cited

De Roo, Harvey. "A Little Like Flying: An Interview with Carol Shields." *West Coast Review*, vol. 23, no. 3, 1988, p 54.

Giardini, Anne and Giardini, Nicholas, eds. *Startle and Illuminate: Carol Shields on Writing.* Toronto: Random House, 2016.

Shields, Carol. "Be Bold All the Way Through." *Startle and Illuminate: Carol Shields on Writing.* Ed Anne Giardini and Nicholas Giardini. Toronto: Random House, 2016a. 141–8.

———. "Boxcars, Coat Hangers and Other Devices." *Startle and Illuminate: Carol Shields on Writing.* Ed Anne Giardini and Nicholas Giardini. Toronto: Random House, 2016b. 15–22.

———. "Myths That Keep You from Writing." *Startle and Illuminate: Carol Shields on Writing.* Ed Anne Giardini and Nicholas Giardini. Toronto: Random House, 2016c. 23–30.

———. "The Short Story (and Women Writers)." *Startle and Illuminate: Carol Shields on Writing.* Ed. Anne Giardini and Nicholas Giardini. Toronto: Random House, 2016d. 97–108.

———. "To Write Is to Raid." *Startle and Illuminate: Carol Shields on Writing.* Ed. Anne Giardini and Nicholas Giardini. Toronto: Random House, 2016e. 31–6.

———. "Writers Are Readers First." *Startle and Illuminate: Carol Shields on Writing.* Ed. Anne Giardini and Nicholas Giardini. Toronto: Random House, 2016f. 1–14.

———. "Writing What We've Discovered—So Far." *Startle and Illuminate: Carol Shields on Writing*. Ed. Anne Giardini and Nicholas Giardini. Toronto: Random House, 2016g. 109–114.

———. "What You Use and What You Protect." *Startle and Illuminate: Carol Shields on Writing*. Ed. Anne Giardini and Nicholas Giardini. Toronto: Random House, 2016h. 49–66.

INDEX

Mrs. Dalloway (character of Woolf), 14, 52, 54
"Mrs. Turner Cutting the Grass," 52, 101
Munro, Alice, 46, 59, 115, 244
  compared to Shields, 97
  "divine Alice," 97
  elegiac fiction, 150
  Friend of my Youth, 221
  "Prue," 99
  twist endings, 99
The Muslim woman, 181
  agency, 15, 207, 208
  intermediality, 207
  in *Unless* (novel), 194, 195, 197, 206–210, 212–214
  See also Islam
Myth, 10, 60, 64, 70
  méconnaissance, 135
  mermaids, 67, 135
  obstacles were overcome and victories realized, vi, 151
  of original desire, 139
  poet as victim, 121
  Ulysses, 60
Myth patterning, 59
"Myths That Keep you from Writing" (essay), 3, 58, 182, 187, 240
  Coral Ann Howells, 7
  essay by Shields, 86
  postmodern version of the carnivalesque, 73

N
Nabokov, Vladimir, *Pale Fire*, 102
Narrative hunger, 127
  concept of, 58, 147–148
  The Stone Diaries, 147
"Narrative Hunger and the Overflowing Cupboard," 22

account or story that serves as witness to the world, 36
the glance, 39n10
"The New New New Fiction" (essay), 5, 224
"The Next Best Kiss," 85
'Nightmare' (Lowther) (poem), 121
Noonan, Gerald, *Studies in Canadian Literature*, 120

O
Oates, Joyce Carol, "An Endangered Species," 74
O'Connor, Flannery, 76
O'Connor, Frank, *The Lonely Voice*, 51
O'Neill, Eugene, 76
"Open Every Question, Every Possibility" (essay), 11, 13, 146, 147, 154
  agenda, 149, 159
  "the full potential" of narrative, 159
  on language, 148
  revisionist agenda, 150
  signs, 147
The Orange Fish, 7, 9
  compared to "Dressing Up for the Carnival," 74
  focus on literature and the arts, 73
  See also "Chemistry"; "Hinterland"
Other, men as Shields's, 195
Otherness, 133, 194–195
  narrator's representation of, 197
  of others, 6, 12
  racialization, 181
  Reta's aversion to, 200
Other (poetry collection), 169
"Others," 6
Other (textual event), 212
Out of Place (Mandel), 150
Ozick, Cynthia, *The Puttermesser Papers*, 221, 224